ECONOMY OF THE PEOPLE'S REPUBLIC OF CHINA

ECONOMY OF THE
PEOPLE'S REPUBLIC OF CHINA

Dr S K Shah

Vij Books India Pvt Ltd

New Delhi (India)

Published by

Vij Books India Pvt Ltd
(Publishers, Distributors & Importers)
2/19, Ansari Road
Delhi – 110 002
Phones: 91-11-43596460, 91-11-47340674
Fax: 91-11-47340674
e-mail: vijbooks@rediffmail.com
www.vijbooks.com

ISBN: 978-93-86457-49-3 (Hardback)
ISBN: 978-93-86457-51-6 (ebook)

Printed and Bound in India

Contents

Contents

Preface

Growth in the People's Republic of China's restructuring economy continued to decelerate in 2016, but the government ensured stability through targeted fiscal and monetary support. Inflation started to rise, and the current account surplus narrowed but remained sizeable. These trends will continue in 2017 and 2018. Structural reform needs to be accelerated to boost productivity and sustain growth as outlined in the current 5-year plan.

Today, China's economy is behaving in a rather similar way to most other countries. This is true even of the government's influence on industry which in some sectors is similar to what we see in some European countries such as France. China uses (thanks to the World Bank) the same measurement yardsticks for GDP, foreign trade, inflation, industrial output, etc. as almost every other country. As such, comparisons are possible and called for.

The People's Republic of China has the second largest economy in the world after the US with a GDP of over $ 7 trillion (2007) when measured on a purchasing power parity (PPP) basis. In November 2007, it became the third largest in the world after the US and Japan with a nominal GDP of US$3.42 trillion (2007) when measured in exchange-rate terms. China has been the fastest-growing major nation for the past quarter of a century with an average annual GDP growth rate above 10%. China's per capita income has grown at an average annual rate of more than 8% over the last three decades drastically reducing poverty, but this rapid growth has been accompanied by rising income inequalities. The country's per capita income is classified as low by world standards, at about $2,000 (nominal, 107th of 179 countries/economies), and $7,800 (PPP, 82nd of 179 countries/economies) in 2006, according to the IMF.

Since the late 1970s and early 1980s, the economic reforms initially began with the shift of farming work to a system of household responsibility to start the phase out of collectivized agriculture, and later expanded to include the gradual liberalization of prices; fiscal decentralization; increased autonomy for state enterprises that increased the authority of local government officials and plant managers in industry thereby permitting a wide variety of private enterprise in services and light manufacturing; the foundation of a diversified banking system; the development of stock markets; the rapid growth of the non-state sector, and the opening of the economy to increased foreign trade and foreign investment. China has generally implemented reforms in a gradualist fashion, including the sale of equity in China's largest state banks to foreign investors and refinements in foreign exchange and bond markets in mid-2000s. As its role in world trade has steadily grown, its importance to the international economy has also increased apace. China's foreign trade has grown faster than its GDP for the past 25 years. As of 2007, most of china's growth came from the Private Sector instead of exports. Particularly the smaller public sector, which was dominated by about 200 large state enterprises concentrated mostly in utilities, heavy industries, and energy resources.

China is a global hub for manufacturing, and is the largest manufacturing economy in the world as well as the largest exporter of goods in the world. China is also the world's fastest growing consumer market and second largest importer of goods in the world. China is a net importer of services products. As of 2016, China is the second largest trading nation in the world and plays a prominent role in international trade , and has increasingly engaged in trade organizations and treaties in recent years. China became a member of the World Trade Organization in 2001. China also has free trade agreements with several nations, including Australia, South Korea, ASEAN, New Zealand, Switzerland and Pakistan. The provinces in the coastal regions of China tend to be more industrialized, while regions in the hinterland are less developed. As China's economic importance has grown, so has attention to the structure and health of the economy.

As the book addresses this crucial issue quite deftly, it is hoped that it would prove to be a source of great information for the reader.

— *Editor*

1

China: Past, Present & Future

The rapid progression of the Chinese economy over the last 30 years has turned the nation into a world superpower, with a population of 1.39bn (2013) and GDP of 8.2tn USD (2012) which is still growing at a rate of 7.7% p.a. (2014). The future of China will have ramifications for not only wider Asia; but the world economy as a whole. In this chapter we will firstly look at the rise of China, uncovering the political, economic and social reforms which have shaped this nation. We will then look towards the issues the nation is currently facing. Finally we will address the issues the country will likely face in the future.

Adam Smith dispelled the benefits of export led growth through Mercantilism in the 18th century; however the export policies and resulting large and unsustainable current account surplus of China, combined with cheap credit and off balance sheet lending has given rise to under-consumption, asset inflation, financial instability as well as social and resource misallocation.

These factors increase the prospect of civil unrest and economic stagnation or worse disintegration, replicating the fate of Japan in the 1980's (*Marroquin 2007*). The Chinese Government and corporates must increase domestic investment in education (*currently 4% of GPD, below the average of developing countries. Tao Yang 2012*) and allow liberal labour flows between urban 'hukou' (*a household registration system*) and agricultural 'hukou' in order to increase the standard of living, productivity, family incomes and therefore domestic consumption.

THE RISE OF CHINA

The two fundamental elucidations that led to the rise of China are Globalization and Internal Reforms, financial and social (*Huang 2012*). In 1978 China was one the poorest countries in the World, with real GDP per capita being only one fourteenth of the U.S. (*Zhu 2012*). 1978 was a pivotal year in the narrative of the rise of China as it was when the general policy of *Gaige Kaifang or* "reform and opening up" after the Cultural Revolution ended; post the death of Chairman Mao Zedong in 1976 (*Zhu 2012*). Market pricing for agricultural production above quotas and decentralisation of local economies, introducing "township and village enterprises" (TVEs) were two of the early reforms.

Grain being sold above quotas at market prices increased the agricultural efficiency and aligned incentives, as noted by (*Zhu 2012*) this reform increased productivity by 47%. The amplified productivity destined these agricultural workers to other sectors. From 1978 to 1984, 49 million or 19% of the work force reallocated from the agricultural sector. As part of the decentralisation programme the majority of the reallocated workers did not move to urban centres but rather set up or went to work in the TVEs. By 2007 employment in the agricultural sector had fallen from 69% in 1978 to 26%. As work in the TVEs and urban centres generated labour productivity that was six times that of the agricultural sector (*Zhu 2012*) the productivity gains were argued by Zhu to be the most imperative reason for Chinas growth in the first two decades of reform.

Globalisation started when Deng Xiaoping opened up China for foreign investment and created explicit exporting nucleuses which were, by and large; funded with foreign investment. In 2001 China joined the World Trade Organisation (WTO), (*Yang* 2012). The export driven policies of an artificially low exchange rate and incentives for exporters in the form of preferential loans and tax rebates aligned to make China the powerhouse exporting economy we see today. The large current account surpluses were initially met with similar increases in investment. However, since the mid 2000's investment has lagged leading to enormous foreign reserves (*Yang* 2012).

THE ISSUES CHINA CURRENTLY FACES

Li, Li, Wu and Xiong (2012) argue the one of the main challenges for China moving forward is the inevitable end to cheap Chinese labour. Since the 1990's wages have increased faster than productivity gains, this is shifting Chinas comparative advantage and moving labour intensive industries to lower wage economies such as Vietnam and India. China will have to move to value added production in order to justify the wage increases or risk being priced out of the market. In order for China to compete on the world stage, investment will need to be focussed towards R&D and education (*Tao Yang 2012*)

As with most countries, China is heavily reliant on its trading partners. However, as China has low domestic consumption (evidence by their consumption to GDP ratio) there is insufficient internal demand to absorb domestic production, leaving China vulnerable to external shocks. The large current account surplus has resulted in the largest accumulation of foreign reserves in the world leaving China susceptible to large losses should rates move against them. The major countries in which China is accumulating reserves from are or have been easing monetary policy, economic theory states if you increase the money supply inflation will result. This inflation will increase nominal rates; all things equal. China, in 2011, held 3.2trillion USD in foreign reserves (*Tao Yang 2012*) with US inflation currently 2% and the 30 year T-Bill offering a yield 3.16% (22.8.2014). A small increase in inflation or currency appreciation will eliminate any real return for China. I theorise the U.S is inflating their way out of debt.

Labour market migration and inequality between rural and urban 'hukou' is one of the mounting pressures within China (*Meng* 2012).

Meng predicts the number of migrants over the next few decades from rural to urban areas could reach 300m, they will need to be housed, clothed, their children educated and work opportunities abundant otherwise China will face civil unrest and increased inequality. Migration within China is still regulated with rural workers being allowed 'quest' status in the urban areas. The rural migrants often take the jobs the urban settlers do not wish to do (*Meng* 2012). This structural segregation threatens to create a social underclass and create labour market distortions and exploitation. Meng notes:

"89 percent of migrant workers are employed as unskilled workers in sales and service or production jobs, while only 40% of urban hukou workers are in this category".

Migrant children are often denied education at local schools and their parents have little access to unemployment services, healthcare and retirement plans.

CHINA: RISE, FALL AND RE-EMERGENCE AS A GLOBAL POWER

First we will outline the main contours of historical China's rise to global economic superiority over West before the 19th century, following closely John Hobson's account in The Eastern Origins of Western Civilization. Since the majority of western economic historians (liberal, conservative and Marxist) have presented historical China as a stagnant, backward, parochial society, an "oriental despotism", some detailed correctives will be necessary. It is especially important to emphasize how China , the world technological power between 1100 and 1800, made the West's emergence possible. It was only by borrowing and assimilating Chinese innovations that the West was able to make the transition to modern capitalist and imperialist economies.

In part two we will analyze and discuss the factors and circumstances which led to China's decline in the 19th century and its subsequent domination, exploitation and pillage by Western imperial countries, first England and then the rest of Europe, Japan and the United States. In part three, we will briefly outline the factors leading to China's emancipation from colonial and neo-colonial rule and analyze its recent rise to becoming the second largest global economic power.

Finally we will look at the past and present threats to China's rise to global economic power, highlighting the similarities between British colonialism of the 18 and 19th centuries and the current US imperial strategies and focusing on the weaknesses and strengths of past and present Chinese responses.

China: The Rise and Consolidation of Global Power 1100 – 1800

In a systematic comparative format, John Hobson provides a wealth of empirical indicators demonstrating China's global economic superiority over the West and in particular England. These are some striking facts:

As early as 1078, China was the world's major producer of steel (125,000 tons); whereas Britain in 1788 produced 76,000 tons.

China was the world's leader in technical innovations in textile manufacturing, seven centuries before Britain's 18th century "textile revolution". China was the leading trading nation, with long distance trade reaching most of Southern Asia, Africa, the Middle East and Europe. China's 'agricultural revolution' and productivity surpassed the West down to the 18th century.

Its innovations in the production of paper, book printing, firearms and tools led to a manufacturing superpower whose goods were transported throughout the world by the most advanced navigational system. China possessed the world's largest commercial ships. In 1588 the largest English ships displaced 400 tons, China's 3,000 tons. Even as late as the end of the 18th century China's merchants employed 130,000 private transport ships, several times that of Britain. China retained this pre-eminent position in the world economy up until the early 19th century.

British and Europeans manufacturers followed China's lead, assimilating and borrowing its more advanced technology and were eager to penetrate China's advanced and lucrative market. Banking, a stable paper money economy, manufacturing and high yields in agriculture resulted in China's per capita income matching that of Great Britain as late as 1750.

China's dominant global position was challenged by the rise of British imperialism, which had adopted the advanced technological, navigational and market innovations of China and other Asian countries in order to bypass earlier stages in becoming a world power.

WESTERN IMPERIALISM AND THE DECLINE OF CHINA

The British and Western imperial conquest of the East, was based on the militaristic nature of the imperial state, its non-reciprocal economic relations with overseas trading countries and the Western imperial ideology which motivated and justified overseas conquest. Unlike China , Britain's industrial revolution and overseas expansion was driven by a military policy. According to Hobson, during the period from 1688-1815 Great Britain was engaged in wars 52% of the time. Whereas the Chinese relied on their open markets and their superior production and sophisticated commercial and banking skills, the British relied on tariff protection, military conquest, the systematic destruction of competitive overseas enterprises as well as the appropriation and plunder of local resources. China's global predominance was based on 'reciprocal benefits' with its trading partners, while Britain relied on mercenary armies of occupation, savage repression and a 'divide and conquer' policy to foment local rivalries. In the face of native resistance, the British (as well as other Western imperial powers) did not hesitate to exterminate entire communities.

Unable to take over the Chinese market through greater economic competitiveness, Britain relied on brute military power. It mobilized, armed and led mercenaries, drawn from its colonies in India and elsewhere to force its exports on China and impose unequal treaties to lower tariffs. As a result China was flooded with British opium produced on its plantations in India – despite Chinese laws forbidding or regulating the importation and sale of the narcotic. China's rulers, long accustomed to its trade and manufacturing superiority, were unprepared for the 'new imperial rules' for global power. The West's willingness to use military power to win colonies, pillage resources and recruit huge mercenary armies commanded by European officers spelt the end for China as a world power.

China had based its economic predominance on 'non-interference in the internal affairs of its trading partners'. In contrast, British imperialists intervened violently in Asia , reorganizing local economies to suit the needs of the empire (eliminating economic competitors including more efficient Indian cotton manufacturers) and seized control of local political, economic and administrative apparatus to establish the colonial state.

Britain's empire was built with resources seized from the colonies and through the massive militarization of its economy. It was thus able to secure military supremacy over China. China's foreign policy was hampered by its ruling elite's excessive reliance on trade relations. Chinese officials and merchant elites sought to appease the British and convinced the emperor to grant devastating extra-territorial concessions opening markets to the detriment of Chinese manufacturers while surrendering local sovereignty. As always, the British precipitated internal rivalries and revolts further destabilizing the country.

Western and British penetration and colonization of China's market created an entire new class: The wealthy Chinese 'compradores' imported British goods and facilitated the takeover of local markets and resources. Imperialist pillage forced greater exploitation and taxation of the great mass of Chinese peasants and workers. China's rulers were obliged to pay the war debts and finance trade deficits imposed by the Western imperial powers by squeezing its peasantry. This drove the peasants to starvation and revolt.

By the early 20th century (less than a century after the Opium Wars), China had descended from world economic power to a broken semi-colonial country with a huge destitute population. The principle ports were controlled by Western imperial officials and the countryside was subject to the rule by corrupt and brutal warlords. British opium enslaved millions.

British Academics: Eloquent Apologists for Imperial Conquest

The entire Western academic profession – first and foremost British imperial historians – attributed British imperial dominance of Asia to English 'technological superiority' and China's misery and colonial status to 'oriental backwardness', omitting any mention of the millennium of Chinese commercial and technical progress and superiority up to the dawn of the 19th century. By the end of the 1920's, with the Japanese imperial invasion, China ceased to exist as a unified country. Under the aegis of imperial rule, hundreds of millions of Chinese had starved or were dispossessed or slaughtered, as the Western powers and Japan plundered its economy. The entire Chinese 'collaborator' comprador elite were discredited before the Chinese people.

What did remain in the collective memory of the great mass of the Chinese people – and what was totally absent in the accounts of prestigious US and British academics – was the sense of China once having been a prosperous, dynamic and leading world power. Western commentators dismissed this collective memory of China's ascendancy as the foolish pretensions of nostalgic lords and royalty – empty Han arrogance.

THE CHINESE COMMUNIST REVOLUTION

The rise of modern China to become the second largest economy in the world was made possible only through the success of the Chinese communist revolution in the mid-20th century. The People's Liberation 'Red' Army defeated first the invading Japanese imperial army and later the US imperialist-backed comprador led Kuomintang "Nationalist" army. This allowed the reunification of China as an independent sovereign state. The Communist government abolished the extra-territorial privileges of the Western imperialists, ended the territorial fiefdoms of the regional warlords and gangsters and drove out the millionaire owners of brothels, the traffickers of women and drugs as well as the other "service providers" to the Euro-American

Empire.

In every sense of the word, the Communist revolution forged the modern Chinese state. The new leaders then proceeded to reconstruct an economy ravaged by imperial wars and pillaged by Western and Japanese capitalists. After over 150 years of infamy and humiliation the Chinese people recovered their pride and national dignity. These socio-psychological elements were essential in motivating the Chinese to defend their country from the US attacks, sabotage, boycotts, and blockades mounted immediately after liberation.

Contrary to Western and neoliberal Chinese economists, China's dynamic growth did not start in 1980. It began in 1950, when the agrarian reform provided land, infrastructure, credits and technical assistance to hundreds of millions of landless and destitute peasants and landless rural workers. Through what is now called "human capital" and gigantic social mobilization, the Communists built roads, airfields, bridges, canals and railroads as well as the basic industries, like coal, iron and steel, to form the backbone of the modern Chinese economy. Communist China's vast free educational and health systems created a healthy, literate and motivated work force. Its highly professional military prevented the US from extending its military empire throughout the Korean peninsula up to China's territorial frontiers. Just as past Western scholars and propagandists fabricated a history of a "stagnant and decadent" empire to justify their destructive conquest, so too their modern counterparts have rewritten the first thirty years of Chinese Communist history, denying the role of the revolution in developing all the essential elements for a modern economy, state and society. It is clear that China's rapid economic growth was based on the development of its internal market, its rapidly growing cadre of scientists, skilled technicians and workers and the social safety net which protected and promoted working class and peasant mobility were products of Communist planning and investments. China's rise to global power began in 1949 with the removal of the entire parasitic financial, compradore and speculative classes who had served as the intermediaries for European, Japanese and US imperialists draining China of its great wealth.

China's Transition to Capitalism

Beginning in 1980 the Chinese government initiated a dramatic shift in its economic strategy: Over the next three decades, it opened the country to large-scale foreign investment; it privatized thousands of industries and it set in motion a process of income concentration based on a deliberate strategy of re-creating a dominant economic class of billionaires linked to overseas capitalists. China's ruling political class embraced the idea of "borrowing" technical know-how and accessing overseas markets from foreign firms in exchange for providing cheap, plentiful labor at the lowest cost.

The Chinese state re-directed massive public subsidies to promote high capitalist growth by dismantling its national system of free public education and health care. They ended subsidized public housing for hundreds of millions of peasants and urban factory workers and provided funds to real estate speculators for the construction of private luxury apartments and office skyscrapers.

China's new capitalist strategy as well as its double digit growth was based on the profound structural changes and massive public investments made possible by the previous communist government. China's private sector "take off" was based on the huge public outlays made since 1949.

The triumphant new capitalist class and its Western collaborators claimed all the credit for this "economic miracle" as China rose to become the world's second largest economy. This new Chinese elite have been less eager to announce China's world-class status in terms of brutal class inequalities, rivaling only the US.

CHINA'S TRADE POLICIES IN WIDER ASIAN PERSPECTIVE

This chapter looks at China's trade-policy developments compared with related trends in India and southeast Asia (the ASEAN countries). The larger backdrop is the historic – but very recent – integration of first China and then India into the global economy; but in between also lies the longer history of southeast-Asian integration into the global economy, which accelerated after the 1970s. Such preliminary observations also raise the question of economic integration *between and among* these different parts of Asia – or the lack thereof – and how that relates to trade policies. Time and space prohibit an even wider comparison with Japan, South Korea and Taiwan, the more developed countries of northeast Asia.

Consider the following questions. How far has economic opening come in China, India and southeast Asia, and how much farther is it likely to go? Where does trade policy in these regions fit in the spectrum between liberalism and intervention? How does it relate to broad trends in domestic and foreign policies? What is China's place in the World Trade Organisation, just four years into accession? What are its negotiating positions and strategies in the Doha Round? How does it interact with other WTO members, particularly the major players? What of China's future in the WTO? How does that compare with India's and the ASEAN countries' longer history in the GATT/WTO and their Doha-Round negotiating positions? What is China's Free-Trade-Agreement (FTA) strategy? Will it become the FTA hub in east Asia? How does that compare with FTA developments in India and the ASEAN countries?

Making a stab at answering these questions will proceed as follows. China, India and southeast Asia in the context of economic globalisation and policy reforms around the world. At their trade-policy frameworks. It summarises recent reforms, links them down to domestic economic policies, and up to foreign policy and trade diplomacy.

The concluding argument of the paper, worth flagging at the outset, is that trade *policy* matters more than trade *negotiations*. There has been huge trade-and-investment liberalisation; but this has happened *unilaterally* for the most part, not through trade negotiations, whether in the WTO or in FTAs. Trade negotiations have distinct and perhaps increasing limitations, and their effects should not be exaggerated. All the more reason, therefore, to rely on the unilateral engine of freer trade, with China setting the late 20th/early 21st-century example much as Britain did in the second half of the 19th century. That will have powerful emulatory effects elsewhere, particularly in Asia. A combined China-and-India effect, with India accelerating liberalisation in response to China, will send even stronger liberalisation signals, not least to southeast Asia.

What makes the crucial difference to economic globalisation today, and probably for next half century, is the dramatic opening of first China and then India. They are the world's second- and fourth-largest economies respectively (at purchasing-power parity): China accounted for 12.5 per cent, and India about 6 per cent, of global GDP in 2003. Together they are home to 40 per cent of humanity (China with a population of 1.37 billion, and India 1.07 billion). With still low levels of per-capita income (China's being 15 per cent, and India's 7 per cent, of US levels, measured at PPP), and huge supplies of cheap, productive labour, they have the potential for stellar catch-up growth rates for decades ahead. Their integration into the world economy, still in its early stages, promises to be more momentous than that of Japan and the east-Asian Tigers, and perhaps on a par with the rise of the US as a global economic power in the late nineteenth century.

Asia was conspicuously absent from the world economy from early modernity to relatively recent times. International economic integration spread from Britain to Western Europe and the British offshoots of Empire, notably north America and Australasia, plus a handful of other lands of recent settlement (such as Argentina). Mostly, Asia came into the fold only in the second half of the 20th century: first with the emergence of Japan in the 1950s (rather its re-emergence after its late nineteenth century rise and then wartime destruction); followed by Hong Kong, Singapore, Taiwan and South Korea; and then the second-generation Tigers of southeast Asia. China and India remained closed during most of this period. Only come the 1980s and 1990s did they wake up and join the fray.

Southeast Asia has a longer history of global economic integration than China or India. This is particularly the case with Singapore and Malaysia: both were tightly integrated into the commercial networks of the British Empire. Notwithstanding vast differences among countries in the region, the older ASEAN members (Singapore, Malaysia, Thailand, Indonesia and Philippines) have integrated further into the world economy since the 1970s, especially through trade and foreign direct investment (FDI) in manufactures. In terms of headline indicators, the ASEAN countries have a combined GDP well below that of China but still ahead of India (at market prices, though below the Indian level in terms of PPP comparisons); a combined population less than half that of China or India; and an average per-capita GDP that is higher than China's or India's.

The rise of east and south Asia (but not west or north Asia) is one feature of globalisation today; the other is its extremely partial and uneven nature. China, India and southeast Asia figure prominently in that story too. A recent World Bank report identifies 24 "new-globalising" developing countries with a total population of 2.9 billion. Between 1980 and 1997, this group registered a doubling of their trade-to-GDP ratio, a two-thirds increase in real per- capita income, and a one-third cut in average import tariffs. In the same period, the 49 "less-globalised" developing countries in the sample, with a combined population of 1.1 billion, saw a decline in their trade-to-GDP ratio, a rise of just 10 per cent in real per-capita income, and an 11 per cent cut in average import tariffs. The former also registered a better reading on the rule of law than the latter. These figures are, of course, yet further empirical support for the proposition that relatively liberal trade policies and openness to trade, combined with market-oriented institutions at home, lead to higher rates of growth than is the case for economies that remain relatively closed. That is what distinguishes the West, and more recently Japan, the east-Asian Tigers, and now China and India, from most other countries in the developing world. But what is really striking about this group of 24 new globalisers is that, first, Asia makes up 85 per cent of its population, and second, that India and China alone make up 75 per cent.

Now turn to China specifically. Between 1980 and 2003, its real income per head rose by over 300 per cent. Its export and import volumes have grown by 11-13 per cent a year since 1980, and by 35-40 per cent annually in the last few years. Manufactures account for 90 per cent of merchandise exports. China's ratio of trade in goods to GDP, at market prices, now stands at about 70 per cent. This is truly exceptional.

The most-peopled country in the world has, in quick time, acquired the trade openness of a much smaller country (such as South Korea). It is far more open than roughly equivalent large countries like the US, India and Japan, with trade-to-GDP ratios of about 20 per cent. China's share of world merchandise exports was 6 per cent in 2003, up from 1.2 per cent in 1980. China has just overtaken Japan as the world's third-largest trading nation.

China's trade openness is intimately bound up with its openness to inward investment. The stock of FDI in China was over $550 billion in 2004 from $25 billion in 1990. It was about 40 per cent of Chinese GDP, compared with 1.5 per cent for Japan, just over 5 per cent for India and 13 per cent for the US. FDI inflows in 2004, at $60 billion, were over one-third of the total going to all developing countries. The bulk of FDI stock is in manufacturing, and it is estimated that China is home to about 7 per cent of global manufacturing production. Foreign-owned firms generate over 50 per cent of exports (on a par with small, highly open economies like Estonia, Costa Rica and Malaysia) and 60 per cent of imports. The latter figures are especially striking, and bear repetition: *foreign affiliates generate one-half of total exports and an even greater share of imports.*

This astounding combination of trade-and-FDI penetration means that China is already well integrated into the world economy, indeed more so than other developing countries (except highly open, small-to-medium economies, most of them in east Asia), and much more so than the giant rival on its eastern flank, Japan.

China's global integration dwarfs that of India, but the latter has come far by its own standards, especially since the early 1990s. Real incomes have increased by 125 per cent since 1980 (less than half the increase in China). Exports and imports have picked up since the early 1990s, albeit from a very low base. India accounts for less than 1 per cent of world manufacturing exports, putting it in 30th position globally. It has a 1.4-per-cent share of world commercial-services exports, in 19th position globally (though Chinese commercial-services exports are about double the Indian level). FDI has increased from a low base, with an inward investment stock of about \$36 billion by 2004. FDI inflows were \$6 billion in 2004 – about 10 per cent of Chinese levels.

What about southeast Asia? Its figures mirror China's but not India's. Its trade levels in 2003 were a little ahead of China's but well ahead of India's. Basically, China has been catching up fast with southeast-Asian trade shares; and, with higher growth in trade volumes, it will rapidly overtake southeast Asia. ASEAN countries are highly open to the world economy, with an average trade/GDP ratio of 134.5 per cent, about double that of China. This masks differences within the region: Singapore is at one extreme; Malaysia is also extremely trade dependent; and even Thailand, Philippines and Vietnam have trade/GDP ratios of over 100 per cent. FDI inflows, which have not maintained their pre-Asian-crisis rate of increase, pale in comparison with inflows to China but are still some way ahead of Indian levels.

There are increasing economic links between China, India and southeast Asia, though from a low base. The main link is between China and southeast Asia. China's share in ASEAN exports nearly tripled, and its share of ASEAN imports more than quadrupled, between 1993 and 2003. Trade in manufactures accounted for most of this increase. ASEAN trade with India, though increasing, is about 20-25 per cent of ASEAN-China trade levels.

What do these comparisons tell us about relative specialisation in the current and emerging international division of labour? The main point is that China has clear-cut comparative advantage in labour-intensive manufactured exports; and this will remain the case for some time ahead, given a huge pool of cheap labour pouring from the countryside into the cities, particularly on the coast. Less often mentioned is China's growing exploitation of comparative advantage in labour-intensive agricultural exports such as fruits and vegetables. At the same time, it is sucking in ever-increasing land-intensive agricultural imports as domestic resources shift further to industrial production. It has recently become a net importer of farm produce. Such rapid specialisation is forging complementary trade relationships with agricultural and other commodity producers in Australasia, Latin America and Africa. In manufactures, as China integrates into global supply chains, it is forging very strong links with the USA, EU and other east-Asian countries, including ASEAN. Much of this is in the form of vertically-integrated, intra-industry trade: China imports capital-intensive components for labour-intensive processing and export to the rest of the world. Finally, rising real incomes are driving domestic demand for sophisticated foreign consumer products and services.

The net effect of China's insertion into the global economy is to intensify competition, and with it the need for mutual adjustment and adaptation. More pressure will bear down on low-value, low-wage industries in the West that compete directly with Chinese exports. More pressure is already being felt in developing countries that compete directly with Chinese manufactured exports for third-country export markets. Competition is particularly keen in the global market for clothing.

Now turn to India. China should be the shadow of India's future. With an abundance of cheap labour, India should become a powerhouse for manufacturing exports, occupying low-wage niches (e.g. in textiles and clothing) vacated by China as real incomes rise there. This should apply to labour-intensive agricultural exports too. That is the story of fast-paced, catch-up growth in developing countries in the last half-century.

But this is not happening in India. Its major problem is that only 10 million people are employed in the formal manufacturing sector, out of a total employable population that is rising to 450 million. Industry has a less than 30 per-cent share of GDP, compared with a figure of 50 per cent or more in China and other east-Asian developing countries. External protection, strangulating domestic labour-market regulation, poor infrastructure and other bad business-climate conditions are to blame. Agriculture accounts for 60 per cent of employment but only 20 per cent of GDP. Growth and employment generation are hindered by high external protection, poor infrastructure, other barriers to internal trade, small plots of land, and otherwise pervasive government intervention.

That leaves services, with a share of 50 per cent of GDP (high by developing-country standards and much higher than the share of services in China's GDP). India does have comparative advantage in labour-intensive areas of services, which it is exploiting in business-process outsourcing and software exports. But this is not the panacea often advertised. IT-related services will generate an extra 1 million jobs and account for 1 per cent of GDP by 2010, according to the most optimistic projections. The jobs created require relatively high qualifications and are well paid by Indian standards. But they are a drop in the ocean compared with the wealth-creation and employment-generation potential in manufacturing and, to a lesser extent, in agriculture.

Where does southeast Asia fit into this comparative-advantage picture? It will maintain strong trade-and-FDI links with the USA and Europe. But its future also seems to lie in complementary trade, especially of the intra-industry manufacturing variety, with China and other parts of northeast Asia (Japan, Korea and Taiwan). This will bring in associated FDI. Production-sharing arrangements in IT-related sectors figure prominently, with different parts of the value chain in different locations. But, to exploit these niches fully, the older ASEAN countries need to improve infrastructure, education, skills *and* governance in order to compensate for eroded advantage in cheap labour. They also need to liberalise highly protected markets in agriculture and services. The newer and much poorer ASEAN countries (Cambodia, Vietnam, Laos and Myanmar) can exploit comparative advantage in cheap labour, especially as relative incomes rise in China. However, for some ASEAN countries with an eroding labour-cost advantage, there are areas where trade with China is more frictional than complementary, e.g. in agriculture, textiles and clothing. Finally, the older ASEAN countries should be able to export more commercial services to an opening and expanding Chinese market, gain from expanding travel and tourism, and invest in large Chinese infrastructure projects.

ASEAN trade with India is much less developed. Trade-and-FDI links are increasing in services and pockets of manufacturing (e.g. cars and car parts). However, for bilateral trade to really take off, India will have to burst its self-imposed chains in manufacturing. That would lead to much stronger, complementary trade and associated FDI between China, India and southeast Asia in goods and services, and with it a more rational, integrated Asian division of labour. But that appears to be on the distant horizon. In all, China's, India's and southeast Asia's integration into the world economy creates vast opportunities. In China and southeast Asia, catch-up growth based on inward investment and manufactured exports, underpinned by trade-and-investment liberalisation, has massively benefited the poor. That has happened to a lesser extent in India because it has been far less successful in exploiting comparative advantage. The task for public policy is to grasp these opportunities by keeping borders open, or opening them where they are closed, while managing the necessary adjustments. The emerging complementary commercial relationships between China, India and southeast Asia, and between them and other countries, in both developed and developing worlds, will hopefully make this political task realistic and manageable. But protectionist danger lurks behind every free-trade opportunity. These dangers are bound to increase as China's advance gathers pace; and they will increase further if India accelerates its pace of global integration. They will come from declining industries in rich countries and directly competing industries in other poor countries.

Last, the growth story told here masks large and in some cases increasing problems with regional income disparities, environmental pollution, and health, education and social-security systems. That is more the case in China and India, but less so in the richer southeast-Asian countries. Reversing or even slowing down integration into the world economy is not the lesson to draw. That would deprive people of further growth and poverty reduction, and more generally of further improvements to human welfare. Rather the challenge is to bring globalisation's benefits to the parts of these regions they have not yet reached, while devoting more public and private resources to health care, pollution control and other public goods.

CHINA: FROM IMPERIAL DEPENDENCY TO WORLD CLASS COMPETITOR

China's sustained growth in its manufacturing sector was a result of highly concentrated public investments, high profits, technological innovations and a protected domestic market. While foreign capital profited, it was always within the framework of the Chinese state's priorities and regulations. The regime's dynamic 'export strategy' led to huge trade surpluses, which eventually made China one of the world's largest creditors especially for US debt. In order to maintain its dynamic industries, China has required huge influxes of raw materials, resulting in large-scale overseas investments and trade agreements with agro-mineral export countries in Africa and Latin America. By 2010 China displaced the US and Europe as the main trading partner in many countries in Asia, Africa and Latin America.

Modern China's rise to world economic power, like its predecessor between 1100-1800, is based on its gigantic productive capacity: Trade and investment was governed by a policy of strict non-interference in the internal relations of its trading partners. Unlike the US , China did initiate brutal wars for oil; instead it signed lucrative contracts. And China does not fight wars in the interest of overseas Chinese, as the US has done in the Middle East for Israel.

The seeming imbalance between Chinese economic and military power is in stark contrast to the US where a bloated, parasitic military empire continues to erode its own global economic presence. US military spending is twelve times that of China. Increasingly the US military plays the key role shaping policy in Washington as it seeks to undercut China's rise to global power.

China's Rise to World Power: Will History Repeat Itself?

China has been growing at about 9% per annum and its goods and services are rapidly rising in quality and value. In contrast, the US and Europe have wallowed around 0% growth from 2007-2012. China's innovative techno-scientific establishment routinely assimilates the latest inventions from the West (and Japan) and improves them, thereby decreasing the cost of production. China has replaced the US and European controlled "international financial institutions" (the IMF, World Bank, the Inter-American Development Bank) as the principle lender in Latin America. China continues to lead as the prime investor in African energy and mineral resources. China has replaced the US as the principle market for Saudi Arabian, Sudanese and Iranian petroleum and it will soon replace the US as the principle market for Venezuela petroleum products. Today China is the world's biggest manufacturer and exporter, dominating even the US market, while playing the role of financial life line as it holds over $1.3 trillion in US Treasury notes.

Under growing pressure from its workers, farmers and peasants, China's rulers have been developing the domestic market by increasing wages and social spending to rebalance the economy and avoid the specter of social instability. In contrast, US wages, salaries and vital public services have sharply declined in absolute and relative terms.

Given the current historical trends it is clear that China will replace the US as the leading world economic power, over the next decade, if the US empire does not strike back and if China's profound class inequalities do not lead to a major social upheaval. Modern China's rise to global power faces serious challenges. In contrast to China's historical ascent on the world stage, modern Chinese global economic power is not accompanied by any imperialist undertakings. China has seriously lagged behind the US and Europe in aggressive war-making capacity.

This may have allowed China to direct public resources to maximize economic growth, but it has left China vulnerable to US military superiority in terms of its massive arsenal, its string of forward bases and strategic geo-military positions right off the Chinese coast and in adjoining territories.

In the nineteenth century British imperialism demolished China's global position with its military superiority, seizing China's ports – because of China's reliance on 'mercantile superiority'.

The conquest of India , Burma and most of Asia allowed Britain to establish colonial bases and recruit local mercenary armies. The British and its mercenary allies encircled and isolated China , setting the stage for the disruption of China's markets and the imposition of the brutal terms of trade. The British Empire's armed presence dictated what China imported (with opium accounting for over 50% of British exports in the 1850s) while undermining China's competitive advantages via tariff policies.

Today the US is pursuing similar policies: US naval fleet patrols and controls China's commercial shipping lanes and off-shore oil resources via its overseas bases. The Obama-Clinton White House is in the process of developing a rapid military response involving bases in Australia , Philippines and elsewhere in Asia. The US is intensifying its efforts to undermine Chinese overseas access to strategic resources while backing 'grass roots' separatists and 'insurgents' in West China, Tibet, Sudan, Burma, Iran, Libya, Syria and elsewhere. The US military agreements with India and the installation of a pliable puppet regime in Pakistan have advanced its strategy of isolating China. While China upholds its policy of "harmonious development" and "non-interference in the internal affairs of other countries", it has stepped aside as US and European military imperialism have attacked a host of China's trading partners to essentially reverse China's peaceful commercial expansion.

China's lack of a political and ideological strategy capable of protecting its overseas economic interests has been an invitation for the US and NATO to set-up regimes hostile to China. The most striking example is Libya where US and NATO intervened to overthrow an independent government led by President Gadhafi, with whom China had signed multi-billion dollar trade and investments agreements. The NATO bombardment of Libyan cities, ports and oil installation forced the Chinese to withdraw 35,000 Chinese oil engineers and construction workers in a matter of days. The same thing happened in Sudan where China had invested billions to develop its oil industry. The US, Israel and Europe armed the South Sudanese rebels to disrupt the flow of oil and attack Chinese oil workers. In both cases China passively allowed the US and European military imperialists to attack its trade partners and undermine its investments.

Under Mao Tse Tung, China had an active policy countering imperial aggression: It supported revolutionary movements and independent Third World governments. Today's capitalist China does not have an active policy of supporting governments or movements capable of protecting China's bilateral trade and investment agreements. China's inability to confront the rising tide of US military aggression against its economic interests, is due to deep structural problems. China's foreign policy is shaped by big commercial, financial and manufacturing interests who rely on their 'economic competitive edge' to gain market shares and have no understanding of the military and security underpinnings of global economic power. China's political class is deeply influenced by a new class of billionaires with strong ties to Western equity funds and who have uncritically absorbed Western cultural values. This is illustrated by their preference for sending their own children to elite universities in the US and Europe. They seek "accommodation with the West" at any price.

This lack of any strategic understanding of military empire-building has led them to respond ineffectively and ad hoc to each imperialist action undermining their access to resources and markets. While China's "business first" outlook may have worked when it was a minor player in the world economy and US empire builders saw the "capitalist opening" as a chance to easily takeover China's public enterprises and pillage the economy. However, when China (in contrast to the former USSR) decided to retain capital controls and develop a carefully calibrated, state directed "industrial policy" directing western capital and the transfer of technology to state enterprises, which effectively penetrated the US domestic and overseas markets, Washington began to complain and talked of retaliation.

China's huge trade surpluses with the US provoked a dual response in Washington : It sold massive quantities of US Treasury bonds to the Chinese and began to develop a global strategy to block China's advance. Since the US lacked economic leverage to reverse its decline, it relied on its only "comparative advantage" – its military superiority based on a world wide system of attack bases, a network of overseas client regimes, military proxies, NGO'ers, intellectuals and armed mercenaries.

Washington turned to its vast overt and clandestine security apparatus to undermine China's trading partners. Washington depends on its long-standing ties with corrupt rulers, dissidents, journalists and media moguls to provide the powerful propaganda cover while advancing its military offensive against China's overseas interests.

China has nothing to compare with the US overseas 'security apparatus' because it practices a policy of "non-interference". Given the advanced state of the Western imperial offensive, China has taken only a few diplomatic initiatives, such as financing English language media outlets to present its perspective, using its veto power on the UN Security Council to oppose US efforts to overthrow the independent Assad regime in Syria and opposing the imposition of drastic sanctions against Iran.

It sternly repudiated US Secretary of State Hilary Clinton's vitriolic questioning of the 'legitimacy' of the Chinese state when it voted against the US-UN resolution preparing an attack on Syria.

Chinese military strategists are more aware and alarmed at the growing military threat to China. They have successfully demanded a 19% annual increase in military spending over the next five years (2011-2015). Even with this increase, China's military expenditures will still be less than one-fifth of the US military budget and China has not one overseas military base in stark contrast to the over 750 US installations abroad. Overseas Chinese intelligence operations are minimal and ineffective. Its embassies are run by and for narrow commercial interests who utterly failed to understand NATO's brutal policy of regime change in Libya and inform Beijing of its significance to the Chinese state.

There are two other structural weaknesses undermining China's rise as a world power. This includes the highly 'Westernized' intelligentsia which has uncritically swallowed US economic doctrine about free markets while ignoring its militarized economy. These Chinese intellectuals parrot the US propaganda about the 'democratic virtues' of billion-dollar Presidential campaigns, while supporting financial deregulation which would have led to a Wall Street takeover of Chinese banks and savings. Many Chinese business consultants and academics have been educated in the US and influenced by their ties to US academics and international financial institutions directly linked to Wall Street and the City of London.

They have prospered as highly-paid consultants receiving prestigious positions in Chinese institutions. They identify the 'liberalization of financial markets' with "advanced economies" capable of deepening ties to global markets instead of as a major source of the current global financial crisis. These "Westernized intellectuals" are like their 19th century comprador counterparts who underestimated and dismissed the long-term consequences of Western imperial penetration. They fail to understand how financial deregulation in the US precipitated the current crisis and how deregulation would lead to a Western takeover of China's financial system- the consequences of which would reallocate China's domestic savings to non-productive activities (real estate speculation), precipitate financial crisis and ultimately undermine China's leading global position.

These Chinese yuppies imitate the worst of Western consumerist life styles and their political outlooks are driven by these life styles and Westernized identities which preclude any sense of solidarity with their own working class.

There is an economic basis for the pro-Western sentiments of China's neo-compradors. They have transferred billions of dollars to foreign bank accounts, purchased luxury homes and apartments in London , Toronto , Los Angeles , Manhattan , Paris , Hong Kong and Singapore. They have one foot in China (the source of their wealth) and the other in the West (where they consume and hide their wealth).

Westernized compradores are deeply embedded in China's economic system having family ties with the political leadership in the party apparatus and the state. Their connections are weakest in the military and in the growing social movements, although some "dissident" students and academic activists in the "democracy movements" are backed by Western imperial NGO's. To the extent that the compradors gain influence, they weaken the strong economic state institutions which have directed China's ascent to global power, just as they did in the 19th century by acting as intermediaries for the British Empire. Proclaiming 19th Century "liberalism" British opium addicted over 50 million Chinese in less than a decade. Proclaiming "democracy and human rights" US gunboats now patrol off China's coast. China's elite-directed rise to global economic power has spawned monumental inequalities between the thousands of new billionaires and multi-millionaires at the top and hundreds of millions of impoverished workers, peasants and migrant workers at the bottom.

China s rapid accumulation of wealth and capital was made possible through the intense exploitation of its workers who were stripped of their previous social safety net and regulated work conditions guaranteed under Communism. Millions of Chinese households are being dispossessed in order to promote real estate developer/speculators who then build high rise offices and the luxury apartments for the domestic and foreign elite. These brutal features of ascendant Chinese capitalism have created a fusion of workplace and living space mass struggle which is growing every year. The developer/speculators' slogan "to get rich is wonderful" has lost its power to deceive the people. In 2011 there were over 200,000 popular encompassing urban coastal factories and rural villages. The next step, which is sure to come, will be the unification of these struggles into new national social movements with a class-based agenda demanding the restoration of health and educational services enjoyed under the Communists as well as a greater share of China's wealth. Current demands for greater wages can turn to demands for greater work place democracy. To answer these popular demands China's new compradore-Westernized liberals cannot point to their 'model' in the US empire where American workers are in the process of being stripped of the very benefits Chinese workers are struggling to regain.

China , torn by deepening class and political conflict, cannot sustain its drive toward global economic leadership. China's elite cannot confront the rising global imperial military threat from the US with its comprador allies among the internal liberal elite while the country is a deeply divided society with an increasingly hostile working class. The time of unbridled exploitation of China's labor has to end in order to face the US military encirclement of China and economic disruption of its overseas markets. China possesses enormous resources. With over $1.5 trillion dollars in reserves China can finance a comprehensive national health and educational program throughout the country.

China can afford to pursue an intensive 'public housing program' for the 250 million migrant workers currently living in urban squalor. China can impose a system of progressive income taxes on its new billionaires and millionaires and finance small family farmer co-operatives and rural industries to rebalance the economy. Their program of developing alternative energy sources, such as solar panels and wind farms – are a promising start to addressing their serious environmental pollution. Degradation of the environment and related health issues already engage the concern of tens of millions. Ultimately China's best defense against imperial encroachments is a stable regime based on social justice for the hundreds of millions and a foreign policy of supporting overseas anti-imperialist movements and regimes – whose independence are in China's vital interest. What is needed is a pro-active policy based on mutually beneficial joint ventures including military and diplomatic solidarity. Already a small, but influential, group of Chinese intellectuals have raised the issue of the growing US military threat and are "saying no to gunboat diplomacy".

Modern China has plenty of resources and opportunities, unavailable to China in the 19th century when it was subjugated by the British Empire. If the US continues to escalate its aggressive militaristic policy against China , Beijing can set off a serious fiscal crisis by dumping a few of its hundreds of billions of dollars in US Treasury notes. China , a nuclear power should reach out to its similarly armed and threatened neighbor, Russia , to confront and confound the bellicose rantings of US Secretary of State, Hilary Clinton. Russian President-to-be Putin vows to increase military spending from 3% to 6% of the GDP over the next decade to counter Washington's offensive missile bases on Russia's borders and thwart Obama's 'regime change' programs against its allies, like Syria.

China has powerful trading, financial and investment networks covering the globe as well as powerful economic partners.These links have become essential for the continued growth of many of countries throughout the developing world. In taking on China , the US will have to face the opposition of many powerful market-based elites throughout the world. Few countries or elites see any future in tying their fortunes to an economically unstable empire-based on militarism and destructive colonial occupations. In other words, modern China , as a world power, is incomparably stronger than it was in early 18th century. The US does not have the colonial leverage that the ascendant British Empire possessed in the run-up to the Opium Wars.

Moreover, many Chinese intellectuals and the vast majority of its citizens have no intention of letting its current "Westernized compradors" sell out the country. Nothing would accelerate political polarization in Chinese society and hasten the coming of a second Chinese social revolution more than a timid leadership submitting to a new era of Western imperial pillage.

STRUCTURE AND SIZE OF FINANCIAL SYSTEM IN CHINA

Until introduction of reforms in 1978, China's financial sector was essentially a monobank with the People's Bank of China (PBC) as the only bank. The PBC managed the deposits of state-owned enterprises (SOEs) and mobilised household savings. The current structure of the Chinese financial system reflects the significant institutional changes that have taken place over the last decade or so. The Chinese financial system, as it exists today, comprises commercial banks, co-operative banks, non-bank financial institutions and the capital market.

As at end-September 2004, the Chinese commercial banking system consisted of four wholly owned state-owned commercial banks (SOCBs), 12 nation-wide joint stock commercial banks (JSCBs), 112 city commercial banks (with business restricted to home city) and 162 foreign banks' branches and 14 subsidiaries or joint venture entities. The four state-owned commercial banks were originally established in the 1980s to serve different economic sectors and to extend loans for policy objectives.

In 1994, they were reestablished as commercial banks and officially absolved of their policy lending responsibilities. Since then they have expanded their operations beyond their original sectors and have come into competition with one another. JSCBs, which were initially created to provide specialised products, now offer a full range of financial services. They are partially owned by local government and state owned enterprises (SOEs) and in some cases by the corporate sector. Since 1994, China has set up three policy related banks under the State Council to assume the policy lending roles previously performed by the SOCBs. Policy banks operate on a no-profit no-loss basis and they do not compete with commercial banks. Unlike the SOCBs and other commercial banks, policy banks fund themselves through central bank loans, government deposits and issuance of government guaranteed bonds held by commercial banks. Policy banks primarily extend long-term loans for infrastructure projects. China also has four rural commercial banks.

The co-operative banking structure in China comprises 709 urban credit co-operatives and nearly 34,000 rural credit co-operatives. Chinese non-banking financial institutions consist of four asset management companies, 59 trust and investment companies, 74 finance companies, 12 financial leasing companies, four auto financing companies and several postal saving institutions.

The capital market in China is of recent origin. There are two stock exchanges, *viz.*, Shanghai Securities Exchange (SHSE) and Shenzhan Securities Exchange (SZSE). Until the establishment of SHSE, there was no capital market in China because the financial system was highly centralised.

Initially, Chinese firms issued four different classes of shares, *viz.*, State Shares, Legal Person Shares, 'A' Shares and Employees Shares. State and Legal Person Shares are non-tradable. Employees Shares are not tradable for a certain period after the issuance. Only 'A' shares are tradable upon issuing.

In 1992, the Chinese stock markets were opened to international investors with the aim of helping companies to obtain foreign financing and introduce a level of sophistication into the stock markets. For foreign investors, 'B' shares were created.

'B' shares can be owned only by foreign investors and have the same rights as 'A' shares which are owned only by the Chinese citizens. The recent data indicate that on an average State Shares, Legal Person Shares and A-Shares account for 30 per cent each of the total shares, with the remaining shares being accounted for by the 'B' shares and employees shares.

In addition to the above, around 70 Chinese firms have dual listing overseas, mainly in Hong Kong ('H' Shares) and New York ('N' Shares). The 'H' shares were introduced to facilitate the direct listings of Chinese companies on the Stock Exchange of Hong Kong, while 'N' shares were introduced for listing at New York Stock Exchange.

Listing on either SHSE or SZSE is through government consent. The State Planning Commission and the Securities Regulatory Commission set the quota for the total number of shares to be issued over the year after which is subsequently allocated among provinces. The number of listed firms on the two national stock exchanges increased to 1,378 as at end-October 2004 with the combined market capitalisation of two stock exchanges being at RMB 3,874 billion (US $ 468 billion) or 29.2 per cent of GDP.

Reforms in the Chinese Financial Sector

Financial sector reforms in China have been based on the following five broad tenets: First, a central bank was created and developed which has resulted in more effective conduct of monetary policy. Second, a diverse network of government financial intermediaries has been established. Third, measures have been initiated to develop the financial markets. Fourth, a system of financial regulation and supervision has been put in place. Finally, the financial sector is gradually and cautiously being opened up.

Following Shuangning (2004), various reforms introduced could be broadly divided into three phases.

Phase I (1978-1994): In 1978, the People's Bank of China (PBC) became independent of the Ministry of Finance. Until then, the PBC was responsible for a wide range of activities such as the conduct of monetary policy, exchange policy, foreign reserve management, deposit taking, commercial lending activities and the financing of development projects. During the Phase I, a two-tier banking system was created in which the PBC emerged as the central bank, while the Bank of China (BOC), the China Construction Bank (CCB), the Agricultural Bank of China (ABC) and the Industrial and Commercial Bank of China (ICBC) emerged as the specialised banks. The ABC specialised in rural credit; the CCB in fixed asset management, while the BOC in the foreign exchange business. With the restructuring of the PBC as the central bank, the ICBC was set up to serve a target client base consisting of industrial and commercial enterprises. In 1984, the PBC was specifically designated as the central bank of China. In 1992, the securities business supervision was transferred from the PBC to the newly established China Securities Regulatory Commission (CSRC) to supervise stock listing and trading activities.

Phase II (1994-1998): During Phase II, three policy banks, *viz.*, the China Development Bank, the Agricultural Development Bank of China and the Export-Import Bank of China were set up in 1994 to undertake the policy driven financing earlier assigned to specialised banks. Specialised banks, in turn, became commercial banks engaging in commercial financial business only. In 1994, the Company Law containing provisions on issuance, transacting and listing of public securities became effective.

Phase III (1998 onwards): This phase witnessed several significant reform initiatives, as set out below:

- As part of its WTO accession, China has committed to open the banking sector to foreign institutions by December 2006. Accordingly, China has been gradually opening its financial sector to foreign competition. 13 cities have been opened for foreign banks to conduct renminbi business. 100 eligible foreign banks were permitted to conduct renminbi business and 55 of them were allowed to provide renminbi services to the Chinese enterprises. Foreign banks have so far been allowed to provide 12 categories of services in China. The permitted equity holding in Chinese financial institutions by a single foreign investor has been raised from 15 per cent to 20 per cent, while the maximum foreign equity holding remains at 25 per cent.

- In 1998, the China Insurance Regulatory Commission (CIRC) was set up to take over the function of insurance business supervision from the central bank, *i.e.*, PBC. In 1999, the securities laws became operational, aimed at standardising the issuing and trading of securities, protecting investors and promoting the development of the socialist market economy. The Government's intention in developing the equity market was to improve the performance of relatively promising SOEs, regulating problematic ones through mergers and acquisition and raising funds to finance companies and budget.

- In 1999-2000, China set up three asset management companies (AMCs) for offloading RMB 1.4 billion of NPLs representing about 40 per cent of the estimated total NPLs of the big four banks. NPL transfers represented 'policy based' loans; the government took responsibility for bank losses related to policy lending prior to 1996 but not for loans made after 1996.

- In March 2003, the Chinese government made another big move in reforming the financial supervisory regime by creating the China Banking Regulatory Commission (CBRC) to assume the responsibility of supervising all banking institutions. The PBC is now expected to concentrate only on monetary policy matters. The Bank of Communications has further diversified its ownership to include a foreign strategic investor.

- A joint mechanism has been developed among the CBRC, the CSRC and the CIRC for co-operation among themselves.

- Among the specialised banks-turned commercial banks, the Bank of China (BOC) and the China Construction Bank (CCB) have completed the corporatisation process, *viz.*, corporate restructuring into shareholding banks. The BOC and the CCB were chosen to launch joint-stock restructuring on a pilot basis. The Chinese government invested US $ 45 billion from the official foreign exchange reserves at the end of 2003 into the BOC and the CCB to boost their capital aimed at building good corporate governance. The two banks are required to write off or dispose of their asset losses *via* market means. The CBRC promulgated Guidelines on Corporate Governance Reforms and Supervision of these two banks setting ten requirements for them to reform their management regime and systems, improve their corporate governance and operating mechanisms and thereby boost their profit-earning capacity. The CBRC also set seven benchmarks to assess the operational performance of the BOC and the CCB, requiring them to reach or surpass the average performance of the world's top 100 banks by the year 2007. The CBRC has asked the other two state-owned banks, *i.e.*, the ICBC and the ABC to follow the corporate governance guidelines to speed up the internal reforms and get ready for ownership restructuring.

China has introduced several monetary policy reforms as well moving from direct instruments of monetary control towards indirect system of monetary management.

Major Challenges faced by the Financial Sector in China

As part of its accession to the WTO, China has promised to open banking business in all places and in all currencies to foreign banks by 2006. After December 2006, foreign and domestic banks should be able to provide products to all customers in China throughout the country. With this, the banking system in China will face serious challenges; First, there is a large stock of NPLs in comparison with the international standards. Secondly, there is still a gap between the management and operational capacity of the wholly state-owned commercial banks and that of the world's leading banks. Third, the regulatory and supervisory system is not yet prepared for the complexities of the new situation.

The key focus of further reforms in the Chinese financial system is on resolution of NPLs problem. This requires concrete action plan on two fronts, *i.e*, to resolve the existing stock of NPLs and to avoid accumulation of further NPLs. The flow problem perhaps could be tackled by further enhancing commercial orientation of the lending operations of banks. Ceiling on interest rates as and when removed could also allow banks to price their products based on their risk-return perception. To overcome the stock problem, the authorities need to keep in view the experience of the four AMCs set up, which has not been satisfactory as their losses are expected to surpass the current financial contributions to the AMCs from both the Ministry of Finance and the PBC. Further improvements in bankruptcy and foreclosures would also enable banks to recover NPLs.

The further development of financial markets apart from imparting market discipline into the system, would have several other advantages. A balanced financial system, where both banks and financial markets play important roles, not only helps in averting crises, but also creates competitive conditions which would benefit both savers and investors. The capital market could help in improving allocative efficiency of resources by putting competitive pressures on the banking system. The financing needs of the Chinese economy appear to be far more than the lending capacity of banks. Those enterprises, which are not able to raise funds from the banking system could finance their requirements from the capital market. The capital market could, thus, help in spurring the growth of the private sector.

In China, ownership of shares is based on the status of the investor as well as of that of the company. There is no transferability between 'A' and 'B' shares, even as they are identical in respect of shareholder rights. Because of segmentation, the Chinese capital market is also not much integrated with other capital markets. Further integration with the international capital market could help China in reaping the benefits. The convertibility of state and legal person shares into 'A' class shares and making them tradable along with 'B' shares could also help in integrating its market further.

Administrative controls over raising of capital perhaps could be phsed out in favour of well defined and objective entry and disclosure norms. Reforms of the capital market in China could also include the development of the private debt market, which could provide the financing choices to the borrowers and the opportunity to diversify risk to the savers.

Impact of Reforms in China

Wide ranging reforms introduced in China have had a distinct positive impact. Average return on assets and average return on equity, however, declined significantly between 1996 and 2002, reflecting perhaps the impact of increased competition. Net interest margin, especially in respect of SOCBs declined significantly and is now at reasonable level by international standards, reflecting improvement in the cost of intermediation. A disconcerting feature, however, has been the overall deterioration in the ratio of equity to total asset and capital funds to liabilities ratio in respect of JSCBs; the ratios in respect of SOCBs have improved significantly.

There has been a steady increase in the number of companies listed on the stock exchanges in China. However, the size of the capital market measured both in absolute terms (market capitalisation) and in relation to the size of the economy has shrunk quite significantly in recent years. Liquidity in the stock market measured in terms of traded value ratio (turnover as percentage of GDP) has declined significantly during the last three years. The turnover ratio (turnover as percentage of market capitalization), after declining in 2002 and 2003 however, improved in 2004.

THE ISSUES CHINA WILL FACE IN THE FUTURE

Rebalancing the Chinese economy from export driven growth to consumer led growth is going to provide numerous challenges for China moving forward. The imbalances, rapid credit growth, and social policies most pressing to China in the future have been highlighted herewith.

Inflation and the 'Shadow Banking Crisis'

Decades of investment into the urban centres has led to the accumulation of billions in off balance sheet financing for companies and infrastructure projects. Some estimate the amount of off balance sheet lending is of a similar size to the regulated on balance sheet lending. Jamil Anderlini wrote in the Financial Times in April 2014

"After the 2008 collapse of Lehman Brothers and the ensuing global crisis, the Peoples Bank of China PBOC ordered the banks to lend indiscriminately in massive amounts to prop up slowing Chinese growth"

The relaxed and unregulated lending has the potential to lead to a liquidity and refinancing crisis, the magnitude of which China has not seen before. 50% of capital flows in China are now unregulated (*Anderlini 2014*). Current policies of increasing domestic consumption combined with a financial crisis could see interest rates spike as witnesses earlier this year. *"People familiar with the matter said relations between the two bodies (regulators & PBOC) turned especially nasty in June, when the central bank allowed liquidity to dry up in the interbank market. That sent short-term interest rates soaring and confronted investors with the prospect of a Chinese financial crisis for the first time in a decade.China's banks are feeding unwanted assets into the country's "shadow banking system" on an unprecedented scale, reinforcing suspicions that bank balance sheets reflect only a fraction of the actual credit risk lurking in the financial system"(Anderlini 2014).*

Resistance to reforms

Some in China view the increasing inequality as a result of reform, increasing the likelihood of resistance to future reforms. The current legislation regarding labour force flows, discriminate against a large part of the population, people in power or currently benefiting from the legislation e.g. urban 'hukou' or corrupt government officials will have motivation to resist change. (*Zengke 2000*)

Increasing wage pressures

Wages in China have been increasing faster than productivity gains since the 1990's. I predict this will continue in the future, diminishing the comparative advantage of the Chinese labour force. As China transitions to a middle wage economy, pressure will be put on policy makers for an increased standard of living, namely through reduced pollution and increased provisions for education and healthcare.

Currency appreciation

Many international markets wish for the Renminbi to appreciate, the advantage a low exchange has on an exporting economy is clear, with the 'Bigmac' index implying the Chinese currency is undervalued by 44% (2014). Currency speculation and freer capital flows, could appreciate the nominal exchange rate lowering Chinese competitiveness.

Increasing inequality

Liberal policies have led to reduced poverty in China. In 1990 60% of the population lived below the poverty line, by 2008 that number had fallen to 13% (*World Bank 2012*).Rising wages have not been dispersed equally, with the rural workers being discriminated against and left behind in the economic progression of China. Without careful management the disparity between rich and poor could lead to civil unrest and political upheaval.

Ageing Population

Chinas rampant population explosion during the 1950's after the Cultural Revolution led to the implementation of the one child policy in 1979. This policy achieved its goal of slowing the population growth but has led to unintended consequences as male children were favoured. The ageing population will put constraints on domestic consumption and healthcare.

In conclusion China is in a transitional phase; much like that of Japan and Korea two decades prior. The augmentation of China has been a leading illustration of neoliberal economic policy and the affects it has on progression.

The growing pains apparent pose jeopardies for China and the world going forward. China's evolution will be one scrutinised closely by the international community.

The development of social policies such as healthcare, subsidised education, pensions and welfare that are mutually inclusive to both urban and rural 'hukou' will assist the people of China to rebalance the economy. The increasing divide between urban and rural 'hukou' has the potential to destabilise the current regime and distinct consideration needs to be given in order to avoid a social underclass and minimise labour market distortions.

The suspicions of a 'Shadow Banking Crisis' are well justified, as are the apprehensions around inequality and discrimination. Social policy reform and financial reform are required to assist China through this transitional phase, the execution of which will prove delicate and challenging.

CHINA 2020: LOOKING TOWARD CHINA'S ECONOMIC FUTURE

The second presenter focused on the future of Chinese economic growth and its implications for internal domestic stability. First, he offered three basic scenarios for China—one in which China will become the world's second largest economy by the year 2020, another in which China experiences a slowdown over the next two decades, which in turns causes a loss of legitimacy for the CCP and possibly leads to disorder, and finally a scenario of economic stagnation.

The presenter noted that the high-growth scenario that is often touted in the popular press is probably not realistic; if it were likely,

China's gross domestic product (GDP) would have to reach $11.2 trillion in the year 2020 (compared with the U.S. at $15.4 trillion and Japan at $9.4 trillion).

Four major factors are barriers to high economic growth in China. First, there is the problem of low productivity growth. The presenter asserted that China's productivity growth is much less than is commonly believed and that it is difficult to convert China's high savings rate into useful capital that can then fuel additional productivity. Secondly, there is the problem of "animosity, bureaucracy and corruption".

Animosity refers to growing internal ethnic cleavages in China — such as the Uyghur separatist movement in China's western region. The impediment that bureaucracy presents is related to the "local-central" divide that persists between local governments and Beijing. Local governments often pursue policies that circumvent national directives. Corruption makes the problem worse. China is increasingly recognized as one of the most corrupt countries in the world.

A third factor is reliance on exports to fuel economic growth. Much of the enthusiasm about China's economic growth is rooted in the fact that exports have played such a prominent role. From 1987 to 1995, the real rate of Chinese export growth was 18.1% a year, which was significantly higher than the overall growth of the economy. Yet continued export growth at this rate is not realistic.

If China's exports to the United States, for example, were to continue at their present growth rate, they would constitute almost 80% of U.S. imports and the U.S. would likely have a trade deficit of 48% of GDP, an unlikely scenario. A similar dilemma involves foreign direct investment (FDI). Since 1980, foreign investment in China has grown at a rate of 35% a year; in 1995, moreover, foreign direct investment totaled about $35 billion. However, current evidence suggests that this trend is reversing.

Investors are realizing that China is not as profitable as they once believed. Moreover, continued FDI at past rates is not realistic: "With 35% annual growth, China's receipts of foreign capital will exceed all of Japan's foreign investment in two years and in ten years China would have to receive all of the international capital invested in the whole world."

Other constraints to economic growth in China include energy demand and environmental degradation. Regarding energy, China is already the world's largest energy consumer in the world, consuming 850 million metric tons of oil equivalent. China's energy demand is expected to jump significantly over the next 25 years. To satisfy its growing energy needs, China will most likely increase its dependence on imported energy.

In fact, China will likely become the world's largest energy importer by 2010, with most imports coming from the Persian Gulf and Siberian Russia. Growing energy demand and consumption portends massive environmental consequences. Roughly 300,000 Chinese citizens in urban areas annually suffer premature deaths due to outdoor or indoor pollution.

If environmental standards continued to be ignored by Beijing, the "cumulative effect of deteriorating air and water quality will sharply reduce both the country's productive capacity and the living standards of the Chinese people."

Overall, the presenter proposed three scenarios for the future of Chinese economic growth: the "medium growth" scenario, the "low growth" scenario, and the "economic stagnation" scenario. The presenter argued that the "low growth" scenario was the most likely. Under this scenario, China's real growth would average about 4% a year and by 2020 China's GDP would likely total about $2.6 trillion. This GDP would make China the fifth largest economy, placing it squarely between Korea ($3.2 trillion) and France ($2.4 trillion).

The presenter noted that if the "low growth" scenario actually takes place, it could be devastating for the Chinese Communist Party which, as a substitute for its loss of ideological legitimacy, has maintained a bargain with the Chinese people "to deliver the goods." If the CCP is not able to improve the material welfare of the Chinese people, it will likely face opposition to its rule—most likely from provincial governments—and this could in turn lead to political instability.

The People's Liberation Army: Social and Political Implications of Restructuring

Most of the analysts who follow the People's Liberation Army (PLA) focus on China's military purchases from Russia and the PLA's threat to Taiwan while ignoring the volatility of the internal security problem in China. Members of the PLA are facing the same economic difficulties that other segments of the Chinese population are facing. The demographics of an aging population leave a smaller manpower pool available for military service, a problem exacerbated by the one-child policy. If the government cannot provide the expected social and health safety net for the elderly, leaving the burden on families, the incentive for a young person to serve in the military is lower.

Military pay is barely sufficient to sustain the soldier, let alone a family, and military service takes the child away from the family. Because pay is so low in the security organs of China, whether it be the PLA, People's Armed Police (PAP), or the Public Security Bureau, the incentive to engage in corruption is quite high. In short the leadership cannot isolate the members of its security organs from some of the same problems caused by economic re-structuring that members of the population at large are facing.

If any of the difficulties mentioned earlier grow to the point where the intervention of any of China's security branches is required, the loyalty of those branches in a crisis may be suspect.

Low pay and outside opportunities have created both recruiting and retention problems for the PAP and the PLA. If a family member leaves the farm, he or she tends to migrate to the urban labor market and thereby avoids military or paramilitary service.

The disincentives to join the military and the incentives to avoid conscription are higher now than they ever have been in China for four reasons.

- With the high losses incurred against the attack on Vietnam, it became clear that it was dangerous to send a child into military service.
- Sending a son or daughter into military service is a poor economic choice.
- Due to the actions of the PLA in 1989, entering the military is a distasteful political option.
- As the Party slowly loses its mantle of legitimacy, doing anything for the Party or state organs of power increasingly becomes a meaningless political choice.

The degree of loyalty to the party within the PAP may be more highly suspect than that of the PLA. Following basic training, PAP troops are generally not isolated from the general population as are the troops of the PLA. Because they are not confined to the barracks, they have opportunities to mingle with the populace. They generally enjoy close relationships with the local families and children where they work. Generally speaking, because of this familiarity, the PAP was reluctant or failed to use force against the population in Beijing in 1989. That is why the PLA was tapped to restore order. To avoid using the PLA in the future, the Central Military Commission has increased the numbers of the PAP by converting whole divisions of the PLA to the PAP.

Thus the Party's leadership hopes that if it again becomes necessary to suppress large segments of the total population, they can depend on the new PAP units.

In addition to suspect loyalty, there is another internal security problem looming in the background. The PLA has demobilized thousands of soldiers who have received basic military training. Moreover, workers in the countryside and in the cities have either served in the military or have received militia training. China now has a large group of people who know how to use violence and manage force in an organized way.

Many people in this large pool are disgruntled due to the economic and social problems mentioned earlier. The problem is further compounded by the previously mentioned state of affairs in the SOEs. The potential for labor unrest in the SOEs is high. The one million-plus officers and soldiers in the reserve forces of the PLA are primarily located in the state or collectively owned enterprises of one form or another. The presenter ended this session with the following questions:

"In the past, the CCP has always been able to call on the PLA to suppress unrest when it was ordered to do so. And in the near term, it can probably count on the PLA again.

But if the PLA faces parts of the PAP and its own reserve divisions, will it act resolutely? Or will things devolve into a general breakdown of the government? This is the dilemma that China's leaders face, and they are riding a tiger they are having difficulty controlling as they liberalize the economy."

Conclusion

Throughout the seminar, two themes remained constant: Because China faces so many internal problems and many nations in the region have experience in managing similar problems, there is ample opportunity for other countries to share their expertise with China. Such cooperation may create an atmosphere that could be extended to more sensitive realms of security as nuclear non-proliferation and border disputes. Secondly, all participants agreed that China is still far away from a Soviet style collapse; however, should China be unable to solve one or more of the many challenges it faces, the result will be some decrease in the internal stability of China. Restructuring the economy has created a degree of fragmentation in China.

Fragmentation can be a destabilizing factor for any regime. The leadership will react but how? Will it become more strict or perhaps even more intolerant of opposition? Will it divert attention away from internal problems by whipping up an already nascent nationalism? The very scale of China (large population, geographic size and location, etc.) implies that any degree of instability in China will likely affect the region as a whole. Hence there is even more incentive for China's neighbors to work with China on cooperative solutions to the challenges that China faces.

2

Economy History of China

The People's Republic of China (PRC) is the world's second largest economy by nominal GDP and by purchasing power parity after the United States. It is the world's fastest-growing major economy, with growth rates averaging 10% over the past 30 years. China is also the largest exporter and second largest importer of goods in the world. On a per capita income basis, China ranked 90th by nominal GDP and 91st by GDP (PPP) in 2011, according to the International Monetary Fund (IMF). The provinces in the coastal regions of China tend to be more industrialized, while regions in the hinterland are less developed. As China's economic importance has grown, so has attention to the structure and health of the economy.

OVERVIEW

In the modern era, China's influence in the world economy was minimal until the late 1980s. At that time, economic reforms initiated after 1978 began to generate significant and steady growth in investment, consumption and standards of living. As of 2012 China is a major importer of raw materials, manufacturer of basic goods, and exporter of consumer goods. The economy is dominated by large, profitable, state owned enterprises, but private enterprises also play a major role in the economy. State-owned enterprises are a major source of profit and power for members of the Communist Party of China and their families and are favoured by the government. Since 1978 hundreds of millions have been lifted out of poverty – yet hundred of millions of rural population as well as millions of migrant workers remain unattended: According to China's official statistics, the poverty rate fell from 53% in 1981 to 2.5% in 2005. However, in 2009, as many as 150 million Chinese were living on less than $1.25 a day The infant mortality rate fell by 39.5% between 1990 and 2005, and maternal mortality by 41.1%. Access to telephones during the period rose more than 94-fold, to 57.1%, as did in many developing countries such as Peru or Nigeria.

In the 1949 revolution, China's economic system was officially made into a communist system. Since the wide-ranging reforms of the 1980s and afterwards, many scholars assert that China can be defined as one of the leading examples of state capitalism today.

China has generally implemented reforms in a gradualist fashion. As its role in world trade has steadily grown, its importance to the international economy has also increased apace. China's foreign trade has grown faster than its GDP for the past 25 years. China's growth comes both from huge state investment in infrastructure and heavy industry and from private sector expansion in light industry instead of just exports, whose role in the economy appears to have been significantly overestimated. The smaller but highly concentrated public sector, dominated by 159 large SOEs, provided key inputs from utilities, heavy industries, and energy resources that facilitated private sector growth and drove investment, the foundation of national growth. In 2008 thousands of private companies closed down and the government announced plans to expand the public sector to take up the slack caused by the global financial crisis. In 2010, there were approximately 10 million small businesses in China.

The PRC government's decision to permit China to be used by multinational corporations as an export platform has made the country a major competitor to other Asian export-led economies, such as South Korea, Singapore, and Malaysia. China has emphasized raising personal income and consumption and introducing new management systems to help increase productivity. The government has also focused on foreign trade as a major vehicle for economic growth. The restructuring of the economy and resulting efficiency gains have contributed to a more than tenfold increase in GDP since 1978. Some economists believe that Chinese economic growth has been in fact understated during much of the 1990s and early 2000s, failing to fully factor in the growth driven by the private sector and that the extent at which China is dependent on exports is exaggerated despite the lack of full convertibility of the RMB. Nevertheless, key bottlenecks continue to constrain growth. Available energy is insufficient to run at fully installed industrial capacity, and the transport system is inadequate to move sufficient quantities of such critical items ascoal.

The two most important sectors of the economy have traditionally been agriculture and industry, which together employ more than 70 percent of the labor force and produce more than 60 percent of GDP. The two sectors have differed in many respects. Technology, labor productivity, and incomes have advanced much more rapidly in industry than in agriculture. Agricultural output has been vulnerable to the effects of weather, while industry has been more directly influenced by the government. The disparities between the two sectors have combined to form an economic-cultural-social gap between the rural and urban areas. China is the world's largest producer of rice and is among the principal sources of wheat, corn (maize), tobacco, soybeans, peanuts(groundnuts), and cotton. The country is one of the world's largest producers of a number of industrial and mineral products, including cotton cloth, tungsten, and antimony, and is an important producer of cotton yarn, coal, crude oil, and a number of other products. Its mineral resources are probably among the richest in the world but are only partially developed.

China has acquired highly sophisticated foreign production facilities and through "localization policies" also built a number of advanced engineer ingplants capable of manufacturing an increasing range of sophisticated equipment, including nuclear weapons and satellites, but most of its industrial output still comes from relatively ill-equipped factories. The technological level and quality standards of its industry as a whole are still disastrous, notwithstanding a marked change since 2000, spurred in part by foreign investment. A report by UBS in 2009 concluded that China has experienced total factor productivity growth of 4 per cent per year since 1990, one of the fastest improvements in world economic history.

China's increasing integration with the international economy and its growing efforts to use market forces to govern the domestic allocation of goods have exacerbated this problem. Over the years, large subsidies were built into the price structure, and these subsidies grew substantially in the late 1970s and 1980s.By the early 1990s these subsidies began to be eliminated, in large part due to China's admission into the World Trade Organization (WTO) in 2001, which carried with it requirements for further economic liberalization and deregulation. China's ongoing economic transformation has had a profound impact not only on China but on the world. The market-oriented reforms

China has implemented over the past two decades have unleashed individual initiative and entrepreneurship, whilst retaining state domination of the economy.

HISTORY

By 1949, continuous foreign invasions, frequent revolutions and restorations, and civil wars had left the country with a fragile economy with little infrastructure. As Communist ascendancy seemed inevitable, almost all hard and foreign currency in China country were transported to Taiwan in 1948, making the war-time inflation even worse.

Since the formation of the PRC, an enormous effort was made towards creating economic growth and entire new industries were created. Tight control of budget and money supply reduced inflation by the end of 1950. Though most of it was done at the expense of suppressing the private sector of small to big businesses by the Three-anti/five-anti campaigns between 1951 to 1952. The campaigns were notorious for being anti-capitalist, and imposed charges that allowed the government to punish capitalists with severe fines. In the beginning of the Communist party's rule, the leaders of the party had agreed that for a nation such as China, which does not have any heavy industry and minimal secondary production, capitalism is to be utilized to help the building of the "New China" and finally merged into communism.

The new government nationalized the country's banking system and brought all currency and credit under centralized control. It regulated prices by establishing trade associations and boosted government revenues by collecting agricultural taxes. By the mid-1950s, the communists had ruined the country's railroad and highway systems, barely brought the agricultural and industrial production to their prewar levels, by bringing the bulk of China's industry and commerce under the direct control of the state.

Meanwhile, in fulfilment of their revolutionary promise, China's communist leaders completed land reform within two years of coming to power, eliminating landlords and redistribute their land and other possessions to peasant households.

Mao tried in 1958 to push China's economy to new heights. Under his highly touted "Great Leap Forward", agricultural collectives were reorganized into enormous communes where men and women were assigned in military fashion to specific tasks. Peasants were told to stop relying on the family, and instead adopted a system of communal kitchens, mess halls, and nurseries. Wages were calculated along the communist principle of "From each according to his ability, to each according to his need", and sideline production was banned as incipient capitalism. All Chinese citizens were urged to boost the country's steel production by establishing "backyard steel furnaces" to help overtake the West. The Great Leap Forward quickly revealed itself as a giant step backwards. Over-ambitious targets were set, falsified production figures were duly reported, and Chinese officials lived in an unreal world of miraculous production increases. By 1960, agricultural production in the countryside had slowed dangerously and large areas of China were gripped by a devastating famine.

For the next several years, China experienced a period of relative stability. Agricultural and industrial production returned to normal levels, and labor productivity began to rise. Then, in 1966, Mao proclaimed a Cultural Revolution to "put China back on track". Under orders to "Destroy the Four Olds" (old thoughts, culture, customs and habits), universities and schools closed their doors, and students, who became Mao's "Red Guards", were sent throughout the country to make revolution, beating and torturing anyone whose rank or political thinking offended. By 1969 the country had descended into anarchy, and factions of the Red Guards had begun to fight among themselves.

1978–1990

Reforms began with Li Xiannian and Deng Xiaoping, Chinese leaders in 80s. Unlike Mao, Deng and Li were pragmatic leaders, known less for their ideological commitment than for their slogan: "Who cares if a cat is black or white, as long as it catches the mice." Once they consolidated their power, they began to put their pragmatic policies to work, determined to bring China back from the devastation that the Cultural Revolution had wrought.

Since 1978, China began to make major reforms to its economy. The Chinese leadership adopted a pragmatic perspective on many political and socioeconomic problems, and quickly began to introduce aspects of a capitalist economic system. Political and social stability, economic productivity, and public and consumer welfare were considered paramount and indivisible. In these years, the government emphasized raising personal income and consumption and introducing new management systems to help increase productivity. The government also had focused on foreign trade as a major vehicle for economic growth. In the 1980s, China tried to combine central planning with market-oriented reforms to increase productivity, living standards, and technological quality without exacerbating inflation, unemployment, and budget deficits. Reforms began in the agricultural, industrial, fiscal, financial, banking, price setting, and labor systems.

A decision was made in 1978 to permit foreign direct investment in several small "special economic zones" along the coast. The country lacked the legal infrastructure and knowledge of international practices to make this prospect attractive for many foreign businesses, however. In the early 1980s steps were taken to expand the number of areas that could accept foreign investment with a minimum of red tape, and related efforts were made to develop the legal and other infrastructures necessary to make this work well.This additional effort resulted in making 14 coastal cities and three coastal regions "open areas" for foreign investment. All of these places provide favoured tax treatment and other advantages for foreign investment. Laws on contracts, patents, and other matters of concern to foreign businesses were also passed in an effort to attract international capital to spur China's development. The largely bureaucratic nature of China's economy, however, posed a number of inherent problems for foreign firms that wanted to operate in the Chinese environment, and China gradually had to add more incentives to attract foreign capital.

Reform in the Countryside

When Deng came into power, China's vast peasantry was still organized in communes, work brigades, and production teams. Procurement prices were too low to cover even production costs, and ceilings were set on the amount of grain that producers could keep for consumption. Deng changed all that. He allowed farmers to produce on their own and sanctioned the sale of surplus production and other cash crops in newly freed markets. State procurement prices were raised, and prices for many agricultural goods were left to the dictates of the market. Beginning with the poor mountain areas of Anhui and then spreading across the country, Deng and his officials broke up the communes established by Mao and replaced them with a complicated system of leases that eventually brought effective land tenure back to the household level (even though ownership of land remained collective). The Household Responsibility System allowed peasants to lease land for a fixed period from the collective, provided they delivered to the collective a minimum quota of produce, usually basic grain.

They could then sell any surplus they produced, either to the state at government procurement prices or on the newly free market. They were also free to retain any profits they might earn. Within a decade, grain production had grown by roughly 30%, and production of cotton, sugarcane, tobacco, and fruit had doubled.

RURAL INDUSTRIALIZATION AND ENTERPRISE REFORM

As the reforms fuelled production increases that surprised even the reformers, the scale of change grew bolder, and by the mid-1980s, the party leadership had begun the more complicated and politically delicate task of transforming the country's cumbersome system of central planning and state-owned enterprise. Prior to 1978, enterprises were almost all owned by the state in one form or another. At the top of each sector were the State-owned Enterprises (SOEs), answerable to the national government. Below these were other enterprises reporting to provincial, municipal, or county authorities. Private enterprises, meaning family-run shops, were not allowed until after 1978, and even then they were limited to seven employees.

China's SOEs were typical of large industrial firms in a centrally planned economy. Inefficient, overstaffed, and with outdated technology, they functioned not only as industrial units but also as social agencies, providing housing, daycare, education, and health care for the workers and their families. The largest enterprises included hundreds of thousands of employees, only a small proportion of whom were directly engaged in production.

The update of this system was that Chinese workers could expect both lifetime employment and an extensive, firm-based welfare system—the so-called "iron rice bowl". All welfare entitlements in this system were accounted for as costs of production and were deducted from revenues before the calculation of the profits that were to be remitted to the state. There was no national social security system because none was needed.

1990–2000

In the 1990s, the Chinese economy continued to grow at a rapid pace, at about 9.5%, accompanied by a rapidly increasing inflation, which reached over 20 percent in 1994. The Asian financial crisis affected China at the margin, mainly through decreased foreign direct investment and a sharp drop in the growth of its exports. However,

China had huge reserves, a currency that was not freely convertible, and capital inflows that consisted overwhelmingly of long-term investment. For these reasons it remained largely insulated from the regional crisis and its commitment not to devalue had been a major stabilizing factor for the region. However, China faced slowing growth and rising unemployment based on internal problems, including a financial system burdened by huge amounts of bad loans, and massive layoffs stemming from aggressive efforts to reform state-owned enterprises (SOEs).

Despite China's impressive economic development during the past two decades, reforming the state sector and modernizing the banking system remained major hurdles. Over half of China's state-owned enterprises were inefficient and reporting losses. During the15th National Communist Party Congress that met in September 1997, President Jiang Zemin announced plans to sell, merge, or close the vast majority of SOEs in his call for increased "non-public ownership" (*feigong you* or privatization.) The 9th National People's Congress endorsed the plans at its March 1998 session. In 2000, China claimed success in its three year effort to make the majority of large state owned enterprises (SOEs) profitable.

2000–2010

Following the Chinese Communist Party's Third Plenum, held in October 2003, Chinese legislators unveiled several proposed amendments to the state constitution. One of the most significant was a proposal to provide protection for private property rights. Legislators also indicated there would be a new emphasis on certain aspects of overall government economic policy, including efforts to reduce unemployment (now in the 8–10% range in urban areas), to rebalance income distribution between urban and rural regions, and to maintain economic growth while protecting the environment and improving social equity. The National People's Congress approved the amendments when it met in March 2004. The Fifth Plenum in October 2005 approved the 11th Five-Year Economic Program (2006–2010) aimed at building a "harmonious society" through more balanced wealth distribution and improved education, medical care, and social security. On March 2006, the National People's Congress approved the 11th Five-Year Program. The plan called for a relatively conservative 45% increase in GDP and a 20% reduction in energy intensity (energy consumption per unit of GDP) by 2010.

China's economy grew at an average rate of 10% per year during the period 1990–2004, the highest growth rate in the world. China's GDP grew 10.0% in 2003, 10.1%, in 2004, and even faster 10.4% in 2005 despite attempts by the government to cool the economy. China's total trade in 2010 surpassed $2.97 trillion, making China the world's second-largest trading nation after the U.S. Such high growth is necessary if China is to generate the 15 million jobs needed annually—roughly the size of Ecuador or Cambodia—to employ new entrants into the national job market.

On January 14, 2009, as confirmed by the World Bank the NBS published the revised figures for 2007 fiscal year in which growth happened at 13 percent instead of 11.9 percent (provisional figures). China's gross domestic product stood at US$3.38 trillion whileGermany's GDP was USD $3.32 trillion for 2007. This made China the world's third largest economy by gross domestic product. Based on these figures, in 2007 China recorded its fastest growth since 1994 when the GDP grew by 13.1 percent.

China launched its Economic Stimulus Plan to specifically deal with the Global financial crisis of 2008–2009. It has primarily focused on increasing affordable housing, easing credit restrictions for mortgage and SMEs, lower taxes such as those on real estate sales and commodities, pumping more public investment into infrastructure development, such as the rail network, roads and ports. By the end of 2009 it appeared that the Chinese economy was showing signs of recovery. At the 2009 Economic Work Conference in December 'managing inflation expectations' was added to the list of economic objectives, suggesting a strong economic upturn and a desire to take steps to manage it.

2010–present

By 2010 it was evident to outside observers such as *The New York Times* that China was poised to move from export dependency to development of an internal market. Wages were rapidly rising in all areas of the country and Chinese leaders were calling for an increased standard of living. In 2010, China's GDP was valued at $5.87 trillion, surpassed Japan's $5.47 trillion, and became the world's second largest economy after the U.S. China could become the world's largest economy (by nominal GDP) sometime as early as 2020.

China is the largest creditor nation in the world and owns approximately 20.8% of all foreign-owned US Treasury securities. It has also appeared that Noopolitik and the knowledge economy had become salient interests of the PRC's economic policy across the 2000s, through which the country made clear its move from "Made in China" to "Innovated in China" as notes Adam Segal. Idriss Aberkane thus argued "With China's cosmopolitan and highly educated diaspora, it is no surprise that as of 2010, five of the top twenty most visited websites in the world are indexed in Mandarin. They include PRC-born behemoths such as Baidu.com, Taobao.com, andSina.com.cn, and video sharing Tudou.com, which has gained users in both North America and Europe."

The Institute of Economic Research of Renmin University of China has conducted several studies and released several reports regarding China's economy. "Under the influences of 2009's stimulus policies, the spread of the economic bubble and implementation of the "12th Five-Year Plan", China was at a key stage of steering the economic recovery to stable growth. While prices increased steadily, China's GDP went back to the high-level growth rate and its economic structure gradually became market-oriented.". The foremost authorities on the Chinese economy — those within the Chinese think-tanks and government — give a unique, first-hand perspective. Their works, translated into English for a Western audience, are published only through an independent Hong Kong publishing house,Enrich Professional Publishing (EPP), and can be found at academic libraries throughout the world. The World Bank's chief economist Justin Lin in 2011 stated that China, which became the world's second largest economy in 2010, may become the world's largest economy in 2030, overtaking the United States, if current trends continue. Challenges include income inequality and pollution. The Standard Chartered Bank in a 2011 report suggested that China may become the world's largest economy in 2020. A 2007 OECD rapport by Angus Maddison estimated that if using purchasing power parity conversions, then China will overtake the United States in 2015. James Wolfensohn, former World Bank president, estimated in 2010 that by 2030 two-thirds of the world's middle class will live in China. The Director of the China Centre for Economic Reform at Peking University Yao Yang in 2011 stated that "Assuming that the Chinese and U.S. economies grow, respectively, by 8% and 3% in real terms, that China's inflation rate is 3.6% and America's is 2% (the averages of the last decade), and that the renminbi appreciates against the dollar by 3% per year (the average of the last six years), China would become the world's largest economy by 2021. By that time, both countries' GDP will be about $24 trillion."

In 2011, the IMF warned that government controlled banks could be building up imbalances that could hamper growth and leave the system "severely impacted". In 2011, the IMF predicted that China's GDP (purchasing power parity adjusted) would overtake that of the United States in 2016.

Government Role

Since 1949 the government, under socialist political and economic system, has been responsible for planning and managing the national economy. In the early 1950s, the foreign trade system was monopolized by the state. Nearly all the domestic enterprises were state-owned and the government had set the prices for key commodities, controlled the level and general distribution of investment funds, determined output targets for major enterprises and branches, allocated energy resources, set wage levels and employment targets, operated the wholesale and retail networks, and steered the financial policy and banking system. In the countryside from the mid-1950s, the government established cropping patterns, set the level of prices, and fixed output targets for all major crops.

Since 1978 when economic reforms were instituted, the government's role in the economy has lessened by a great degree. Industrial output by state enterprises slowly declined, although a few strategic industries, such as the aerospace industry have today remained predominantly state-owned. While the role of the government in managing the economy has been reduced and the role of both private enterprise and market forces increased, the government maintains a major role in the urban economy.

With its policies on such issues as agricultural procurement the government also retains a major influence on rural sector performance. The State Constitution of 1982specified that the state is to guide the country's economic development by making broad decisions on economic priorities and policies, and that the State Council, which exercises executive control, was to direct its subordinate bodies in preparing and implementing the national economic plan and the state budget. A major portion of the government system (bureaucracy) is devoted to managing the economy in a top-down chain of command with all but a few of the more than 100 ministries, commissions, administrations, bureaus, academies, and corporations under the State

Council being concerned with economic matters. Each significant economic sector is supervised by one or more of these organizations, which includes the People's Bank of China, National Development and Reform Commission, Ministry of Finance, and the ministries of agriculture; coal industry; commerce; communications; education; light industry; metallurgical industry; petroleum industry; railways; textile industry; and water resources and electric power. Several aspects of the economy are administered by specialized departments under the State Council, including the National Bureau of Statistics, Civil Aviation Administration of China, and the tourism bureau. Each of the economic organizations under the State Council directs the units under its jurisdiction through subordinate offices at the provincial and local levels.

The whole policy-making process involves extensive consultation and negotiation. Economic policies and decisions adopted by the National People's Congress and the State Council are to be passed on to the economic organizations under the State Council, which incorporates them into the plans for the various sectors of the economy. Economic plans and policies are implemented by a variety of direct and indirect control mechanisms. Direct control is exercised by designating specific physical output quotas and supply allocations for some goods and services.

Indirect instruments — also called "economic levers" — operate by affecting market incentives. These included levying taxes, setting prices for products and supplies, allocating investment funds, monitoring and controlling financial transactions by the banking system, and controlling the allocation of key resources, such as skilled labor, electric power, transportation, steel, and chemicals (including fertilizers). The main advantage of including a project in an annual plan is that the raw materials, labor, financial resources, and markets are guaranteed by directives that have the weight of the law behind them. In reality, however, a great deal of economic activity goes on outside the scope of the detailed plan, and the tendency has been for the plan to become narrower rather than broader in scope. A major objective of the reform program was to reduce the use of direct controls and to increase the role of indirect economic levers. Major state-owned enterprises still receive detailed plans specifying physical quantities of key inputs and products from their ministries. These corporations, however, have been increasingly affected by prices and allocations that were determined through market interaction and only indirectly influenced by the central plan. Total economic enterprise in China is apportioned along lines of directive planning (mandatory), indicative planning (indirect implementation of central directives), and those left to market forces.

In the early 1980s during the initial reforms enterprises began to have increasing discretion over the quantities of inputs purchased, the sources of inputs, the variety of products manufactured, and the production process. Operational supervision over economic projects has devolved primarily to provincial, municipal, and county governments. The majority of state-owned industrial enterprises, which were managed at the provincial level or below, were partially regulated by a combination of specific allocations and indirect controls, but they also produced goods outside the plan for sale in the market. Important, scarce resources — for example, engineers or finished steel — may have been assigned to this kind of unit in exact numbers. Less critical assignments of personnel and materials would have been authorized in a general way by the plan, but with procurement arrangements left up to the enterprise management.

In addition, enterprises themselves are gaining increased independence in a range of activity. While strategically important industry and services and most of large-scale construction have remained under directive planning, the market economy has gained rapidly in scale every year as it subsumes more and more sectors. Overall, the Chinese industrial system contains a complex mixture of relationships. The State Council generally administers relatively strict control over resources deemed to be of vital concern for the performance and health of the entire economy. Less vital aspects of the economy have been transferred to lower levels for detailed decisions and management. Furthermore, the need to coordinate entities that are in different organizational hierarchies generally causes a great deal of informal bargaining and consensus building.

Consumer spending has been subject to a limited degree of direct government influence but is primarily determined by the basic market forces of income levels and commodity prices. Before the reform period, key goods were rationed when they were in short supply, but by the mid-1980s availability had increased to the point that rationing was discontinued for everything except grain, which could also be purchased in the free markets. Collectively owned units and the agricultural sector were regulated primarily by indirect instruments. Each collective unit was "responsible for its own profit and loss," and the prices of its inputs and products provided the major production incentives.

Vast changes were made in relaxing the state control of the agricultural sector from the late 1970s. The structural mechanisms for implementing state objectives—the people's communes and their subordinate teams and brigades—have been either entirely eliminated or greatly diminished. Farm incentives have been boosted both by price increases for state-purchased agricultural products, and it was permitted to sell excess production on a free market. There was more room in the choice of what crops to grow, and peasants are allowed to contract for land that they will work, rather than simply working most of the land collectively. The system of procurement quotas (fixed in the form of contracts) has been being phased out, although the state can still buy farm products and control surpluses in order to affect market conditions.

Foreign trade is supervised by the Ministry of Commerce, customs, and the Bank of China, the foreign exchange arm of the Chinese banking system, which controls access to the foreign currency required for imports. Ever since restrictions on foreign trade were reduced, there have been broad opportunities for individual enterprises to engage in exchanges with foreign firms without much intervention from official agencies.

Though private sector companies still dominate small and medium sized businesses, the government still plays a large part in the bigger industries. The fact that government accounts for a third of the GDP shows this. Foreign owned companies hold significant stakes. The public sector is mainly made up of State-Owned Enterprises (SOEs).

LABOUR SHORTAGES AND RISING EXPORT COSTS

By 2005, there were signs of stronger demand for workers being able to choose employment that offered higher wages and better working conditions, enabling some to move away from the restrictive dormitory life and boring marriage work that have characterized export industries in provinces such as Guangdong and Fujian. Minimum wages began rising toward the equivalent of 100 U.S. dollars a month as companies scrambled for employees, with some paying as much as $150 a month on average. The labour shortage was partially driven by the demographic trends, as the proportion of people of working age fell as the result of strict family planning.

It was reported in *The New York Times* in April 2006 that labour costs continued to increase and a shortage of unskilled labour had developed with a million or more employees being sought.

Operations that relied on cheap labour were contemplating relocations to cities in the interior or to other low-cost countries such as Vietnam or Bangladesh. Many young people were attending college rather than opting for minimum-wage factory work. The demographic shift resulting from the one-child policy continued to reduce the supply of young entry-level workers. Also, government efforts to advance economic development in the interior of the country were beginning to be effective at creating better opportunities there.

A follow-up article in *The New York Times* in late August 2007 reported acceleration of this trend. The minimum wage a young unskilled factory worker could be hired at had increased to $200 with experienced workers commanding more. There was strong demand for young workers willing to work long hours and live in dormitory conditions, while older workers, over forty, were considered unsuitable.

Rising wages were being, to a certain extent, offset by increases in productivity, but in 2007, a slight rise in the cost of imports from China was recorded by the United States government: "After falling since its inception in December 2003, the price index for imports from China rose 0.4 percent in July 2007, the largest monthly increase since the index was first published in December 2003. The July increase was the third consecutive monthly advance. Over the past year, import prices from China increased 0.9 percent." By February 2008, concerns were being raised that rising wages and inflation in China were beginning to create inflationary pressure in the United States and Europe, which had depended on cheap prices for consumer goods from China exerting downward pressure on prices.

On January 1, 2008, China introduced a new Labour Law, increasing the rights of the workforce, this caused many foreign and private companies, whose operations in China were based on low wages, to move to countries with lower labour costs, like Thailand, Vietnam or Bangladesh. In the summer of 2008 the growth in export orders began to fall sharply as the sub-prime crisis in export markets reduced demand in Guangdong province, particularly in toy and textile manufacture. According to Chinese Government sources 20 million jobs in 67,000 factories were reported to have been lost. The government initially was happy to see factories close down in labour intensive low wage factories, and the Labour law was seen as a means of helping to eradicate them, but the global financial crisis led to a far more rapid process of private sector collapse in Guangdong than was expected, raising fears of a contagious spread of social unrest.

In early 2010 a labour shortage developed in coastal areas with many migrant workers not returning after the new year holiday. Wages rose rapidly with temp agencies charging over $1.00 US per hour for factory workers in Guangzhou. Following the strikes in 2010 at Japanese auto plants, the shortage continued with many factories unable to fully staff their factories. Failure to return from the new year holiday has become an annual occurrence, resulting in labour shortages and increases in wages as companies struggle to fill empty slots. According to Fan Gang, professor of economics at Beijing University and director of China's National Economic Research Institute, due to the large volume of workers engaged in relatively unremunerative agricultural work there is considerable room for increased nominal wages in China without changing the competitive position of the Chinese export industry for the next few decades. Lower wages in other countries may not represent productivity comparable to the increasing productivity of Chinese workers. The alternative view is that China is near the Lewisian turning point where surplus agricultural labour has been exhausted and a shortage of labour results in increases in wages.

3

Chinese Economic Development

China's socialist market economy is the world's second largest economy by nominal GDP, and the world's largest economy by purchasing power parity according to the IMF, although China's National Bureau of Statistic denies this claim. Until 2015 China was the world's fastest-growing major economy, with growth rates averaging 10% over 30 years. Due to historical and political facts of China's developing economy, China's public sector accounts for a bigger share of the national economy than the burgeoning private sector. On a per capita income basis, China ranked 71st by GDP (nominal) and 78th by GDP (PPP) in 2016, according to the International Monetary Fund (IMF).

China is a global hub for manufacturing, and is the largest manufacturing economy in the world as well as the largest exporter of goods in the world. China is also the world's fastest growing consumer market and second largest importer of goods in the world. China is a net importer of services products. As of 2016, China is the second largest trading nation in the world and plays a prominent role in international trade , and has increasingly engaged in trade organizations and treaties in recent years. China became a member of the World Trade Organization in 2001. China also has free trade agreements with several nations, including Australia, South Korea, ASEAN, New Zealand, Switzerland and Pakistan. The provinces in the coastal regions of China tend to be more industrialized, while regions in the hinterland are less developed. As China's economic importance has grown, so has attention to the structure and health of the economy.

To avoid the long-term socioeconomic cost of environmental pollution in China, it has been suggested by Nicholas Stern and Fergus Green of the Grantham Research Institute on Climate Change and the Environment that the economy of China be shifted to more advanced industrial development with high-tech, low carbon emissions with better allocation of national resources to innovation and R&D for sustainable economic growth in order to reduce the impact of China's heavy industry. This is in accord with the planning goals of the central government. Xi Jinping's Chinese Dream is described as achieving the "Two 100s": the material goal of China becoming a "moderately well-off society" by 2021, the 100th anniversary of the Chinese Communist Party, and the modernization goal of China becoming a fully developed nation by 2049, the 100th anniversary of the founding of the People's Republic.

The internationalization of the Chinese economy continues to affect the standardized economic forecast officially launched in China by the Purchasing Managers Index in 2005. By 2009, China became the sole Asian nation to have a GDP (PPP) above the $10-trillion mark (along with the United States and the European Union). By the end of 2015, China became the world's first ever nation to have a GDP (PPP) above the $20-trillion mark, doubling its overall output in the fastest time possible (6 years). As China's economy grows, so does China's Renminbi, which undergoes the process needed for its internationalization. China initiated the founding of the Asian Infrastructure Investment Bank in 2015.

REGIONAL ECONOMIES

China's unequal transportation system — combined with important differences in the availability of natural and human resources and in industrial infrastructure — has produced significant variations in the regional economies of China.

Economic development has generally been more rapid in coastal provinces than in the interior, and there are large disparities in per capita income between regions. The three wealthiest regions are along the southeast coast, centered on the Pearl River Delta; along the east coast, centered on the Lower Yangtze River; and near the Bohai Gulf, in the Beijing–Tianjin region. It is the rapid development of these areas that is expected to have the most significant effect on the Asian regional economy as a whole, and Chinese government policy is designed to remove the obstacles to accelerated growth in these wealthier regions.

Hong Kong and Macau

In accordance with the One Country, Two Systems policy, the economies of the former British colony of Hong Kong, and Portuguese colony of Macau, are separate from the rest of China, and each other. Both Hong Kong and Macau are free to conduct and engage in economic negotiations with foreign countries, as well as participating as full members in various international economic organizations such as the World Customs Organization, the World Trade Organization and the Asia-Pacific Economic Cooperation forum, often under the names "Hong Kong, China" and "Macau, China".

DEVELOPMENT

China, having been through a long period of economic downturn before 1978, has recently become one of the world's major economic powers, following the implementation of economic reform from 1979. China shows a great development potential from its remarkable economic growth rate in these years.

China has in place the "five-year-plan" strategy in order to achieve continuous economic development. The Thirteenth Five-Year Plan (2016–2020) is currently being implemented.

Like Japan and South Korea before it, for nearly 30 years China has indeed been growing, thrusting its citizens into prosperity and its goods across the world. Between 1978 and 2005, China's per capita GDP had grown from $153 to $1284, while its current account surplus had increased over twelve-fold between 1982 and 2004, from $5.7 billion to $71 billion. During this time, China had also become an industrial powerhouse, moving beyond initial successes in low-wage sectors like clothing and footwear to the increasingly sophisticated production of computers, pharmaceuticals, and automobiles.

Just how long the trajectory could continue, however, remained unclear. According to the 11th five-year plan, China needed to sustain an annual growth rate of 8% for the foreseeable future. Only with such levels of growth, the leadership argued, could China continue to develop its industrial prowess, raise its citizen's standard of living, and redress the inequalities that were cropping up across the country. Yet no country had ever before maintained the kind of growth that

China was predicting. Moreover, China had to some extent already undergone the easier parts of development. In the 1980s, it had transformed its vast and inefficient agricultural sector, freeing its peasants from the confines of central planning and winning them to the cause of reform. In the 1990s, it had likewise started to restructure its stagnant industrial sector, wooing foreign investors for the first time. These policies had catalysed the country's phenomenal growth. Instead, China had to take what many regarded as the final step toward the market, liberalizing the banking sector and launching the beginnings of a real capital market. According to an article in Journal of the Asia Pacific Economy authored by Mete Feridun of University of Greenwich Business School and his co-author Abdul Jalil from Wuhan University in China, financial development leads to a reduction in the income inequality in China. This process, however, would not be easy. As of 2004, China's state-owned enterprises were still only partially reorganized, and its banks were dealing with the burden of over \$205 billion (1.7 trillion RMB) in non-performing loans, monies that had little chance of ever being repaid. The country had a floating exchange rate, and strict controls on both the current and capital accounts.

In mid-2014 China announced it was taking steps to boost the economy, which at the time was running at a rate 7.4% per annum, but was slowing. The measures included plans to build a multi-tier transport network, comprising railways, roads and airports, to create a new economic belt alongside the Yangtze River.

In 2024 China will become the world's largest economy, according to the global information provider IHS Inc. NYSE:IHS. "Over the next 10 years, China's economy is expected to rebalance toward more rapid growth in consumption, which will help the structure of the domestic economy," Rajiv Biswas, IHS chief Asia economist, said in a statement by the company based in Englewood, Colo.

Regional development

These strategies are aimed at the relatively poorer regions in China in an attempt to prevent widening inequalities:

- China Western Development, designed to increase the economic situation of the western provinces through capital investment and development of natural resources.
- Revitalize Northeast China, to rejuvenate the industrial bases in Northeast China. It covers the three provinces of Heilongjiang,

Jilin, and Liaoning, as well as the five eastern prefectures of Inner Mongolia.

- Rise of Central China Plan, to accelerate the development of its central regions. It covers six provinces: Shanxi, Henan, Anhui, Hubei, Hunan, and Jiangxi.
- Third Front, focused on the southwestern provinces.

Foreign investment abroad:

- Go Global, to encourage its enterprises to invest overseas.

Key national projects

The "West-to-East Electricity Transmission", the "West-to-East Gas Transmission", and the "South–North Water Transfer Project" are the government's three key strategic projects, aimed at realigning overall of 12 billion cu m per year. Construction of the "South-to-North Water Diversion" project was officially launched on 27 December 2002 and completion of Phase I is scheduled for 2010; this will relieve serious water shortfall in northern China and realize a rational distribution of the water resources of the Yangtze, Yellow, Huaihe, and Haihe river valleys.

MACROECONOMIC TRENDS

In January 1985, the State Council of China approved to establish a SNA (System of National Accounting), use the gross domestic product (GDP) to measure the national economy. China started the study of theoretical foundation, guiding, and accounting model etc., for establishing a new system of national economic accounting. In 1986, as the first citizen of the People's Republic of China to receive a Ph.D. in economics from an overseas country, Dr. Fengbo Zhang headed Chinese Macroeconomic Research – the key research project of the seventh Five-Year Plan of China, as well as completing and publishing the China GDP data by China's own research. The summary of the above has been included in the book Chinese Macroeconomic Structure and Policy (1988) Editor: Fengbo Zhang, collectively authored by the Research Center of the State Council of China. This is the first GDP data which was published by China. The State Council of China issued "The notice regarding implementation of System of National Accounting" in August 1992, the SNA system officially is introduced to China, replaced Soviet Union's MPS system, Western economic indicator GDP became China's most important economic indicator (WikiChina: China GDP, The First China GDP).

Systemic issues and environment

The government has in recent years struggled to contain the social strife and environmental damage related to the economy's rapid transformation; collect public receipts due from provinces, businesses, and individuals; reduce corruption and other economic crimes; sustain adequate job growth for tens of millions of workers laid off from state-owned enterprises, migrants, and new entrants to the work force; and keep afloat the large state-owned enterprises, most of which had not participated in the vigorous expansion of the economy and many of which had been losing the ability to pay full wages and pensions. From 50 to 100 million surplus rural workers were adrift between the villages and the cities, many subsisting through part-time low-paying jobs. Popular resistance, changes in central policy, and loss of authority by rural cadres have weakened China's population control program.

Other major problems concern the labor force and the pricing system. There is large-scale underemployment in both urban and rural areas, and the fear of the disruptive effects of major, explicit unemployment is strong. The prices of certain key commodities, especially of industrial raw materials and major industrial products, are determined by the state. In most cases, basic price ratios were set in the 1950s and are often irrational in terms of current production capabilities and demands. Over the years, large subsidies were built into the price structure, and these subsidies grew substantially in the late 1970s and 1980s. By the early 1990s, these subsidies began to be eliminated, in large part due to China's admission into the World Trade Organization (WTO) in 2001, which carried with it requirements for further economic liberalization and deregulation.

By 2010, rapidly rising wages and a general increase in the standard of living had put increased energy use on a collision course with the need to reduce carbon emissions in order to control global warming. There were diligent efforts to increase energy efficiency and increase use of renewable sources; over 1,000 inefficient power plants had been closed, but projections continued to show a dramatic rise in carbon emissions from burning fossil fuels.

National debt

The International Monetary Fund, the Federal Reserve Bank of St. Louis and other sources, such as the Article IV Consultation Reports, state that, at the end of 2014, the "general government gross debt"-to-GDP ratio for China was 41.44 percent. With China's 2014 GDP being US$ 10,356.508 trillion, this makes the government debt of China approximately US$ 4.3 trillion.

By the mid-2010s, many analysts have expressed concern over the overall "size" of the Chinese government debt.

An 2015 International Monetary Fund report concluded that China's public debt is relatively low "and on a stable path in all standard stress tests except for the scenario with contingent liability shocks," such as "a large-scale bank recapitalization or financial system bailout to deal, for example, with a potential rise in NPLs from deleveraging."

"Shadow banking" has risen in China, posing risks to the financial system.

Chinese authorities have dismissed analysts' worries, insisting that "the country still has room to increase government debt." Former Fed Chairman Ben Bernanke, earlier in 2016, commented that "the...debt pile facing China [is] an 'internal' problem, given the majority of the borrowings was issued in local currency. Many economists have expressed the same views as Bernanke.

Regulatory environment and tax system

Though China's economy has expanded rapidly, its regulatory environment has not kept pace. Since Deng Xiaoping's open market reforms, the growth of new businesses has outpaced the government's ability to regulate them. This has created a situation where businesses, faced with mounting competition and poor oversight, take drastic measures to increase profit margins, often at the expense of consumer safety. This issue became more prominent in 2007, with a number of restrictions being placed on problematic Chinese exports by the United States.

From the 1950s to the 1980s, the central government's revenues derived chiefly from the profits of the state enterprises, which were remitted to the state. Some government revenues also came from taxes, of which the most important was the general industrial and commercial tax.

The trend, however, has been for remitted profits of the state enterprises to be replaced with taxes on those profits. Initially, this tax system was adjusted so as to allow for differences in the market capitalization and pricing situations of various firms, but more-uniform tax schedules were introduced in the early 1990s. In addition, personal income and value-added taxes were implemented at that time.

Inflation

Shortages of gasoline and diesel fuel developed in the fall of 2007 due to reluctance of refineries to produce fuel at low prices set by the state. These prices were slightly increased in November 2007 with fuel selling for $2.65 a gallon, still slightly below world prices. Price controls were in effect on numerous basic products and services, but were ineffective with food, prices of which were rising at an annual rate of 18.2% in November 2007. The problem of inflation has caused concern at the highest levels of the Chinese government. On 9 January 2008, the government of China issued the following statement on its official website: "The Chinese government decided on Wednesday to take further measures to stabilize market prices and increase the severity of punishments for those guilty of driving up prices through hoarding or cheating."

Pork is an important part of the Chinese economy with a per capita consumption of a fifth of a pound per day. The worldwide rise in the price of animal feed associated with increased production of ethanol from corn resulted in steep rises in pork prices in China in 2007. Increased cost of production interacted badly with increased demand resulting from rapidly rising wages. The state responded by subsidizing pork prices for students and the urban poor and called for increased production. Release of pork from the nation's strategic pork reserve was considered.

By January 2008, the inflation rate rose to 7.1%, which BBC News described as the highest inflation rate since 1997, due to the winter storms that month. China's inflation rate jumped to a new decade high of 8.7 percent in February 2008 after severe winter storms disrupted the economy and worsened food shortages, the government said 11 March 2008. Throughout the summer and fall, however, inflation fell again to a low of 6.6% in October 2008.

By November 2010, the inflation rate rose up to 5.1%, driven by an 11.7% increase in food prices year on year. According to the bureau, industrial output went up 13.3 percent. As supplies have run short, prices for fuel and other commodities have risen.

Investment cycles

Chinese investment has always been highly cyclical. Ever since the 1958 Great Leap Forward, growth in fixed capital formation has typically peaked about every five years. Recent peaks occurred in 1978, 1984, 1988, 1993, 2003, and 2009. The corresponding troughs were in 1981, 1986, 1989, 1997, and 2005. In China, the majority of investment is carried out by entities that are at least partially state-owned. Most of these are under the control of local governments. Thus booms are primarily the result of perverse incentives at the local-government level. Unlike entrepreneurs in a free-enterprise economy, Chinese local officials are motivated primarily by political considerations. As their performance evaluations are based, to a large extent, on GDP growth within their jurisdictions, they have a strong incentive to promote large-scale investment projects. They also don't face any real bankruptcy risk. When localities get into trouble, they are invariably bailed out by state-owned banks. Under these circumstances, overinvestment is inevitable.

A typical cycle begins with a relaxation of central government credit and industrial policy. This allows local governments to push investment aggressively, both through state-sector entities they control directly and by offering investment-promotion incentives to private investors and enterprises outside their jurisdictions. The resulting boom puts upward pressure on prices and may also result in shortages of key inputs such as coal and electricity (as was the case in 2003). Once inflation has risen to a level at which it begins to threaten social stability, the central government will intervene by tightening enforcement of industrial and credit policy. Projects that went ahead without required approvals will be halted. Bank lending to particular types of investors will be restricted. Credit then becomes tight and investment growth begins to decline.

Eventually such centrally-imposed busts alleviate shortages and bring inflation down to acceptable levels. At that point, the central government yields to local-government demands for looser policy and the cycle begins again.

SECTORS

Agriculture

China is the world's largest producer and consumer of agricultural products – and some 300 million Chinese farm workers are in the industry, mostly laboring on pieces of land about the size of U.S farms. Virtually all arable land is used for food crops. China is the world's largest producer of rice and is among the principal sources of wheat, corn (maize), tobacco, soybeans, potatoes, sorghum, peanuts, tea, millet, barley, oilseed, pork, and fish. Major non-food crops, including cotton, other fibers, and oilseeds, furnish China with a small proportion of its foreign trade revenue. Agricultural exports, such as vegetables and fruits, fish and shellfish, grain and meat products, are exported to Hong Kong. Yields are high because of intensive cultivation, for example, China's cropland area is only 75% of the U.S. total, but China still produces about 30% more crops and livestock than the United States. China hopes to further increase agricultural production through improved plant stocks, fertilizers, and technology.

According to the government statistics issued in 2005, after a drop in the yield of farm crops in 2000, output has been increasing annually.

According to the United Nations World Food Program, in 2003, China fed 20 percent of the world's population with only 7 percent of the world's arable land. China ranks first worldwide in farm output, and, as a result of topographic and climatic factors, only about 10–15 percent of the total land area is suitable for cultivation.

Of this, slightly more than half is unirrigated, and the remainder is divided roughly equally between paddy fields and irrigated areas. Nevertheless, about 60 percent of the population lives in the rural areas, and until the 1980s a high percentage of them made their living directly from farming. Since then, many have been encouraged to leave the fields and pursue other activities, such as light manufacturing, commerce, and transportation; and by the mid-1980s farming accounted for less than half of the value of rural output. Today, agriculture contributes only 13% of China's GDP.

Animal husbandry constitutes the second most important component of agricultural production. China is the world's leading producer of pigs, chickens, and eggs, and it also has sizable herds of sheep and cattle.

Since the mid-1970s, greater emphasis has been placed on increasing the livestock output. China has a long tradition of ocean and freshwater fishing and of aquaculture. Pond raising has always been important and has been increasingly emphasized to supplement coastal and inland fisheries threatened by overfishing and to provide such valuable export commodities as prawns.

Environmental problems such as floods, drought, and erosion pose serious threats to farming in many parts of the country. The wholesale destruction of forests gave way to an energetic reforestation program that proved inadequate, and forest resources are still fairly meagre. The principal forests are found in the Qin Mountains and the central mountains and on the Sichuan–Yunnan plateau. Because they are inaccessible, the Qinling forests are not worked extensively, and much of the country's timber comes from Heilongjiang, Jilin, Sichuan, and Yunnan.

Western China, comprising Tibet, Xinjiang, and Qinghai, has little agricultural significance except for areas of floriculture and cattle raising. Rice, China's most important crop, is dominant in the southern provinces and many of the farms here yield two harvests a year.

In the north, wheat is of the greatest importance, while in central China wheat and rice vie with each other for the top place. Millet and kaoliang (a variety of grain sorghum) are grown mainly in the northeast and some central provinces, which, together with some northern areas, also provide considerable quantities of barley.

Most of the soybean crop is derived from the north and the northeast; corn (maize) is grown in the center and the north, while tea comes mainly from the warm and humid hilly areas of the south. Cotton is grown extensively in the central provinces, but it is also found to a lesser extent in the southeast and in the north. Tobacco comes from the center and parts of the south. Other important crops are potatoes, sugar beets, and oilseeds.

There is still a relative lack of agricultural machinery, particularly advanced machinery. For the most part the Chinese peasant or farmer depends on simple, nonmechanized farming implements. Good progress has been made in increasing water conservancy, and about half the cultivated land is under irrigation.

In the late 1970s and early 1980s, economic reforms were introduced. First of all this began with the shift of farming work to a system of household responsibility and a phasing out of collectivized agriculture.

Later this expanded to include a gradual liberalization of price controls; fiscal decentralization; massive privatization of state enterprises, thereby allowing a wide variety of private enterprises in the services and light manufacturing; the foundation of a diversified banking system (but with large amounts of state control); the development of a stock market; and the opening of the economy to increased foreign trade and foreign investment.

Housing and construction

The real estate industry is about 20% of the Chinese economy.

ENERGY AND MINERAL RESOURCES

Energy

Electricity:
- *production:* 2.8344 trillion kWh (2006)
- *consumption:* 2.8248 trillion kWh (2006)
- *exports:* 11.19 billion kWh (2005)
- *imports:* 5.011 billion kWh (2005)

Electricity – production by source:
- *thermal:* 77.8% (68.7% from coal) (2006)
- *hydro:* 20.7% (2006)
- *other:* 0.4% (2006)
- *nuclear:* 1.1% (2006)

Oil:
- *production:* 3,631,000 bbl/d (577,300 m^3/d) (2005)
- *consumption:* 6,534,000 bbl/d (1,038,800 m^3/d) (2005) and expected 9,300,000 bbl/d (1,480,000 m^3/d) in 2030
- *exports:* 443,300 bbl/d (70,480 m^3/d) (2005)
- *imports:* 3,181,000 bbl/d (505,700 m^3/d) (2005)
- *net imports:* 2,740,000 barrels per day (436,000 m^3/d) (2005)
- *proved reserves:* 16.3 Gbbl (2.59×10^9 m^3) (1 January 2006)

Natural gas:
- *production:* 47.88 km^3 (2005 est.)
- *consumption:* 44.93 km^3 (2005 est.)
- *exports:* 2.944 km^3 (2005)
- *imports:* 0 m^3 (2005)
- *proved reserves:* 1,448 km^3 (1 January 2006 est.)

Since 1980, China's energy production has grown dramatically, as has the proportion allocated to domestic consumption. Some 80 percent of all power is generated from fossil fuel at thermal plants, with about 17 percent at hydroelectric installations; only about two percent is from nuclear energy, mainly from plants located in Guangdong and Zhejiang. Though China has rich overall energy potential, most have yet to be developed. In addition, the geographical distribution of energy puts most of these resources relatively far from their major industrial users. Basically the northeast is rich in coal and oil, the central part of north China has abundant coal, and the southwest has immense hydroelectric potential. But the industrialized regions around Guangzhou and the Lower Yangtze region around Shanghai have too little energy, while there is relatively little heavy industry located near major energy resource areas other than in the southern part of the northeast.

China, due in large part to environmental concerns, has wanted to shift China's current energy mix from a heavy reliance on coal, which accounts for 70–75% of China's energy, toward greater reliance on oil, natural gas, renewable energy, and nuclear power. China has closed thousands of coal mines over the past five to ten years to cut overproduction. According to Chinese statistics, this has reduced coal production by over 25%.

Since 1993, China has been a net importer of oil, a large portion of which comes from the Middle East. Imported oil accounts for 20% of the processed crude in China. Net imports are expected to rise to 3.5 million barrels (560,000 m^3) per day by 2010. China is interested in diversifying the sources of its oil imports and has invested in oil fields around the world. China is developing oil imports from Central Asia and has invested in Kazakhstani oil fields. Beijing also plans to increase China's natural gas production, which currently accounts for only 3% of China's total energy consumption and incorporated a natural gas strategy in its 10th Five-Year Plan (2001–2005), with the goal of expanding gas use from a 2% share of total energy production to 4% by 2005 (gas accounts for 25% of U.S. energy production). Analysts expect China's consumption of natural gas to more than double by 2010.

The 11th Five-Year Program (2006–10), announced in 2005 and approved by the National People's Congress in March 2006, called for greater energy conservation measures, including development of renewable energy sources and increased attention to environmental protection. Guidelines called for a 20% reduction in energy consumption per unit of GDP by 2010. Moving away from coal towards cleaner energy sources including oil, natural gas, renewable energy, and nuclear power is an important component of China's development program. Beijing also intends to continue to improve energy efficiency and promote the use of clean coal technology. China has abundant hydroelectric resources; the Three Gorges Dam, for example, will have a total capacity of 18 gigawatts when fully on-line (projected for 2009). In addition, the share of electricity generated by nuclear power is projected to grow from 1% in 2000 to 5% in 2030. China's renewable energy law, which went into effect in 2006, calls for 10% of its energy to come from renewable energy sources by 2020.

Mining

Outdated mining and ore-processing technologies are being replaced with modern techniques, but China's rapid industrialization requires imports of minerals from abroad. In particular, iron ore imports from Australia and the United States have soared in the early 2000s as steel production rapidly outstripped domestic iron ore production. Also China has become increasingly active in several African countries to mine the reserves it requires for economic growth, particularly in countries such as the Democratic Republic of the Congo and Gabon.

The major areas of production in 2004 were coal (nearly 2 billion tons), iron ore (310 million tons), crude petroleum (175 million tons), natural gas (41 million cubic meters), antimony ore (110,000 tons), tin concentrates (110,000 tons), nickel ore (64,000 tons), tungsten concentrates (67,000 tons), unrefined salt (37 million tons), vanadium (40,000 tons), and molybdenum ore (29,000 tons). In order of magnitude, produced minerals were bauxite, gypsum, barite, magnesite, talc and related minerals, manganese ore, fluorspar, and zinc. In addition, China produced 2,450 tons of silver and 215 tons of gold in 2004. The mining sector accounted for less than 0.9% of total employment in 2002 but produced about 5.3% of total industrial production.

Hydroelectric resources

China has an abundant potential for hydroelectric power production due to its considerable river network and mountainous terrain. Most of the total hydroelectric capacity is situated in the southwest of the country, where coal supplies are poor but demand for energy is rising swiftly. The potential in the northeast is fairly small, but it was there that the first hydroelectric stations were built — by the Japanese during its occupation of Manchuria. Due to considerable seasonal fluctuations in rainfall, the flow of rivers tends to drop during the winter, forcing many power stations to operate at less than normal capacity, while in the summer, on the other hand, floods often interfere with generation.

Thirteen years in construction at a cost of $24 billion, the immense Three Gorges Dam across the Yangtze River was essentially completed in 2006 and will revolutionize electrification and flood control in the area.

Coal

China is well endowed with mineral resources, the most important of which is coal. China's mineral resources include large reserves of coal and iron ore, plus adequate to abundant supplies of nearly all other industrial minerals. Although coal deposits are widely scattered (some coal is found in every province), most of the total is located in the northern part of the country. The province of Shanxi, in fact, is thought to contain about half of the total; other important coal-bearing provinces include Heilongjiang, Liaoning, Jilin, Hebei, and Shandong. Apart from these northern provinces, significant quantities of coal are present in Sichuan, and there are some deposits of importance in Guangdong, Guangxi, Yunnan, and Guizhou. A large part of the country's reserves consists of good bituminous coal, but there are also large deposits of lignite. Anthracite is present in several places (especially Liaoning, Guizhou, and Henan), but overall it is not very significant.

To ensure a more even distribution of coal supplies and to reduce the strain on the less than adequate transportation network, the authorities pressed for the development of a large number of small, locally run mines throughout the country. This campaign was energetically pursued after the 1960s, with the result that thousands of small pits have been established, and they produce more than half the country's coal. This output, however, is typically expensive and is used for local consumption. It has also led to a less than stringent implementation of safety measures in these unregulated mines, which cause several thousands of deaths each year.

Coal makes up the bulk of China's energy consumption (70% in 2005), and China is the largest producer and consumer of coal in the world. As China's economy continues to grow, China's coal demand is projected to rise significantly. Although coal's share of China's overall energy consumption will decrease, coal consumption will continue to rise in absolute terms. China's continued and increasing reliance on coal as a power source has contributed significantly to putting China on the path to becoming the world's largest emitter of acid rain-causing sulfur dioxide and greenhouse gases, including carbon dioxide. As of 2015 falling coal prices resulted in layoffs at coal mines in the northeast.

Oil and natural gas

Main article: Petroleum industry in the People's Republic of China

China's onshore oil resources are mostly located in the Northeast and in Xinjiang, Gansu, Qinghai, Sichuan, Shandong, and Henan provinces. Oil shale is found in a number of places, especially at Fushun in Liaoning, where the deposits overlie the coal reserves, as well as in Guangdong. High quality light oil has been found in the Pearl River estuary of the South China Sea, the Qaidam Basin in Qinghai, and the Tarim Basin in Xinjiang. The country consumes most of its oil output but does export some crude oil and oil products. China has explored and developed oil deposits in the South China Sea and East China Sea, the Yellow Sea, the Gulf of Tonkin, and the Bohai Sea.

In 2013, the pace of China's economic growth exceeded the domestic oil capacity and floods damaged the nation's oil fields in the middle of the year. Consequently, China imported oil to compensate for the supply reduction and surpassed the US in September 2013 to become the world's largest importer of oil.

The total extent of China's natural gas reserves is unknown, as relatively little exploration for natural gas has been done. Sichuan accounts for almost half of the known natural gas reserves and production. Most of the rest of China's natural gas is associated gas produced in the Northeast's major oil fields, especially Daqing oilfield. Other gas deposits have been found in the Qaidam Basin, Hebei, Jiangsu, Shanghai, and Zhejiang, and offshore to the southwest of Hainan Island. According to an article published in Energy Economics in 2011 by economists Mete Feridun (University of Greenwich) and Abdul Jalil (Wuhan University in China), financial development in China has not taken place at the expense of environmental pollution and financial development has led to a decrease in environmental pollution. Authors conclude that carbon emissions are mainly determined by income, energy consumption and trade openness and their findings confirm the existence of an Environmental Kuznets Curve in the case of China.

Metals and nonmetals

Iron ore reserves are found in most provinces, including Hainan. Gansu, Guizhou, southern Sichuan, and Guangdong provinces have rich deposits. The largest mined reserves are located north of the Yangtze River and supply neighboring iron and steel enterprises. With the exception of nickel, chromium, and cobalt, China is well supplied with ferroalloys and manganese. Reserves of tungsten are also known to be fairly large. Copper resources are moderate, and high-quality ore is present only in a few deposits. Discoveries have been reported from Ningxia. Lead and zinc are available, and bauxite resources are thought to be plentiful.

China's antimony reserves are the largest in the world. Tin resources are plentiful, and there are fairly rich deposits of gold. China is the world's fifth largest producer of gold and in the early 21st century became an important producer and exporter of rare metals needed in high-technology industries. The rare earth reserves at the Bayan Obi mine in Inner Mongolia are thought to be the largest in any single location in the world.

China also produces a fairly wide range of nonmetallic minerals. One of the most important of these is salt, which is derived from coastal evaporation sites in Jiangsu, Hebei, Shandong, and Liaoning, as well as from extensive salt fields in Sichuan, Ningxia, and the Qaidam Basin. There are important deposits of phosphate rock in a number of areas; Jiangxi, Guangxi, Yunnan and Hubei. Production has been accelerating every year. As of 2013 China is producing 97,000,000 metric tons of phosphate rock a year. Pyrites occur in several places; Liaoning, Hebei, Shandong, and Shanxi have the most important deposits. China also has large resources of fluorite (fluorspar), gypsum, asbestos, and has the world's largest reserves and production of cement, clinker and limestone.

INDUSTRY AND MANUFACTURING

Industry and construction account for 46.8 % of China's GDP. Between the years 2011 and 2013, China used more cement than the United States consumed during the entire 20th century. In 2009 around 8% of the total manufacturing output in the world came from China itself and China ranked third worldwide in industrial output that year (first was EU and second United States). Research by IHS Global Insight states that in 2010 China contributed to 19.8% of world's manufacturing output and became the largest manufacturer in the world that year, after the US had held that position for about 110 years.

In November 2012 the State Council of the People's Republic of China mandated a "social risk assessment" for all major industrial projects. This requirement followed mass public protests in some locations for planned projects or expansions.

Major industries include mining and ore processing; iron and steel; aluminium; coal; machinery; armaments; textiles and apparel; petroleum; cement; chemical; fertilizers; food processing; automobiles and other transportation equipment including rail cars and locomotives, ships, and aircraft; consumer products including footwear, toys, and electronics; telecommunications and information technology.

China has become a preferred destination for the relocation of global manufacturing facilities. Its strength as an export platform has contributed to incomes and employment in China.

Since the founding of the People's Republic, industrial development has been given considerable attention; as of 2011 46% of China's national output continued to be devoted to investment; a percentage far higher than any other nation.

Among the various industrial branches the machine-building and metallurgical industries have received the highest priority. These two areas alone now account for about 20–30 percent of the total gross value of industrial output.

In these, as in most other areas of industry, however, innovation has generally suffered at the hands of a system that has rewarded increases in gross output rather than improvements in variety, sophistication and quality. China, therefore, still imports significant quantities of specialized steels. Overall industrial output has grown at an average rate of more than 10 percent per year, having surpassed all other sectors in economic growth and degree of modernization. Some heavy industries and products deemed to be of national strategic importance remain state-owned, but an increasing proportion of lighter and consumer-oriented manufacturing firms are privately held or are private-state joint ventures.

The predominant focus of development in the chemical industry is to expand the output of chemical fertilizers, plastics, and synthetic fibers. The growth of this industry has placed China among the world's leading producers of nitrogenous fertilizers.

In the consumer goods sector the main emphasis is on textiles and clothing, which also form an important part of China's exports. Textile manufacturing, a rapidly growing proportion of which consists of synthetics, account for about 10 percent of the gross industrial output and continues to be important, but less so than before. The industry tends to be scattered throughout the country, but there are a number of important textile centers, including Shanghai, Guangzhou, and Harbin.

Automotive industry

By 2006 China had become the world's third largest automotive vehicle manufacturer (after US and Japan) and the second largest consumer (only after US). Automobile manufacturing has soared during the reform period. In 1975 only 139,800 automobiles were produced annually, but by 1985 production had reached 443,377, then jumped to nearly 1.1 million by 1992 and increased fairly evenly each year up until 2001, when it reached 2.3 million.

In 2002 production rose to nearly 3.25 million and then jumped to 4.44 million in 2003, 5.07 million in 2004, 5.71 million in 2005, 7.28 million in 2006, 8.88 million in 2007, 9.35 million in 2008 and 13.83 million in 2009. China has become the number-one automaker in the world in 2009. Domestic sales have kept pace with production. After respectable annual increases in the mid- and late 1990s, passenger car sales soared in the early 2000s. In 2006, a total of 7.22 million automobiles were sold, including 5.18 million units of passenger cars and 2.04 million units of commercial vehicles.

In 2010, China became the world's largest automotive vehicle manufacturer as well as the largest consumer ahead of the United States with an estimated 18 million new cars sold. However, new car sales grew only by an estimated 1% between 2011 and 2012 due to the escalation in the Spratly Islands dispute which involved Japan, the world's third largest producer of vehicles.

China's automotive industry has been so successful that it began exporting car parts in 1999. China began to plan major moves into the automobile and components export business starting in 2005. A new Honda factory in Guangzhou was built in 2004 solely for the export market and was expected to ship 30,000 passenger vehicles to Europe in 2005. By 2004, 12 major foreign automotive manufacturers had joint-venture plants in China. They produced a wide range of automobiles, minivans, sport utility vehicles, buses, and trucks. In 2003 China exported US$4.7 billion worth of vehicles and components. The vehicle export was 78,000 units in 2004, 173,000 units in 2005, and 340,000 units in 2006. The vehicle and component export is targeted to reach US$70 billion by 2010.

The market for domestically produced cars, under a local name, is likely to continue to grow both inside China and outside. Companies such as Geely, Qiantu and Chery are constantly evaluating new international locations, both in developing and developed countries.

Other industries

Substantial investments were made in the manufacture of solar panels and wind generators by a number of companies, supported by liberal loans by banks and local governments. However, by 2012 manufacturing capacity had far outstripped domestic and global demand for both products, particularly solar panels which were subjected to anti-dumping penalties by both the United States and Europe. The global oversupply has resulted in bankruptcies and production cutbacks both inside and outside China. China has budgeted $50 billion to subsidize production of solar power over the two decades following 2015 but, even at the sharply reduced price resulting from oversupply, as of 2012 cost of solar power in China remained three times that of power produced by conventional coal-fired power plants.

China is the world's biggest sex toy producer and accounts for 70% of the worldwide sex toys production. In the country, 1,000 manufacturers are active in this industry, which generates about two billion dollars a year.

As of 2011, China was the world's largest market for personal computers

Services

The output of China's services in 2010 ranks third worldwide — after the United States and Japan — and high power and telecom density has ensured that the country has remained on a high-growth trajectory over the long term. In 2010 the services sector produced 43% of China's annual GDP, second only to manufacturing. However, its proportion of GDP is still low compared to the ratio in more developed countries, and the agricultural sector still employs a larger workforce.

Prior to the onset of economic reforms in 1978, China's services sector was characterized by state-operated shops, rationing, and regulated prices — with reform came private markets, individual entrepreneurs, and a commercial sector. The wholesale and retail trade has expanded quickly, with numerous shopping malls, retail shops, restaurant chains and hotels constructed in urban areas. Public administration remains a main component of the service sector, while tourism has become a significant factor in employment and a source of foreign exchange.

Chengdu, China, is home to the world's largest building — the New Century Global Center, which, at 100 m (328 ft) high, 500 m

(1,640 ft) long, and 400 m (1,312 ft) wide, houses retail outlets, a 14-theater cinema, offices, hotels, the Paradise Island waterpark, an artificial beach, a 150 m (164 yd)-long LED screen, skating rink, pirate ship, fake Mediterranean village, 24-hour artificial sun, and 15,000-spot parking lot.

Telecommunications

China possesses a diversified communications system that links all parts of the country by Internet, telephone, telegraph, radio, and television.

China's number of Internet users or netizens topped 137 million by the end of 2006, an increase of 23.4% from a year before and 162 million by June 2007, making China the second-largest Internet user after the United States, according to China's Ministry of Information Industry (MII). China's mobile phone penetration rate was 34% in 2007. In 2006, mobile phone users sent 429 billion text messages (on average 967 text messages per user). For 2006, the number of fixed-lines grew by 79%, mainly in the rural areas.

Tourism

China's tourism industry is one of the fastest-growing industries in the national economy and is also one of the industries with a very distinct global competitive edge. According to the World Travel and Tourism Council, travel and tourism directly contributed CNY 1,362 billion (US$216 billion) to the Chinese economy (about 2.6% of GDP). In 2011, total international tourist arrivals was 58 million, and international tourism receipts were US$48 billion.

Domestic tourism market makes up more than 90% of the country's tourism traffic, and contributes more than 70% of total tourism revenue. In 2002, domestic tourists reached 878 million and tourism revenue was $46.9 billion. A large middle class with strong consumption power is emerging in China, especially in major cities. China's outbound tourists reached 20.22 million in 2003, overtaking Japan for the first time.

It is forecast by the World Tourism Organisation that China's tourism industry will take up to 8.6% of world market share to become the world's top tourism industry by 2020.

Chinese business-travel spending is also forecast to be the highest in the world by 2014, overtaking the United States. According to a

Global Business Travel Association study, total business-travel spending is expected to reach US$195 billion in 2012.

Luxury goods

Luxury spending in China has skyrocketed, an indicator of the country's newfound wealth. For example, the Chinese bottled water industry is forecast to more than double in size in 2008, becoming a $10.5 billion industry. Meanwhile, as those who once had no recourse but low-quality tap water take advantage of its availability in supermarkets, those who had little or no running water are now capitalising on its availability. Tap water production and supply is expected to grow by 29.3% in 2008, to $11.9 billion. China's automotive industry is expected to expand by 29.5% to nearly $200 billion. Also, consumption of chocolate and other confectionery is to increase by 24.3%, as the industry expands to $4.6 billion. Additionally China's fast food industry has been growing at a 20.8% annual rate as major players such as McDonald's enter the market. The LVMH Group, who own major luxury brands including Louis Vuitton apparel, Moët & Chandon wines and champagne and Hennessy cognacs, reported earnings growth of over 25% in 2007 in China, with the country accounting for around 16% of LVMH's global business.

After an October 2012 ban on government agencies purchasing luxury goods, often used as "gifts", sales of luxury goods in China remained strong but slowed, even falling slightly for some luxury retailers in the 4th quarter of 2012, with sales of shark fins and edible swallow nests (once staples of lavish government banquets) down sharply.

Retail sales in China account for only 7% of global retail sales of luxury consumer goods; however, Chinese buyers account for 25% of global retail sales of luxury consumer goods. Many shops in international travel destinations have specialized staff devoted to Chinese customers.

Cybercrime

As of 2016, computer crime is a lucrative illicit practice in China. An academic study released in August 2012 by the University of California (UC) Institute on Global Conflict and Cooperation, claimed that China's "cyber black market" involved over 90,000 participants, cost the local economy 5.36 billion yuan (£536m), negatively impacted upon 110 million internet users (22%), and affected 1.1 million websites

(20%) in 2011. In July 2012, China's State Council released a set of information security guidelines as a measure to combat cyber crime that included increased auditing, security reporting, and monitoring, and a commitment to "reduce the number of internet connection points".

LABOR AND WELFARE

One of the hallmarks of China's socialist economy was its promise of employment to all able and willing to work and job-security with virtually lifelong tenure. Reformers targeted the labor market as unproductive because industries were frequently overstaffed to fulfill socialist goals and job-security reduced workers' incentive to work. This socialist policy was pejoratively called the iron rice bowl.

In 1979–1980, the state reformed factories by giving wage increases to workers, which was immediately offset by sharply rising inflation rates of 6–7%. The reforms also dismantled the iron rice bowl, which meant it witnessed a rise in unemployment in the economy. In 1979 there were 20 million unemployed people. Official Chinese statistics reveal that 4.2% of the total urban workforce was unemployed in 2004, although other estimates have reached 10%. As part of its newly developing social security legislation, China has an unemployment insurance system. At the end of 2003, more than 103.7 million people were participating in the plan, and 7.4 million laid-off employees had received benefits.

China's estimated employed labor force in 2005 totaled 791.4 million persons, about 60% of the total population. During 2003, 49% of the labor force worked in agriculture, forestry, and fishing; 22% in mining, manufacturing, energy, and construction industries; and 29% in the services sector and other categories. In 2004 some 25 million persons were employed by 743,000 private enterprises. Urban wages rose rapidly from 2004 to 2007, at a rate of 13 to 19% per year with average wages near $200/month in 2007. By 2016 the average monthly wage for workers engaged in manufacturing goods for export was $424. This wage, combined with other costs of doing business in China, had, more or less, equalized any Chinese cost advantage with respect to developed economies.

The All-China Federation of Trade Unions (ACFTU) was established in 1925 to represent the interests of national and local trade unions and trade union councils. The ACFTU reported a membership of 130 million, out of an estimated 248 million urban workers, at the end of 2002. Chinese trade unions are organized on a broad industrial basis. Membership is open to those who rely on wages for the whole or a large part of their income, a qualification that excludes most agricultural workers.

In 2010, the issues of manufacturing wages caused a strike at a Honda parts plant. This resulted in wage increases both at the struck plant and other industrial plants.

The 2010 census found that China was now half urban and rapidly aging due to the one child policy. This is expected to lead to increased demand for labor to take care of an elderly population and a reduced supply of migrant labor from the countryside.

Due to worsening pollution, the corruption and political uncertainties of the one-party state and the limited economic freedom in an economy dominated by large state-owned enterprises, many skilled professionals are either leaving the country or preparing safety nets for themselves abroad. In the decade up to 2014, 10 million Chinese emigrated to other countries, taking assets and their technical skills. Perceived corruption continued to grow worse in China as it dropped from 75th to 80th place in Transparency International's index of state corruption.

A law approved February 2013 will mandate a nationwide minimum wage at 40% average urban salaries to be phased in fully by 2015.

EXTERNAL TRADE

International trade makes up a sizeable portion of China's overall economy. Being a Second World country at the time, a meaningful segment of China's trade with the Third World was financed through grants, credits, and other forms of assistance. The principal efforts were made in Asia, especially to Indonesia, Burma, Pakistan, and Ceylon, but large loans were also granted in Africa (Ghana, Algeria, Tanzania) and in the Middle East (Egypt). However, after Mao Zedong's death in 1976, these efforts were scaled back. After which, trade with developing countries became negligible, though during that time, Hong Kong and Taiwan both began to emerge as major trading partners.

Since economic reforms began in the late 1970s, China sought to decentralize its foreign trade system to integrate itself into the international trading system. On November 1991, China joined the

Asia-Pacific Economic Cooperation (APEC) group, which promotes free trade and cooperation in the economic, trade, investment, and technology spheres. China served as APEC chair in 2001, and Shanghai hosted the annual APEC leaders meeting in October of that year.

After reaching a bilateral WTO agreement with the EU and other trading partners in summer 2000, China worked on a multilateral WTO accession package. China concluded multilateral negotiations on its accession to the WTO in September 2001. The completion of its accession protocol and Working Party Report paved the way for its entry into the WTO on 11 December 2001, after 16 years of negotiations, the longest in the history of the General Agreement on Tariffs and Trade. However, U.S. exporters continue to have concerns about fair market access due to China's restrictive trade policies and U.S. export restrictions.

The vast majority of China's imports consists of industrial supplies and capital goods, notably machinery and high-technology equipment, the majority of which comes from the developed countries, primarily Japan and the United States. Regionally, almost half of China's imports come from East and Southeast Asia, and about one-fourth of China's exports go to the same destinations. About 80 percent of China's exports consist of manufactured goods, most of which are textiles and electronic equipment, with agricultural products and chemicals constituting the remainder. Out of the five busiest ports in the world, three are in China. The U.S. trade deficit with China reached $232.5 billion in 2006, as imports grew 18%. China's share of total U.S. imports has grown from 7% to 15% since 1996.

Trade volume between China and Russia reached $29.1 billion in 2005, an increase of 37.1% compared with 2004. A spokesman for the Ministry of Commerce, Van Jingsun, said that the volume of trade between China and Russia could exceed 40 billion dollars in 2007. China's export of machinery and electronic goods to Russia grew 70%, which is 24% of China's total export to Russia in the first 11 months of 2005. During the same time, China's export of high-tech products to Russia increased by 58%, and that is 7% of China's total exports to Russia. Also at that time period, border trade between the two countries reached $5.13 billion, growing 35% and accounting for nearly 20% of the total trade. Most of China's exports to Russia remain apparel and footwear. Russia is China's eighth largest trade partner and China is now Russia's fourth largest trade partner, and China now has over 750 investment projects in Russia, involving $1.05 billion.

China's contracted investment in Russia totaled $368 million during January–September 2005, twice that in 2004.

Chinese imports from Russia are mainly those of energy sources, such as crude oil, which is mostly transported by rail, and electricity exports from neighboring Siberian and Far Eastern regions. In the near future, exports of both of these commodities are set to increase, as Russia is building the Eastern Siberia-Pacific Ocean oil pipeline with a branch going to the Chinese border, and Russian power grid monopoly UES is building some of its hydropower stations with a view of future exports to China.

Export growth has continued to be a major component supporting China's rapid economic growth. To increase exports, China pursued policies such as fostering the rapid development of foreign-invested factories, which assembled imported components into consumer goods for export and liberalizing trading rights. In its 11th Five-Year Program, adopted in 2005, China placed greater emphasis on developing a consumer demand-driven economy to sustain economic growth and address imbalances.

FOREIGN INVESTMENT

China's investment climate has changed dramatically with more than two decades of reform. In the early 1980s, China restricted foreign investments to export-oriented operations and required foreign investors to form joint-venture partnerships with Chinese firms. The Encouraged Industry Catalogue sets out the degree of foreign involvement allowed in various industry sectors. From the beginning of the reforms legalizing foreign investment, capital inflows expanded every year until 1999. Foreign-invested enterprises account for 58–60% of China's imports and exports.

Since the early 1990s, the government has allowed foreign investors to manufacture and sell a wide range of goods on the domestic market, eliminated time restrictions on the establishment of joint ventures, provided some assurances against nationalization, allowed foreign partners to become chairs of joint venture boards, and authorized the establishment of wholly foreign-owned enterprises, now the preferred form of FDI. In 1991, China granted more preferential tax treatment for Wholly Foreign Owned Enterprises and contractual ventures and for foreign companies, which invested in selected economic zones or in projects encouraged by the state, such as energy, communications and transportation.

China also authorized some foreign banks to open branches in Shanghai and allowed foreign investors to purchase special "B" shares of stock in selected companies listed on the Shanghai and Shenzhen Securities Exchanges. These "B" shares sold to foreigners carried no ownership rights in a company. In 1997, China approved 21,046 foreign investment projects and received over $45 billion in foreign direct investment. China revised significantly its laws on Wholly Foreign-Owned Enterprises and China Foreign Equity Joint Ventures in 2000 and 2001, easing export performance and domestic content requirements.

Foreign investment remains a strong element in China's rapid expansion in world trade and has been an important factor in the growth of urban jobs. In 1998, foreign-invested enterprises produced about 40% of China's exports, and foreign exchange reserves totalled about $145 billion. Foreign-invested enterprises today produce about half of China's exports (the majority of China's foreign investment come from Hong Kong, Macau and Taiwan), and China continues to attract large investment inflows. However, the Chinese government's emphasis on guiding FDI into manufacturing has led to market saturation in some industries, while leaving China's services sectors underdeveloped. From 1993 to 2001, China was the world's second-largest recipient of foreign direct investment after the United States. China received $39 billion FDI in 1999 and $41 billion FDI in 2000. China is now one of the leading FDI recipients in the world, receiving almost $80 billion in 2005 according to World Bank statistics. In 2006, China received $69.47 billion in foreign direct investment. By 2011, with the U.S. seeing a decline in foreign investment following the 2008 financial crisis, China overtook it as the top destination for FDI, receiving over $280 billion that year.

Amid slowing economic conditions and a weakening yuan in 2015, December of that year saw a 5.8% drop in FDI to China. While China's rank as the top receiver of FDI continued through 2014, the slowing of inbound investment in 2015 combined with a massive rebound in foreign investment to the United States resulted in the U.S. reclaiming its position as the top investment destination. Data from the American Chamber of Commerce in China's *2016 China Business Climate Survey* confirms this trend, although it also demonstrates that China remains a top investment destination. This survey of over 500 members found that "China remains a top three investment priority for six out of ten member companies," though this is a decline from the 2012 high of eight out of ten respondents considering China a top priority.

Foreign exchange reserves totaled $155 billion in 1999 and $165 billion in 2000. Foreign exchange reserves exceeded $800 billion in 2005, more than doubling from 2003. Foreign exchange reserves were $819 billion at the end of 2005, $1.066 trillion at the end of 2006, $1.9 trillion by June 2008. In addition, by the end of September 2008 China replaced Japan for the first time as the largest foreign holder of US treasury securities with a total of $585 billion, vs Japan $573 billion. China has now surpassed those of Japan, making China's foreign exchange reserves the largest in the world.

As part of its WTO accession, China undertook to eliminate certain trade-related investment measures and to open up specified sectors that had previously been closed to foreign investment. New laws, regulations, and administrative measures to implement these commitments are being issued. Major remaining barriers to foreign investment include opaque and inconsistently enforced laws and regulations and the lack of a rules-based legal infrastructure. Warner Bros., for instance, withdrew its cinema business in China as a result of a regulation that requires Chinese investors to own at least a 51 percent stake or play a leading role in a foreign joint venture.

Another major development in the history of foreign investment in China was the establishment of the Shanghai Free Trade Zone in September 2013. The Zone is considered a testing ground for a number of economic and social reforms. Critically, foreign investment is controlled via a "negative list" approach, where FDI is permitted in all sectors unless explicitly prohibited by the inclusion of a given sector on the Negative List published by the Shanghai Municipal Government.

Chinese investment abroad

Outward foreign direct investment is a new feature of Chinese globalization, where local Chinese firms seek to make investments in both developing and developed countries. It was reported in 2011 that there was increasing investment by capital rich Chinese firms in promising firms in the United States. Such investments offer access to expertise in marketing and distribution potentially useful in exploiting the developing Chinese domestic market.

After three decades of opening up and reforming, China has been through rapid changes from a planning economy to a market economy.

According to the IMF, China's 2013 GDP is US$9.18 trillion, after the United States (US$17.37 trillion) but far ahead of Japan (US$4.9trillion), the third largest economy.

Since 2005 when Levono acquired IBM's ThinkPad, Chinese companies have been actively expanding outside of China, in both developed and developing countries. In 2013, Chinese companies invested US$90 billion globally in non-financial sectors, 16% more than 2012.

Between January 2009 and December 2013, China contributed a total of $161.03bn in outward FDI, creating almost 300,000 jobs. Western Europe was the largest regional recipient of Chinese outward FDI, with Germany receiving the highest number of FDI projects for any country globally.

There are two ways Chinese companies choose to enter a foreign market: organic growth and Merge & Acquisition (M&A). Many Chinese companies would prefer M&A for the following reasons:

- Fast. M&A is the fastest way for a company to expand into another country by acquiring brand, distribution, talents, and technology. Chinese CEOs has been used to growing at 50%+ speed and do not want to spend capital.

- China market. China has become the world's second largest economy. Many Chinese acquire foreign companies and then bring their products/services to China, anything from premium cars to fashion clothing to meat to Hollywood movies.

- Cheap capital access. The huge Chinese domestic market help many Chinese companies accumulated financial capital to do M&A. Chinese government also provides long-term, low-interest capital for companies to expand abroad.

- Low risk. M&A helped Chinese companies avoid risk of failure of organic growth as they got an established company with everything in place.

- Cheap labor. Some companies may move part of the manufacturing in high labor cost countries to China to reduce the cost and make the product more attractive in price.

- Trade and policy barrier. Chinese companies in many sectors face quota limitation and high tax, which prevent them from being competitive in foreign markets.

- Depressed assets. 2008-2010 global economic crisis created liquidity problems for a lot of western companies and reduced their market value. Chinese companies believe it is a great opportunity for them to buy these depressed assets at discount. China's direct foreign investment in non-financial sector growth from US $25 billion in 2007 to US$90 billion in 2013, more than three times.

At the beginning, state-owned enterprises dominate the foreign acquisition and most of the money goes to oil and minerals. Since 2005, more and more private companies start to acquire non raw material foreign companies. Below is a list of Chinese companies' M&A deals;

- In 2005, Lenovo acquired IBM's PC business Thinkpad at US$1.25 billion.
- In 2007, China PingAn acquired Fortis Insurance International at US$2.7 billion.
- In 2010, Geely acquired Volvo at US$1.8 billion.
- In 2011, Hainan Airline acquired 20% of NH Hotels at US$600 million.
- In 2011, China Bluestar acquired Norway's Elkem at US$2 billion.
- In 2012, Sany acquired Germany's Putzmeister at $US420 million.
- In 2012, Wanda acquired AMC Theater at US$2.6 billion.
- In 2012, Wanxiang acquired A123 at US$450 million.
- In 2012, China Investment Fund (New China Turst, China Aviation Industrial Fund and P3 Investments) acquired 80.1% of International Lease Finance co. from AIG at US$5.28 billion.
- In 2013, Shuanghui acquired Smithfield at US$4.7 billion
- In 2013, Fuxing acquired France's Club MedCLM.PA at 540 million Euros.
- In 2013, Fuxing acquired One Chase ManhattanPlaza at US$750 million.
- In 2014, Lenovo acquired Motorola from Google at US$2.9 billion
- In 2014, Wangxiang acquired Fisker at US$150 million

However, the fast growth and M&A deals did not change consumers' low quality and low price perception of Chinese goods and brands. According to market consecutive researches by The Monogram Group, a Chicago-based advertising agency, in 2007, 2009,

2011 and 2012, American consumers' willingness to purchase Chinese products across all categories except PC remained the same or became worse during 2007 -2012. The only sector that American's were more likely to purchase is PC, maybe due to the brand building of Lenovo.

Moreover, many M&A deals have been proven to be failed because companies underestimated the challenges and failed to restructure the company.

Case 1: Shanghai Auto acquired 48.9% of Korean Ssangyong at US$500 million in 2004, making it the most ambitious acquisition in Chinese auto industry at the time. Shanghai Auto wanted the brand and technology to expand its footprint in China. However, the cultural difference, the objection to transfer the technology and the failed sales of new SUV model put Shanghai Auto's ambition of expansion in jeopardy. It caused huge conflict between Ssangyong employees and Shanghai Auto as things didn't go well as planned. And the 2008 global economic crisis put Ssangyong on a survival mode, let alone expansion. After the negotiation with the labor union to reduce wages failed, Shanghai Auto decided to exit from Ssangyong and didn't get a penny back for their US$500 million investment.

Case 2: In 2004, TCL, the largest TV manufacturer and one of the fastest growing companies in China, acquired TV business including Thomson and RCA brand from Thomson Electronics of France to form a joint vendure called TCL-Thomson Electronics (TTE). For the coming two years, the company recorded huge loss, especially in Europe. Several factors contributed to the failure.

- Failure of Due Diligence. Right after TCL acquired Thomson's TV business, the TV market shifted to LCD technology, put Thomson out of date. As CEO of TCL, Dongsheng Li, said in 2012 "They betted on the wrong thing where the market would go. They thought Thomson's DLP could be the best choice."

- Lack of understanding of rules and regulations. According to the book "Resumption of Trading" by Chong Chen, soon after acquisition, Thomson found it in a situation that they couldn't recruit the talents they wanted and can't fire ones they didn't want.

- Underestimate of the challenges in cultural difference. Xuesong Tong, vice president of TTE, said in an interview with "China Operation" newspaper in 2005: "The French look down upon their Chinese boss. For example, they wanted to share the design model with TTE, but French just dislike it even though it is a popular one in US market. Also, French feel superior in their language and don't want to speak English, which created huge problem in communication. It takes hours to discuss simple issues and can't reach agreement."

- According to Scott Markman, president of Monogram, Chinese companies often moved their business model to developed countries and it doesn't work. Thomson has the problem, they are very good and distribution and operation in China but France and Europe is a totally different world.

Mergers and acquisitions

From 1993 to 2010, Chinese companies have been involved as either an acquiror or acquired company in 25,284 mergers and acquisitions with a total known value of US$969 billion. The number and value of deals hit a new record in 2010. The number of deals that happened in 2010 has been 3,640 which is an increase of 17% compared to 2009. The value of deals in 2010 was US$196 billion which is an increase of 25% compared to the year before.

DEMOGRAPHICS

Since the 1950s medical care, public hygiene and sanitation improved considerably, and epidemics were controlled. Consecutive generations continuously experienced better health. The population growth rate surged as the mortality rate dropped more rapidly than the birth rate. China's massive population has always been a major difficulty for the government as it has struggled to provide for it. In the 1950s, food supply was inadequate and the standard of living was generally low. This spurred the authorities to initiate a major birth control program. The Great Leap Forward industrial plan in 1958–60 was partially responsible for a huge famine that caused the death rate to surpass the birth rate, and by 1960, the overall population was declining. A second population control drive began in 1962 with major efforts focused on promoting late marriages and the use of contraceptives. By 1963 the country was in the beginning of recovery from the famine and the birth rate soared to its highest since 1949 with an annual population growth rate of 3%. In 1966, the Cultural Revolution suspended this second family planning program, but resumed four years later with the third attempt by making later marriage and family size limitation an obligation. Since 1970, the efforts have been much more effective. The third family planning program continued until 1979 when the one child per family policy was implemented. By the early 1980s, China's population reached around 1 billion and by the early 2000s, surpassed 1.3 billion. In the 1980s, the average overall population growth was around 1.5%. In the 1990s, this fell to about 1%. Today it is about 0.6%. China's population growth rate is now among the lowest for a developing country, although, due to its large population, annual net population growth is still considerable. One demographic consequence of the one-child policy is that China is now one of the most rapidly ageing countries in the world.

From 100 million to 150 million surplus rural workers are adrift between the villages and the cities, many subsisting through part-time, low-paying jobs.

According to the latest Forbes China Rich List (2007), China had 66 billionaires, the second largest number after the United States, which had 415. In the 2006 Forbes Rich List it stated that there were 15 Chinese billionaires. In the latest 2007 Hurun Report, it lists 106 billionaires in China.

Labor force

In 2012, for the first time, according to statistics released by China's National Bureau of Statistics in January 2013, the size of the labor force, people aged 15 to 59, in China shrank slightly to 937.27 million people, a decrease of 3.45 million from 2011. This trend, resulting from China's successful one-child policy of population control, is anticipated to continue for at least the next 20 years, to 2030.

On 29 October 2015, Xinhua, China's state news agency, reported a change in the existing law to a two-child policy, citing a statement from the Communist Party of China, and the new law is effective from 1 January 2016 after it was passed in the standing committee of the National People's Congress on 27 December 2015

TRANSPORTATION AND INFRASTRUCTURE

Development of the country's transportation infrastructure is given a high priority because it is so strategically tied to the national economy and national defense. Regardless, the transportation infrastructure is still not fully developed in many aspects and areas, and it constitutes a major hindrance on economic growth and the efficient logistical movement of goods and people. China's transportation policy, influenced by political, military, and economic concerns, have undergone major changes since 1949.

Immediately after the People's Republic was founded, the primary goal was to repair existing transportation infrastructure in order to meet military transport and logistics needs as well as to strengthen territorial integrity. During most of the 1950s, new road and rail links were built, while at the same time old ones were improved. During the 1960s much of the improvement of regional transportation became the responsibility of the local governments, and many small railways were constructed. Emphasis was also placed on developing transportation in remote rural, mountainous, and forested areas, in order to integrate poorer regions of the country and to help promote economies of scale in the agricultural sector.

Before the reform era began in the late 1970s, China's transportation links were mostly concentrated in the coastal areas and access to the inner regions was generally poor. This situation has been improved considerably since then, as railways and highways have been built in the remote and frontier regions of the northwest and southwest. At the same time, the development of international transportation was also pursued, and the scope of ocean shipping was broadened considerably.

Freight haulage is mainly provided by rail transport. The rail sector is monopolized by China Railways, which is controlled by the Ministry of Railways and there is wide variation in services provided. In late 2007 China became one of the few countries in the world to launch its own indigenously developed high-speed train. As rail capacity is struggling to meet demand for the transport of goods and raw materials such as coal, air routes, roads and waterways are rapidly being developed to provide an increasing proportion of China's overall transportation needs.

Some economic experts have argued that the development gap between China and other emerging economies such as Brazil, Argentina and India can be attributed to a large extent to China's early focus on ambitious infrastructure projects: while China invested roughly 9% of its GDP on infrastructure in the 1990s and 2000s, most emerging economies invested only 2% to 5% of their GDP. This considerable spending gap allowed the Chinese economy to grow at near optimal conditions while many South American economies suffered from various development bottlenecks (poor transportation networks, aging power grids, mediocre schools...).

SCIENCE AND TECHNOLOGY

Science and technology in China has in recent decades developed rapidly. The Chinese government has placed emphasis through funding, reform, and societal status on science and technology as a fundamental part of the socio-economic development of the country as well as for national prestige. China has made rapid advances in areas such as education, infrastructure, high-tech manufacturing, academic publishing, patents, and commercial applications and is now in some areas and by some measures a world leader. China is now increasingly targeting indigenous innovation and aims to reform remaining weaknesses. These initiatives are dependent on attracting highly educated overseas Chinese back to China to work in the innovation economy and to teach the next generation of Chinese students.

ECONOMIC HISTORY OF CHINA (1949–PRESENT)

Analysts estimated that investment accounted for about 25 percent of GNP in 1979, a rate surpassed by few other countries. Because of the comparatively low level of GNP, however, even this high rate of investment secured only a small amount of resources relative to the size of the country and the population. In 1978, for instance, only 16 percent of the GNP of the United States went into gross investment, but this amounted to US$345.6 billion, whereas the approximately 25 percent of China's GNP that was invested came to about the equivalent of US$111 billion and had to serve a population 4.5 times the size of that in the United States. The limited resources available for investment prevented China from rapidly producing or importing advanced equipment. Technological development proceeded gradually, and outdated equipment continued to be used as long as possible. Consequently, many different levels of technology were in use simultaneously. Most industries included some plants that were comparable to modern Western facilities, often based on imported equipment and designs. Equipment produced by Chinese factories was generally some years behind standard Western designs. Agriculture received a smaller share of state investment than industry and remained at a much lower average level of technology and productivity. Despite a significant increase in the availability of tractors, trucks, electric pumps, and mechanical threshers, most agricultural activities were still performed by people or animals.

Although the central administration coordinated the economy and redistributed resources among regions when necessary, in practice most economic activity was very decentralized, and there was relatively little flow of goods and services between areas. About 75 percent of the grain grown in China, for instance, was consumed by the families that produced it. One of the most important sources of growth in the economy was the improved ability to exploit the comparative advantages of each locality by expanding transportation capacity. The communications and transportation sectors were growing and improving but still could not carry the volume of traffic required by a modern economy because of the scarcity of investment funds and advanced technology.

Because of limited interaction among regions, the great variety of geographic zones in China, and the broad spectrum of technologies in use, areas differed widely in economic activities, organizational forms, and prosperity. Within any given city, enterprises ranged from tiny, collectively owned handicraft units, barely earning subsistence-level incomes for their members, to modern state-owned factories, whose workers received steady wages plus free medical care, bonuses, and an assortment of other benefits. The agricultural sector was diverse, accommodating well-equipped, "specialized households" that supplied scarce products and services to local markets; wealthy suburban villages specializing in the production of vegetables, pork, poultry, and eggs to sell in free markets in the nearby cities; fishing villages on the seacoast; herding groups on the grasslands of Inner Mongolia; and poor, struggling grain-producing villages in the arid mountains of Shaanxi and Gansu provinces. The economy had progressed in major ways since 1949, but after four to five decades experts in China and abroad agreed that it had a great distance yet to go.

Despite formidable constraints and disruptions, the Chinese economy was never stagnant. Production grew substantially between 1800 and 1949 and increased fairly rapidly after 1949. Before the 1980s, however, production gains were largely matched by population growth, so that productive capacity was unable to outdistance essential consumption needs significantly, particularly in agriculture. Grain output in 1979 was about twice as large as in 1952, but so was the population. As a result, little surplus was produced even in good years. Further, few resources could be spared for investment in capital goods, such as machinery, factories, mines, railroads, and other productive assets. The relatively small size of the capital stock caused productivity per worker to remain low, which in turn perpetuated the economy's inability to generate a substantial surplus.

ECONOMIC POLICIES, 1949–80

When the Communist Party of China came to power in 1949, its leaders' fundamental long-range goals were to transform China into a modern, powerful, socialist nation. In economic terms these objectives meant industrialization, improvement of living standards, narrowing of income differences, and production of modern military equipment. As the years passed, the leadership continued to subscribe to these goals. But the economic policies formulated to achieve them were dramatically altered on several occasions in response to major changes in the economy, internal politics, and international political and economic developments.

An important distinction emerged between leaders who felt that the socialist goals of income equalization and heightened political consciousness should take priority over material progress and those who believed that industrialization and general economic modernization were prerequisites for the attainment of a successful socialist order. Among the prominent leaders who considered politics the prime consideration were Mao Zedong, Lin Biao, and the members of the Gang of Four. Leaders who more often stressed practical economic considerations included Liu Shaoqi, Zhou Enlai, and Deng Xiaoping. For the most part, important policy shifts reflected the alternating emphasis on political and economic goals and were accompanied by major changes in the positions of individuals in the political power structure. An important characteristic in the development of economic policies and the underlying economic model was that each new policy period, while differing significantly from its predecessor, nonetheless retained most of the existing economic organization. Thus the form of the economic model and the policies that expressed it at any given point in Chinese history reflected both the current policy emphasis and a structural foundation built up during the earlier periods.

Recovery from war, 1949–52

In 1949 China's economy was suffering from the debilitating effects of decades of warfare. Many mines and factories had been damaged or destroyed. At the end of the war with Japan in 1945, Soviet troops had dismantled about half the machinery in the major industrial areas of the northeast and shipped it to the Soviet Union. Transportation, communication, and power systems had been destroyed or had deteriorated because of lack of maintenance. Agriculture was disrupted, and food production was some 30 percent below its pre-war peak level. Further, economic ills were compounded by one of the most virulent inflations in world history.

The chief goal of the government for the 1949–52 period was simply to restore the economy to normal working order. The administration moved quickly to repair transportation and communication links and revive the flow of economic activity. The banking system was nationalized and centralized under the People's Bank of China.

To bring inflation under control by 1951, the government unified the monetary system, tightened credit, restricted government budgets at all levels and put them under central control, and guaranteed the value of the currency. Commerce was stimulated and partially regulated by the establishment of state trading companies (commercial departments), which competed with private traders in purchasing goods from producers and selling them to consumers or enterprises.

Transformation of ownership in industry proceeded slowly. About a third of the country's enterprises had been under state control while the Guomindang government was in power (1927–49), as was much of the modernized transportation sector. The Communist Party of China immediately made these units state-owned enterprises upon taking power in 1949. The remaining privately owned enterprises were gradually brought under government control, but 17 percent of industrial units were still completely outside the state system in 1952.

In agriculture a major change in landownership was carried out. Under a nationwide land reform program, titles to about 45 percent of the arable land were redistributed from landlords and more prosperous farmers to the 60 to 70 percent of farm families that previously owned little or no land. Once land reform was completed in an area, farmers were encouraged to cooperate in some phases of production through the formation of small "mutual aid teams" of six or seven households each. Thirty-nine percent of all farm households belonged to mutual aid teams in 1952. By 1952 price stability had been established, commerce had been restored, and industry and agriculture had regained their previous peak levels of production. The period of recovery had achieved its goals.

First Five-Year Plan, 1953–57

Having restored a viable economic base, the leadership under Mao Zedong, Zhou Enlai, and other revolutionary veterans was prepared to embark on an intensive program of industrial growth and socialization. For this purpose the administration adopted the Soviet economic model, based on state ownership in the modern sector, large collective units in agriculture, and centralized economic planning. The Soviet approach to economic development was manifested in the First Five-Year Plan (1953–57). As in the Soviet economy, the main objective was a high rate of economic growth, with primary emphasis on industrial development at the expense of agriculture and particular concentration on heavy industry and capital-intensive technology. Soviet planners helped their Chinese counterparts formulate the plan. Large numbers of Soviet engineers, technicians, and scientists assisted in developing and installing new heavy industrial facilities, including many entire plants and pieces of equipment purchased from the Soviet Union. Government control over industry was increased during this period by applying financial pressures and inducements to convince owners of private, modern firms to sell them to the state or convert them into joint public-private enterprises under state control. By 1956 approximately 67.5 percent of all modern industrial enterprises were state owned, and 32.5 percent were under joint public-private ownership. No privately owned firms remained. During the same period, the handicraft industries were organized into cooperatives, which accounted for 91.7 percent of all handicraft workers by 1956.

Agriculture also underwent extensive organizational changes. To facilitate the mobilization of agricultural resources, improve the efficiency of farming, and increase government access to agricultural products, the authorities encouraged farmers to organize increasingly large and socialized collective units. From the loosely structured, tiny mutual aid teams, villages were to advance first to lower-stage, agricultural producers' cooperatives, in which families still received some income on the basis of the amount of land they contributed, and eventually to advanced cooperatives, or collectives. In the advanced producers' cooperatives, income shares were based only on the amount of labor contributed. In addition, each family was allowed to retain a small private plot on which to grow vegetables, fruit, and livestock for its own use. The collectivization process began slowly but accelerated in 1955 and 1956. In 1957 about 93.5 percent of all farm households had joined advanced producers' cooperatives.

In terms of economic growth the First Five-Year Plan was quite successful, especially in those areas emphasized by the Soviet-style development strategy. A solid foundation was created in heavy industry. Key industries, including iron and steel manufacturing, coal mining, cement production, electricity generation, and machine building were greatly expanded and were put on a firm, modern technological footing. Thousands of industrial and mining enterprises were constructed, including 156 major facilities. Industrial production increased at an average annual rate of 19 percent between 1952 and 1957, and national income grew at a rate of 9 percent a year.

Despite the lack of state investment in agriculture, agricultural output increased substantially, averaging increases of about 4 percent a year. This growth resulted primarily from gains in efficiency brought about by the reorganization and cooperation achieved through collectivization. As the First Five-Year Plan wore on, however, Chinese leaders became increasingly concerned over the relatively sluggish performance of agriculture and the inability of state trading companies to increase significantly the amount of grain procured from rural units for urban consumption.

Great Leap Forward, 1958–60

Before the end of the First Five-Year Plan, the growing imbalance between industrial and agricultural growth, dissatisfaction with inefficiency, and lack of flexibility in the decision-making process convinced the nation's leaders – particularly Mao Zedong – that the highly centralized, industry-based Soviet model was not appropriate for China. In 1957 the government adopted measures to shift a great deal of the authority for economic decision making to the provincial-level, county, and local administrations. In 1958 the Second Five-Year Plan (1958–62), which was intended to continue the policies of the first plan, was abandoned. In its place the leadership adopted an approach that relied on spontaneous heroic efforts by the entire population to produce a dramatic "great leap" in production for all sectors of the economy at once. Further reorganization of agriculture was regarded as the key to the endeavor to leap suddenly to a higher stage of productivity. A fundamental problem was the lack of sufficient capital to invest heavily in both industry and agriculture at the same time. To overcome this problem, the leadership decided to attempt to create capital in the agricultural sector by building vast irrigation and water control works employing huge teams of farmers whose labor was not being fully utilized. Surplus rural labor also was to be employed to support the industrial sector by setting up thousands of small-scale, low-technology, "backyard" industrial projects in farm units, which would produce machinery required for agricultural development and components for urban industries. Mobilization of surplus rural labor and further improvements in agricultural efficiency were to be accomplished by a "leap" to the final stage of agricultural collectivization—the formation of people's communes.

People's communes were created by combining some 20 or 30 advanced producers' cooperatives of 20,000 to 30,000 members on average, although membership varied from as few as 6,000 to over 40,000 in some cases. When first instituted, the communes were envisaged as combining in one body the functions of the lowest level of local government and the highest level of organization in agricultural production. Communes consisted of three organizational levels: the central commune administration; the production brigade (roughly equivalent to the advanced producers' cooperatives, or a traditional rural village), and the production team, which generally consisted of around thirty families. At the inception of the Great Leap Forward, the communes were intended to acquire all ownership rights over the productive assets of their subordinate units and to take over most of the planning and decision making for farm activities. Ideally, communes were to improve efficiency by moving farm families into dormitories, feeding them in communal mess halls, and moving whole teams of laborers from task to task. In practice, this ideal, extremely centralized form of commune was not instituted in most areas.

Ninety-eight percent of the farm population was organized into communes between April and September 1958. Very soon it became evident that in most cases the communes were too unwieldy to carry out successfully all the managerial and administrative functions that were assigned to them. In 1959 and 1960, most production decisions reverted to the brigade and team levels, and eventually most governmental responsibilities were returned to county and township administrations. Nonetheless, the commune system was retained and continued to be the basic form of organization in the agricultural sector until the early 1980s.

During the Great Leap Forward, the industrial sector also was expected to discover and use slack labor and productive capacity to increase output beyond the levels previously considered feasible. Political zeal was to be the motive force, and to "put politics in command" enterprising party branches took over the direction of many factories. In addition, central planning was relegated to a minor role in favor of spontaneous, politically inspired production decisions from individual units.

The result of the Great Leap Forward was a severe economic crisis. In 1958 industrial output did in fact "leap" by 55 percent, and the agricultural sector gathered in a good harvest. In 1959, 1960, and 1961, however, adverse weather conditions, improperly constructed water control projects, and other misallocations of resources that had occurred during the overly centralized communization movement resulted in disastrous declines in agricultural output. In 1959 and 1960, the gross value of agricultural output fell by 14 percent and 13 percent, respectively, and in 1961 it dropped a further 2 percent to reach the lowest point since 1952. Widespread famine occurred, especially in rural areas, according to 1982 census figures, and the death rate climbed from 1.2 percent in 1958 to 1.5 percent in 1959, 2.5 percent in 1960, and then dropped back to 1.4 percent in 1961. From 1958 to 1961, over 14 million people apparently died of starvation, and the number of reported births was about 23 million fewer than under normal conditions. The government prevented an even worse disaster by canceling nearly all orders for foreign technical imports and using the country's foreign exchange reserves to import over 5 million tons of grain a year beginning in 1960. Mines and factories continued to expand output through 1960, partly by overworking personnel and machines but largely because many new plants constructed during the First Five-Year Plan went into full production in these years. Thereafter, however, the excessive strain on equipment and workers, the effects of the agricultural crisis, the lack of economic coordination, and, in the 1960s, the withdrawal of Soviet assistance caused industrial output to plummet by 38 percent in 1961 and by a further 16 percent in 1962.

Readjustment and recovery: "Agriculture First," 1961–65

Faced with economic collapse in the early 1960s, the government sharply revised the immediate goals of the economy and devised a new set of economic policies to replace those of the Great Leap Forward. Top priority was given to restoring agricultural output and expanding it at a rate that would meet the needs of the growing population. Planning and economic coordination were to be revived- -although in a less centralized form than before the Great Leap Forward — so as to restore order and efficient allocation of resources to the economy. The rate of investment was to be reduced and investment priorities reversed, with agriculture receiving first consideration, light industry second, and heavy industry third.

In a further departure from the emphasis on heavy industrial development that persisted during the Great Leap Forward, the government undertook to mobilize the nation's resources to bring about technological advancement in agriculture. Organizational changes in agriculture mainly involved decentralization of production decision making and income distribution within the commune structure. The role of the central commune administration was greatly reduced, although it remained the link between local government and agricultural producers and was important in carrying out activities that were too large in scale for the production brigades. Production teams were designated the basic accounting units and were responsible for making nearly all decisions concerning production and the distribution of income to their members. Private plots, which had disappeared on some communes during the Great Leap Forward, were officially restored to farm families.

Economic support for agriculture took several forms. Agricultural taxes were reduced, and the prices paid for agricultural products were raised relative to the prices of industrial supplies for agriculture. There were substantial increases in supplies of chemical fertilizer and various kinds of agricultural machinery, notably small electric pumps for irrigation. Most of the modern supplies were concentrated in areas that were known to produce "high and stable yields" in order to ensure the best possible results.

In industry, a few key enterprises were returned to central state control, but control over most enterprises remained in the hands of provincial-level and local governments. This decentralization had taken place in 1957 and 1958 and was reaffirmed and strengthened in the 1961-65 period. Planning rather than politics once again guided production decisions, and material rewards rather than revolutionary enthusiasm became the leading incentive for production. Major imports of advanced foreign machinery, which had come to an abrupt halt with the withdrawal of Soviet assistance starting in 1960, were initiated with Japan and West European countries.

During the 1961–65 readjustment and recovery period, economic stability was restored, and by 1966 production in both agriculture and industry surpassed the peak levels of the Great Leap Forward period.

Between 1961 and 1966, agricultural output grew at an average rate of 9.6 percent a year. Industrial output was increased in the same years at an average annual rate of 10.6 percent, largely by reviving plants that had operated below capacity after the economic collapse in 1961. Another important source of growth in this period was the spread of rural, small-scale industries, particularly coal mines, hydroelectric plants, chemical fertilizer plants, and agricultural machinery plants. The economic model that emerged in this period combined elements of the highly centralized, industrially oriented, Soviet-style system of the First Five-Year Plan with aspects of the decentralization of ownership and decision making that characterized the Great Leap Forward and with the strong emphasis on agricultural development and balanced growth of the "agriculture first" policy. Important changes in economic policy occurred in later years, but the basic system of ownership, decision-making structure, and development strategy that was forged in the early 1960s was not significantly altered until the reform period of the 1980s.

Events during the Cultural Revolution decade, 1966–76

The Cultural Revolution was set in motion by Mao Zedong in 1966 and called to a halt in 1968, but the atmosphere of radical leftism persisted until Mao's death and the fall of the Gang of Four in 1976. During this period, there were several distinct phases of economic policy.

High tide of the Cultural Revolution, 1966–69

The Cultural Revolution, unlike the Great Leap Forward, was primarily a political upheaval and did not produce major changes in official economic policies or the basic economic model. Nonetheless, its influence was felt throughout urban society, and it profoundly affected the modern sector of the economy.

Agricultural production stagnated, but in general the rural areas experienced less turmoil than the cities. Production was reduced in the modern nonagricultural sectors in several ways.

The most direct cause of production halts was the political activity of students and workers in the mines and factories.

A second cause was the extensive disruption of transportation resulting from the requisitioning of trains and trucks to carry Chinese Red Guards around the country. Output at many factories suffered from shortages of raw materials and other supplies.

A third disruptive influence was that the direction of factories was placed in the hands of revolutionary committees, consisting of representatives from the party, the workers, and the Chinese People's Liberation Army, whose members often had little knowledge of either management or the enterprise they were supposed to run. In addition, virtually all engineers, managers, scientists, technicians, and other professional personnel were "criticized," demoted, "sent down" to the countryside to "participate in labor," or even jailed, all of which resulted in their skills and knowledge being lost to the enterprise.

The effect was a 14-percent decline in industrial production in 1967. A degree of order was restored by the army in late 1967 and 1968, and the industrial sector returned to a fairly high rate of growth in 1969.

Other aspects of the Cultural Revolution had more far-reaching effects on the economy. Imports of foreign equipment, required for technological advancement, were curtailed by rampant xenophobia.

Probably the most serious and long-lasting effect on the economy was the dire shortage of highly educated personnel caused by the closing of the universities. China's ability to develop new technology and absorb imported technology would be limited for years by the hiatus in higher education.

Resumption of systematic growth, 1970–74

As political stability was gradually restored, a renewed drive for coordinated, balanced development was set in motion under the leadership of Premier Zhou Enlai.

To revive efficiency in industry, Communist Party of China committees were returned to positions of leadership over the revolutionary committees, and a campaign was carried out to return skilled and highly educated personnel to the jobs from which they had been displaced during the Cultural Revolution.

Universities began to reopen, and foreign contacts were expanded. Once again the economy suffered from imbalances in the capacities of different industrial sectors and an urgent need for increased supplies of modern inputs for agriculture. In response to these problems, there was a significant increase in investment, including the signing of contracts with foreign firms for the construction of major facilities for chemical fertilizer production, steel finishing, and oil extraction and refining. The most notable of these contracts was for thirteen of the world's largest and most modern chemical fertilizer plants. During this period, industrial output grew at an average rate of 8 percent a year.

Agricultural production declined somewhat in 1972 because of poor weather but increased at an average annual rate of 3.8 percent for the period as a whole. The party and state leadership undertook a general reevaluation of development needs, and Zhou Enlai presented the conclusions in a report to the Fourth National People's Congress in January 1975. In it he called for the Four Modernizations. Zhou emphasized the mechanization of agriculture and a comprehensive two-stage program for the modernization of the entire economy by the end of the century.

Gang of Four, 1974–76

During the early and mid-1970s, the radical group later known as the Gang of Four attempted to dominate the power center through their network of supporters and, most important, through their control of the media.

More moderate leaders, however, were developing and promulgating a pragmatic program for rapid modernization of the economy that contradicted the set of policies expressed in the media. Initiatives by Zhou Enlai and Deng Xiaoping were vehemently attacked in the press and in political campaigns as "poisonous weeds."

Using official news organs, the Gang of Four advocated the primacy of nonmaterial, political incentives, radical reduction of income differences, elimination of private farm plots, and a shift of the basic accounting unit up to the brigade level in agriculture. They opposed the strengthening of central planning and denounced the use of foreign technology.

In the face of such contradictory policy pronouncements and uncertain political currents, administrators and economic decision makers at all levels were virtually paralyzed. Economic activity slowed, and the incipient modernization program almost ground to a halt. Uncertainty and instability were exacerbated by the death of Zhou Enlai in January 1976 and the subsequent second purge of Deng Xiaoping in April. The effects of the power struggle and policy disputes were compounded by the destruction resulting from the Tangshan earthquake in July 1976. Output for the year in both industry and agriculture showed no growth over 1975. The interlude of uncertainty finally ended when the Gang of Four was arrested in October, one month after Mao's death.

Post-Mao interlude, 1976–78

After the fall of the Gang of Four, the leadership under Hua Guofeng — and by July 1977 the rehabilitated Deng Xiaoping — reaffirmed the modernization program espoused by Zhou Enlai in 1975. They also set forth a battery of new policies for the purpose of accomplishing the Four Modernizations.

The new policies strengthened the authority of managers and economic decision makers at the expense of party officials, stressed material incentives for workers, and called for expansion of the research and education systems. Foreign trade was to be increased, and exchanges of students and "foreign experts" with developed countries were to be encouraged.

This new policy initiative was capped at the Fifth National People's Congress in February and March 1978, when Hua Guofeng presented the draft of an ambitious ten-year plan for the 1976-85 period. The plan called for high rates of growth in both industry and agriculture and included 120 construction projects that would require massive and expensive imports of foreign technology.

Between 1976 and 1978, the economy quickly recovered from the stagnation of the Cultural Revolution. Agricultural production was sluggish in 1977 because of a third consecutive year of adverse weather conditions but rebounded with a record harvest in 1978. Industrial output jumped by 14 percent in 1977 and by 13 percent in 1978.

Reform of the economic system, beginning in 1978

At the milestone Third Plenum of the National Party Congress's 11th Central Committee which opened on December 22, 1978, the party leaders decided to undertake a program of gradual but fundamental reform of the economic system. They concluded that the Maoist version of the centrally planned economy had failed to produce efficient economic growth and had caused China to fall far behind not only the industrialized nations of the West but also the new industrial powers of Asia: Japan, South Korea, Singapore, Taiwan, and Hong Kong.

In the late 1970s, while Japan and Hong Kong rivaled European countries in modern technology, China's citizens had to make do with barely sufficient food supplies, rationed clothing, inadequate housing, and a service sector that was inadequate and inefficient. All of these shortcomings embarrassed China internationally.

The purpose of the reform program was not to abandon communism but to make it work better by substantially increasing the role of market mechanisms in the system and by reducing—not eliminating—government planning and direct control.

The process of reform was incremental. New measures were first introduced experimentally in a few localities and then were popularized and disseminated nationally if they proved successful.

By 1987 the program had achieved remarkable results in increasing supplies of food and other consumer goods and had created a new climate of dynamism and opportunity in the economy. At the same time, however, the reforms also had created new problems and tensions, leading to intense questioning and political struggles over the program's future.

Period of readjustment, 1979–81

The first few years of the reform program were designated the "period of readjustment," during which key imbalances in the economy were to be corrected and a foundation was to be laid for a well-planned modernization drive. The schedule of Hua Guofeng's ten-year plan was discarded, although many of its elements were retained.

The major goals of the readjustment process were to expand exports rapidly; overcome key deficiencies in transportation, communications, coal, iron, steel, building materials, and electric power; and redress the imbalance between light and heavy industry by increasing the growth rate of light industry and reducing investment in heavy industry. Agricultural production was stimulated in 1979 by an increase of over 22 percent in the procurement prices paid for farm products.

The central policies of the reform program were introduced experimentally during the readjustment period. The most successful reform policy, the *contract* responsibility system of production in agriculture, was suggested by the government in 1979 as a way for poor rural units in mountainous or arid areas to increase their incomes. The responsibility system allowed individual farm families to work a piece of land for profit in return for delivering a set amount of produce to the collective at a given price. This arrangement created strong incentives for farmers to reduce production costs and increase productivity. Soon after its introduction the responsibility system was adopted by numerous farm units in all sorts of areas.

Agricultural production was also stimulated by official encouragement to establish free farmers' markets in urban areas, as well as in the countryside, and by allowing some families to operate as "specialized households," devoting their efforts to producing a scarce commodity or service on a profit-making basis.

In industry, the main policy innovations increased the autonomy of enterprise managers, reduced emphasis on planned quotas, allowed enterprises to produce goods outside the plan for sale on the market, and permitted enterprises to experiment with the use of bonuses to reward higher productivity. The government also tested a fundamental change in financial procedures with a limited number of state-owned units: rather than remitting all of their profits to the state, as was normally done, these enterprises were allowed to pay a tax on their profits and retain the balance for reinvestment and distribution to workers as bonuses.

The government also actively encouraged the establishment of collectively owned and operated industrial and service enterprises as a means of soaking up some of the unemployment among young people and at the same time helping to increase supplies of light industrial products. Individual enterprise also was allowed, after having virtually disappeared during the Cultural Revolution, and independent cobblers, tailors, tinkers, and vendors once again became common sights in the cities.

Foreign-trade procedures were greatly eased, allowing individual enterprises and administrative departments outside the Ministry of Foreign Trade (which became the Ministry of Foreign Economic Relations and Trade in 1984) to engage in direct negotiations with foreign firms. A wide range of cooperation, trading and credit arrangements with foreign firms were legalized so that China could enter the mainstream of international trade.

Reform and opening, beginning in 1982

The period of readjustment produced promising results, increasing incomes substantially; raising the availability of food, housing, and other consumer goods; and generating strong rates of growth in all sectors except heavy industry, which was intentionally restrained. On the strength of these initial successes, the reform program was broadened, and the leadership under Deng Xiaoping frequently remarked that China's basic policy was "reform and opening," that is, reform of the economic system and opening to foreign trade.

In agriculture the contract responsibility system was adopted as the organizational norm for the entire country, and the commune structure was largely dismantled. By the end of 1984, approximately 98 percent of all farm households were under the responsibility system, and all but a handful of communes had been dissolved. The communes' administrative responsibilities were turned over to township and town governments, and their economic roles were assigned to townships and villages. The role of free markets for farm produce was further expanded and, with increased marketing possibilities and rising productivity, farm incomes rose rapidly.

In industry the complexity and interrelation of production activities prevented a single, simple policy from bringing about the kind of dramatic improvement that the responsibility system achieved in agriculture. Nonetheless, a cluster of policies based on greater flexibility, autonomy, and market involvement significantly improved the opportunities available to most enterprises, generated high rates of growth, and increased efficiency. Enterprise managers gradually gained greater control over their units, including the right to hire and fire, although the process required endless struggles with bureaucrats and party cadres. The practice of remitting taxes on profits and retaining the balance became universal by 1985, increasing the incentive for enterprises to maximize profits and substantially adding to their autonomy. A change of potentially equal importance was a shift in the source of investment funds from government budget allocations, which carried no interest and did not have to be repaid, to interest-bearing bank loans. As of 1987 the interest rate charged on such loans was still too low to serve as a check on unproductive investments, but the mechanism was in place.

The role of foreign trade under the economic reforms increased far beyond its importance in any previous period. Before the reform period, the combined value of imports and exports had seldom exceeded 10 percent of national income. In 1980 it was 15 percent, in 1984 it was 21 percent, and in 1986 it reached 35 percent. Unlike earlier periods, when China was committed to trying to achieve self-sufficiency, under Deng Xiaoping foreign trade was regarded as an important source of investment funds and modern technology. As a result, restrictions on trade were loosened further in the mid-1980s, and foreign investment was legalized. The most common foreign investments were joint ventures between foreign firms and Chinese units. Sole ownership by foreign investors also became legal, but the feasibility of such undertakings remained questionable.

The most conspicuous symbols of the new status of foreign trade were the four coastal special economic zones, which were created in 1979 as enclaves where foreign investment could receive special treatment. Three of the four zones — the cities of Shenzhen, Zhuhai, and Shantou — were located in Guangdong Province, close to Hong Kong. The fourth, Xiamen, in Fujian Province, was directly across the strait from Taiwan. More significant for China's economic development was the designation in April 1984 of economic development zones in the fourteen largest coastal cities- -including Dalian, Tianjin, Shanghai, and Guangzhou — all of which were major commercial and industrial centers. These zones were to create productive exchanges between foreign firms with advanced technology and major Chinese economic networks.

Domestic commerce also was stimulated by the reform policies, which explicitly endeavored to enliven the economy by shifting the primary burden of the allocation of goods and services from the government plan to the market. Private entrepreneurship and freemarket activities were legalized and encouraged in the 1980s, although the central authorities continuously had to fight the efforts of local government agencies to impose excessive taxes on independent merchants. By 1987 the state-owned system of commercial agencies and retail outlets coexisted with a rapidly growing private and collectively owned system that competed with it vigorously, providing a wider range of consumption choices for Chinese citizens than at any previous time.

Although the reform program achieved impressive successes, it also gave rise to several serious problems. One problem was the challenge to party authority presented by the principles of freemarket activity and professional managerial autonomy. Another difficulty was a wave of crime, corruption, and — in the minds of many older people — moral deterioration caused by the looser economic and political climate. The most fundamental tensions were those created by the widening income disparities between the people who were "getting rich" and those who were not and by the pervasive threat of inflation. These concerns played a role in the political struggle that culminated in party general secretary Hu Yaobang's forced resignation in 1987. Following Hu's resignation, the leadership engaged in an intense debate over the future course of the reforms and how to balance the need for efficiency and market incentives with the need for government guidance and control. The commitment to further reform was affirmed, but its pace, and the emphasis to be placed on macroeconomic and microeconomic levers, remained objects of caution.

China GDP

In 1985, the State Council of China approved to establish a SNA (System of National Accounting), use the GDP to measure the national economy. China started the study of theoretical foundation, guiding, and accounting model etc., for establishing a new system of national economic accounting. In 1986, as the first citizen of the People's Republic of China to receive a Ph.D. in economics from an overseas country, Dr. Fengbo Zhang headed Chinese Macroeconomic Research - the key research project of the seventh Five-Year Plan of China, as well as completing and publishing the China GDP data by China's own research. The summary of the above has been included in the book "Chinese Macroeconomic Structure and Policy" (June 1988) edited by Fengbo Zhang, and collectively authored by the Research Center of the State Council of China. This is the first GDP data which was published by China. The research utilized the World Bank's method as a reference, and made the numerous appropriate adjustments based on China's national condition. The GDP also has been converted to USD based data by utilizing the moving average exchange rate. The research systematically completed China's GDP and GDP per capita from 1952 to 1986 and analyzed growth rate, the change and contribution rates of each component. The research also included international comparisons. Additionally, the research compared MPS (Material Product System) and SNA (System of National Accounting), looking at the results from the two systems from analyzing Chinese economy. This achievement created the foundation for China's GDP research.

The State Council of China issued "The notice regarding implementation of System of National Accounting" in August 1992, the Western SNA system officially is introduced to China, replaced Soviet Union's MPS system, Western economic indicator GDP became China's most important economic indicator. Based on Dr. Fengbo Zhang's research, in 1997, the National Bureau of Statistics of China, in collaboration with Hitotsubashi University of Japan, estimated China's GDP Data from 1952 up to 1995 based on the SNA principal.

Industry

In 1985, industry employed about 17 percent of the labor force but produced more than 46 percent of gross national product (GNP).

It was the fastest growing sector with an average annual growth of 11 percent from 1952 to 1985. There was a wide range of technological levels. There were many small handicraft units and many enterprises using machinery installed or designed in the 1950s and 1960s. There was a significant number of big, up-to-date plants, including textile mills, steel mills, chemical fertilizer plants, and petrochemical facilities but there were also some burgeoning light industries producing consumer goods. China produced most kinds of products made by industrialized nations but limited quantities of high-technology items. Technology transfer was conducted by importing whole plants, equipment, and designs as an important means of progress. Major industrial centers were in Liaoning Province, Beijing-Tianjin-Tangshan area, Shanghai, and Wuhan. Mineral resources included huge reserves of iron ore and there were adequate to abundant supplies of nearly all other industrial minerals. Outdated mining and ore processing technologies were gradually being replaced with modern processes, techniques and equipment.

Agriculture

In 1985, the agricultural sector employed about 63 percent of the labor force and its proportion of GNP was about 33 percent. There was low worker productivity because of scant supplies of agricultural machinery and other modern inputs. Most agricultural processes were still performed by hand. There was very small arable land area (just above 10 percent of total area, as compared with 22 percent in United States) in relation to the size of the country and population. There was intensive use of land; all fields produced at least one crop a year, and wherever conditions permitted, two or even three crops were grown annually, especially in the south.

Grain was the most the important product, including rice, wheat, corn, sorghum, barley, and millet. Other important crops included cotton, jute, oilseeds, sugarcane, and sugar beets. Eggs were also a major product. Pork production increased steadily, and poultry and pigs were raised on family plots. Other livestock were relatively limited in numbers, except for sheep and goats, which grazed in large herds on grasslands of the Inner Mongolia Autonomous Region and the northwest. There was substantial marine and freshwater fishery. Timber resources were mainly located in the northeast and southwest, and much of the country was deforested centuries ago. A wide variety of fruits and vegetables were grown.

Energy resources

China was self-sufficient in nearly all energy forms. Coal and petroleum were exported since the early 1970s. Its coal reserves were among the world's largest, and mining technology was inadequately developed but steadily improved in the late 1980s. Petroleum reserves were very large at the time but of varying quality and in disparate locations. Suspected oil deposits in the northwest and offshore tracts were believed to be among the world's largest. Exploration and extraction was limited by scarcity of equipment and trained personnel. Twenty-seven contracts for joint offshore exploration and production by Japanese and Western oil companies were signed by 1982, but by the late 1980s only a handful of wells were producing oil. Substantial natural gas reserves were in the north, northwest, and offshore. The hydroelectric potential of the country was the greatest in the world and sixth largest in capacity, and very large hydroelectric projects were under construction, with others were in the planning stage. Thermal power, mostly coal fired, produced approximately 68 percent of generating capacity in 1985, and was increased to 72 percent by 1990. Emphasis on thermal power in the late 1980s was seen by policy makers as a quick, shortterm solution to energy needs, and hydroelectric and nuclear power was seen as a long-term solution. Petroleum production growth continued in order to meet the needs of nationwide mechanization and provided important foreign exchange but domestic use was restricted as much as possible until the end of the decade.

Foreign trade

Foreign trade was small by international standards but was growing rapidly in size and importance, as it represented 20 percent of GNP in 1985. Trade was controlled by the Ministry of Foreign Economic Relations and Trade and subordinate units and by the Bank of China, the foreign exchange arm of the central bank. Substantial decentralization and increased flexibility in foreign trade operations occurred since the late 1970s. Textiles were leading the export category. Other important exports included petroleum and foodstuffs. Leading imports included machinery, transport equipment, manufactured goods, and chemicals. Japan was the dominant trading partner, and accounted for 28.9 percent of imports and 15.2 percent of exports in 1986. Hong Kong was a leading market for exports (31.6 percent) but a source of only 13 percent of imports. In 1979 the United States became China's second largest source of imports and in 1986 was the third largest overall trade partner. Western Europe, particularly the Federal Republic of Germany, was also a major trading partner. Tourism was encouraged and growing.

1990–2000

China's economy regained momentum in the early 1990s. During a Chinese New Year visit to southern China in early 1992, China's paramount leader at the time Deng Xiaoping made a series of political pronouncements designed to give new impetus to and reinvigorate the process of economic reform. The 14th National Communist Party Congress later in the year backed up Deng's renewed push for market reforms, stating that China's key task in the 1990s was to create a "socialist market economy". Continuity in the political system but bolder reform in the economic system were announced as the hallmarks of the 10-year development plan for the 1990s.

During 1993, output and prices were accelerating, investment outside the state budget was soaring, and economic expansion was fueled by the introduction of more than 2,000 special economic zones (SEZs) and the influx of foreign capital that the SEZs facilitated. The government approved additional long-term reforms aimed at giving still more play to market-oriented institutions and at strengthening central control over the financial system; state enterprises would continue to dominate many key industries in what was now termed a "socialist market economy". Fearing hyperinflation, the authorities called in speculative loans, raised interest rates, and reevaluated investment projects. The growth rate was thus tempered, and the inflation rate dropped from over 17% in 1995 to 8% in early 1996.

In 1996, the Chinese economy continued to grow at a rapid pace, at about 9.5%, accompanied by low inflation. The economy slowed for the next 3 years, influenced in part by the Asian Financial Crisis, with official growth of 8.9% in 1997, 7.8% in 1998 and 7.1% for 1999. From 1995 to 1999, inflation dropped sharply, reflecting tighter monetary policies and stronger measures to control food prices. The year 2000 showed a modest reversal of this trend. Gross domestic product in 2000 grew officially at 8.0% that year, and had quadrupled since 1978. In 1999, with its 1.25 billion people but a GDP of just $3,800 per capita (PPP), China became the second largest economy in the world after the US. According to several sources, China did not become the second largest economy until 2010. However, according to Gallup polls many Americans rate China's economy as first. Considering

GDP per capita, this is far from accurate. The United States remains the largest economy in the world. However, the trend of China Rising is clear.

The Asian financial crisis affected China at the margin, mainly through decreased foreign direct investment and a sharp drop in the growth of its exports. However, China had huge reserves, a currency that was not freely convertible, and capital inflows that consisted overwhelmingly of long-term investment. For these reasons it remained largely insulated from the regional crisis and its commitment not to devalue had been a major stabilizing factor for the region. However, China faced slowing growth and rising unemployment based on internal problems, including a financial system burdened by huge amounts of bad loans, and massive layoffs stemming from aggressive efforts to reform state-owned enterprises (SOEs).

Despite China's impressive economic development during the past two decades, reforming the state sector and modernizing the banking system remained major hurdles. Over half of China's state-owned enterprises were inefficient and reporting losses. During the 15th National Communist Party Congress that met in September 1997, General secretary, President Jiang Zemin announced plans to sell, merge, or close the vast majority of SOEs in his call for increased "non-public ownership" (*feigongyou* or privatization in euphemistic terms). The 9th National People's Congress endorsed the plans at its March 1998 session. In 2000, China claimed success in its three-year effort to make the majority of large state owned enterprises (SOEs) profitable.

2000–present

Following the Chinese Communist Party's Third Plenum, held in October 2003, Chinese legislators unveiled several proposed amendments to the state constitution. One of the most significant was a proposal to provide protection for private property rights. Legislators also indicated there would be a new emphasis on certain aspects of overall government economic policy, including efforts to reduce unemployment (now in the 8–10% range in urban areas), to rebalance income distribution between urban and rural regions, and to maintain economic growth while protecting the environment and improving social equity. The National People's Congress approved the amendments when it met in March 2004.

The Fifth Plenum in October 2005 approved the 11th Five-Year Economic Program (2006–2010) aimed at building a "socialist harmonious society" through more balanced wealth distribution and improved education, medical care, and social security. On March 2006, the National People's Congress approved the 11th Five-Year Program. The plan called for a relatively conservative 45% increase in GDP and a 20% reduction in energy intensity (energy consumption per unit of GDP) by 2010.

China's economy grew at an average rate of 10% per year during the period 1990–2004, the highest growth rate in the world. China's GDP grew 10.0% in 2003, 10.1%, in 2004, and even faster 10.4% in 2005 despite attempts by the government to cool the economy. China's total trade in 2006 surpassed $1.76 trillion, making China the world's third-largest trading nation after the U.S. and Germany. Such high growth is necessary if China is to generate the 15 million jobs needed annually—roughly the size of Ecuador or Cambodia—to employ new entrants into the job market.

On January 14, 2009 as confirmed by the World Bank the NBS published the revised figures for 2007 financial year in which growth happened at 13 percent instead of 11.9 percent (provisional figures). China's gross domestic product stood at US$3.4 trillion while Germany's GDP was USD $3.3 trillion for 2007. This made China the world's third largest economy by gross domestic product. Based on these figures, in 2007 China recorded its fastest growth since 1994 when the GDP grew by 13.1 percent. China may have already overtaken Germany even earlier as China's informal economy (including the Grey market and underground economy) is larger than Germany's. Louis Kuijs, a senior economist at World Bank China Office in Beijing, said that China's economy may even be (as of January 2009) as much as 15 percent larger than Germany's. According to Merrill Lynch China economist Ting Lu, China is projected to overtake Japan in "three to four years".

Social and economic indicators have improved since various recent reforms were launched, but rising inequality is evident between the more highly developed coastal provinces and the less developed, poorer inland regions. According to UN estimates in 2007, around 130 million people in China—mostly in rural areas of the lagging inland provinces—still lived in poverty, on consumption of less than $1 a day. About 35% of the Chinese population lives under $2 a day.

In the medium-term, economists state that there is ample amount of potential for China to maintain relatively high economic growth rates and is forecasted to be the world's largest exporter by 2010.

Urbanization in China and technological progress and catch-up with developed countries have decades left to run. But future growth is complicated by a rapidly aging population and costs of damage to the environment.

China launched its Economic Stimulus Plan to specifically deal with the Global financial crisis of 2008–2009. It has primarily focused on increasing affordable housing, easing credit restrictions for mortgage and SMEs, lower taxes such as those on real estate sales and commodities, pumping more public investment into infrastructure development, such as the rail network, roads and ports.

Major natural disasters of 2008, such as the 2008 Chinese winter storms, the 2008 Sichuan earthquake, and the 2008 South China floods mildly affected national economic growth but did do major damage to local and regional economies and infrastructure. Growth rates for Sichuan dropped to 4.6% in the 2nd quarter but recovered to 9.5% annual growth for the whole of 2008. Major reconstruction efforts are still continuing after the May 12 earthquake, and are expected to last for at least three years. Despite closures and relocation of some factories because of the 2008 Summer Olympics, the games had a minor impact on Beijing's overall economic growth. The Chinese economy is significantly affected by the 2008-9 global financial crisis due to the export oriented nature of the economy which depends heavily upon international trade. However, government economic-stimulus has been hugely successful by nearly all accounts.

Corporate income tax (CIT): The income tax for companies is set at 25%, although there are some exceptions. When companies invest in industries supported by the Chinese government tax rates are only 15%. Companies that are investing in these industries also get other advantages.

In the online realm, China's e-commerce industry has grown more slowly than the EU and the US, with a significant period of development occurring from around 2009 onwards. According to Credit Suisse, the total value of online transactions in China grew from an insignificant size in 2008 to around RMB 4 trillion (US$660 billion) in 2012. Alipay has the biggest market share in China with 300 million users and control of just under half of China's online payment market in February 2014, while Tenpay's share is around 20 percent, and China UnionPay's share is slightly greater than 10 percent.

According to the 2013 Corruption Perception Index, compiled by global coalition Transparency International, China is ranked 80 out of

177 countries, with a score of 40. The Index scores countries on a scale of 0 (highly corrupt) to 100 (very low corruption) and over half of the nations in the Asia Pacific region emerged with a score lower than 40. Transparency International stated in its final assessment:

If genuine efforts are to be made, the present efforts of the Chinese government should go beyond observing the rule of law. They should embrace political reforms that would allow checks and balances, transparency and independent scrutiny together with acknowledging the role that the civil society can play in countering corruption.

ECONOMIC PLANNING

Until the 1980s the economy was directed and coordinated by means of economic plans that were formulated at all levels of administration. The reform program significantly reduced the role of central planning by encouraging off-plan production by state-owned units and by promoting the growth of collective and individual enterprises that did not fall under the planning system. The government also endeavored to replace direct plan control with indirect guidance of the economy through economic levers, such as taxes and investment support. Despite these changes, overall direction of the economy was still carried out by the central plan, as was allocation of key goods, such as steel and energy.

When China's planning apparatus was first established in the early 1950s, it was patterned after the highly centralized Soviet system. That system basically depended on a central planning bureaucracy that calculated and balanced quantities of major goods demanded and supplied. This approach was substantially modified during the Great Leap Forward (1958–60), when economic management was extensively decentralized. During the 1960s and 1970s, the degree of centralization in the planning system fluctuated with the political currents, waxing in times of pragmatic growth and waning under the influence of the Cultural Revolution and the Gang of Four.

At the national level, planning began in the highest bodies of the central government. National economic goals and priorities were determined by the party's Central Committee, the State Council, and the National People's Congress. These decisions were then communicated to the ministries, commissions, and other agencies under the State Council to be put into effect through national economic plans.

The State Planning Commission worked with the State Economic Commission, State Statistical Bureau, the former State Capital Construction Commission, People's Bank of China, the economic ministries, and other organs subordinate to the State Council to formulate national plans of varying duration and import. Long-range plans as protracted as ten and twelve years also were announced at various times. These essentially were statements of future goals and the intended general direction of the economy, and they had little direct effect on economic activity. As of late 1987 the most recent such long-range plan was the draft plan for 1976-85, presented by Hua Guofeng in February 1978.

The primary form of medium-range plan was the five-year plan, another feature adopted from the Soviet system. The purpose of the five-year plan was to guide and integrate the annual plans to achieve balanced growth and progress toward national goals. In practice, this role was only fulfilled by the First Five-Year Plan (1953-57), which served effectively as a blueprint for industrialization. The second (1958-62), third (1966-70), fourth (1971-75), and fifth (1976-80) five-year plans were all interrupted by political upheavals and had little influence. The Sixth Five-Year Plan (1981-85) was drawn up during the planning period and was more a reflection of the results of the reform program than a guide for reform. The Seventh Five-Year Plan (1986-90) was intended to direct the course of the reforms through the second half of the 1980s, but by mid-1987 its future was already clouded by political struggle.

A second form of medium-range planning appeared in the readjustment and recovery periods of 1949-52, 1963-65, and 1979-81, each of which followed a period of chaos - the civil war, the Great Leap Forward, and the Gang of Four, respectively. In these instances, normal long- and medium-range planning was suspended while basic imbalances in the economy were targeted and corrected. In each case, objectives were more limited and clearly defined than in the five-year plans and were fairly successfully achieved.

The activities of economic units were controlled by annual plans. Formulation of the plans began in the autumn preceding the year being planned, so that agricultural output for the current year could be taken into account. The foundation of an annual plan was a "material balance table." At the national level, the first step in the preparation of a material balance table was to estimate - for each province, autonomous region, special municipality, and enterprise under direct central control - the demand and supply for each centrally controlled good. Transfers of goods between provincial-level units were planned so as to bring quantities supplied and demanded into balance. As a last resort, a serious overall deficit in a good could be made up by imports.

The initial targets were sent to the provincial-level administrations and the centrally controlled enterprises. The provincial-level counterparts of the state economic commissions and ministries broke the targets down for allocation among their subordinate counties, districts, cities, and enterprises under direct provincial-level control. Counties further distributed their assigned quantities among their subordinate towns, townships, and county-owned enterprises, and cities divided their targets into objectives for the enterprises under their jurisdiction. Finally, towns assigned goals to the state-owned enterprises they controlled. Agricultural targets were distributed by townships among their villages and ultimately were reduced to the quantities that villages contracted for with individual farm households.

At each level, individual units received their target input allocations and output quantities. Managers, engineers, and accountants compared the targets with their own projections, and if they concluded that the planned output quotas exceeded their capabilities, they consulted with representatives of the administrative body superior to them. Each administrative level adjusted its targets on the basis of discussions with subordinate units and sent the revised figures back up the planning ladder. The commissions and ministries evaluated the revised sums, repeated the material balance table procedure, and used the results as the final plan, which the State Council then officially approved.

Annual plans formulated at the provincial level provided the quantities for centrally controlled goods and established targets for goods that were not included in the national plan but were important to the province, autonomous region, or special municipality. These figures went through the same process of disaggregation, review, discussion, and reaggregation as the centrally planned targets and eventually became part of the provincial-level unit's annual plan. Many goods that were not included at the provincial level were similarly added to county and city plans.

The final stage of the planning process occurred in the individual producing units. Having received their output quotas and the figures for their allocations of capital, labor, and other supplies, enterprises generally organized their production schedules into ten-day, one-month, three-month, and six-month plans.

The Chinese planning system has encountered the same problems of inflexibility and inadequate responsiveness that have emerged in other centrally planned economies. The basic difficulty has been that it is impossible for planners to foresee all the needs of the economy and to specify adequately the characteristics of planned inputs and products. Beginning in 1979 and 1980, the first reforms were introduced on an experimental basis. Nearly all of these policies increased the autonomy and decision-making power of the various economic units and reduced the direct role of central planning. By the mid-1980s planning still was the government's main mechanism for guiding the economy and correcting imbalances, but its ability to predict and control the behavior of the economy had been greatly reduced.

PRICES

Determination of prices

Until the reform period of the late 1970s and 1980s, the prices of most commodities were set by government agencies and changed infrequently. Because prices did not change when production costs or demand for a commodity altered, they often failed to reflect the true values of goods, causing many kinds of goods to be misallocated and producing a price system that the Chinese government itself referred to as "irrational."

The best way to generate the accurate prices required for economic efficiency is through the process of supply and demand, and government policy in the 1980s increasingly advocated the use of prices that were "mutually agreed upon by buyer and seller," that is, determined through the market. The prices of products in the farm produce free markets were determined by supply and demand, and in the summer of 1985 the state store prices of all food items except grain also were allowed to float in response to market conditions. Prices of most goods produced by private and collectively owned enterprises in both rural and urban areas generally were free to float, as were the prices of many items that state-owned enterprises produced outside the plan. Prices of most major goods produced by state-owned enterprises, however, along with the grain purchased from farmers by state commercial departments for retail sales in the cities, still were set or restricted by government agencies and still were not sufficiently accurate. In 1987 the price structure in China was chaotic. Some prices were determined in the market through the forces of supply and demand, others were set by government agencies, and still others were produced by procedures that were not clearly defined.

In many cases, there was more than one price for the same commodity, depending on how it was exchanged, the kind of unit that produced it, or who the buyer was.

While the government was not pleased with this situation, it was committed to continued price reform. It was reluctant, however, to release the remaining fixed prices because of potential political and economic disruption. Sudden unpredictable price changes would leave consumers unable to continue buying some goods; some previously profitable enterprises under the old price structure would begin to take losses, and others would abruptly become very wealthy.

Role of prices

As a result of the economic reform program and the increased importance of market exchange and profitability, in the 1980s prices played a central role in determining the production and distribution of goods in most sectors of the economy.

Previously, in the strict centrally planned system, enterprises had been assigned output quotas and inputs in physical terms. Under the reform program, the incentive to show a positive profit caused even state-owned enterprises to choose inputs and products on the basis of prices whenever possible.

State-owned enterprises could not alter the amounts or prices of goods they were required to produce by the plan, but they could try to increase their profits by purchasing inputs as inexpensively as possible, and their off-plan production decisions were based primarily on price considerations.

Prices were the main economic determinant of production decisions in agriculture and in private and collectively owned industrial enterprises despite the fact that regulations, local government fees or harassment, or arrangements based on personal connections often prevented enterprises from carrying out those decisions.

Consumer goods were allocated to households by the price mechanism, except for rationed grain. Families decided what commodities to buy on the basis of the prices of the goods in relation to household income.

Problems in price policy

The grain market was a typical example of a situation in which the government was confronted with major problems whether it allowed the irrational price structure to persist or carried out price reform. State commercial agencies paid farmers a higher price for grain than the state received from the urban residents to whom they sold it.

In 1985 state commercial agencies paid farmers an average price of ¥416.4 per ton of grain and then sold it in the cities at an average price of ¥383.3 a ton, for a loss of ¥33.1 per ton. Ninety million tons were sold under this arrangement, causing the government to lose nearly ¥3 billion. If the state reduced the procurement price, farmers would reduce their grain production. Because grain was the staple Chinese diet, this result was unacceptable. If the state increased the urban retail price to equal the procurement price, the cost of the main food item for Chinese families would rise 9 percent, generating enormous resentment. But even this alternative would probably not entirely resolve the problem, as the average free-market price of grain - ¥510.5 a ton in 1987 - indicated that its true value was well above the state procurement price.

There was no clear solution to the price policy dilemma. The approach of the government was to encourage the growth of nonplanned economic activity and thereby expand the proportion of prices determined by market forces. These market prices could then serve as a guide for more accurate pricing of planned items. It was likely that the Chinese economy would continue to operate with a dual price system for some years to come.

Inflation

One of the most striking manifestations of economic instability in China in the 1930s and 1940s was runaway inflation. Inflation peaked during the Chinese civil war of the late 1940s, when wholesale prices in Shanghai increased 7.5 million times in the space of 3 years. In the early 1950s, stopping inflation was a major government objective, accomplished through currency reform, unification and nationalization of the banks, and tight control over prices and the money supply. These measures were continued until 1979, and China achieved a remarkable record of price stability. Between 1952 and 1978, retail prices for consumer goods grew at an average rate of only 0.6 percent a year.

During the reform period, higher levels of inflation appeared when government controls were reduced. The first serious jump in the cost of living for urban residents occurred in 1980, when consumer prices rose by 7.5 percent. In 1985 the increase was 11.9 percent, and in 1986 it was 7.6 percent. There were several basic reasons for this burst of inflation after thirty years of steady prices. First, the years before the reform saw a generally high rate of investment and concentration on the manufacture of producer goods. The resultant shortage of consumer commodities caused a gradual accumulation of excess demand: personal savings were relatively large, and, in the late 1970s and early 1980s, there was a booming market for such expensive consumer durables as watches and television sets. Second, the real value of many items changed as some resources became more scarce and as technology altered both manufacturing processes and products. The real cost of producing agricultural products rose with the increased use of modern inputs. Manufactured consumer goods that were more technologically advanced and more expensive than those previously on the market - such as washing machines and color television sets - became available.

During the early 1980s, both consumer incomes and the amount of money in circulation increased fairly rapidly and, at times, unexpectedly. Consumer incomes grew because of the reform program's emphasis on material incentives and because of the overall expansion in productivity and income-earning possibilities. The higher profits earned and retained by enterprises were passed on to workers, in many cases, in the form of wage hikes, bonuses, and higher subsidies. At the same time, the expanded and diversified role of the banking system caused the amounts of loans and deposits to increase at times beyond officially sanctioned levels, injecting unplanned new quantities of currency into the economy.

NATIONAL GOALS

By 1987, under the stimulus of the reform program, the Chinese economy had made major strides toward achieving modernization and improved living standards. The potential for further improvements in efficiency and productivity was greatly increased by the revival of the education system, the opening of the economy to broader trade and cooperation with other countries, the expanded use of the market to enliven commerce and production, and the increased decision-making power of individual economic units.

4

Globalization and Economic Growth of China

Increase in economic growth began with the sharp rise in GDP in agriculture in the early reform period (1979-1984). Rising incomes stimulated domestic consumption and high savings rates with savings appropriately transferred into physical capital investments in the non-agricultural sector.

From the mid-1980s growth in the non-agricultural sector was stimulated by the growth of *township and village enterprises* (TVEs). Collectivization and the associated self-sufficiency of the commune also seem to have been an important precondition for the growth in the TVEs. This distinctly Chinese institutional development, not replicable elsewhere, was a major factor in contributing to the sharp decline in poverty.

Aided by the growth of TVEs, the average annual growth in the GDP has reached 10 percent annually since 1980. Non-agricultural farm household income has come to exceed agricultural income in many parts of China.

Reforms during the 1990s provided for trade and market liberalization, fiscal and financial expansion, devaluation of the exchange rate, expansion of special economic zones to attract foreign direct investment (FDI) and reform of state-owned enterprises. In 2004 China overtook the United States as the world's largest recipient of FDI; for a long time it has been by far the leading recipient of FDI among developing countries.

GROWTH IN AGRICULTURAL PRODUCTION AND PRODUCTIVITY

The China paper documents the rapid growth in agriculture in the early reform period, 1978 to 1984. The reforms in Chinese agriculture began in 1978. While the collectivization of agriculture is not generally regarded as a sound strategy for agricultural and rural development, there were certain policies under collectivization, e.g. education, health, development of rural infrastructure and agricultural technology, which laid the foundation for subsequent rapid growth in agriculture. Except during the famine years, the country achieved rates of production growth that outpaced the rise in population. From 1961 to 1978 China's cereal yields increased from 1.2 to 2.8. tonnes/ha. Subsequently yields have risen from 2.8 to 5.4 tonnes/ha. Following the adoption of the Household Responsibility System (HRS), agriculture grew at the phenomenal rate of 7 percent. The major policy factor explaining growth during this period, the HRS, gave as incentives the rights of individual farmers to control land and income from their agriculture. The egalitarian nature of these reforms, each household receiving a share of land equal in quality, ensured that the benefits derived from growth in the rural economy were widely shared.

Since 1984 the annual growth in agricultural GDP has been approximately 3 to 4 percent but over a much larger base. The primary engine of agricultural growth during this period has been labour-intensive technological change — in particular the use of modern varieties and inputs such as chemical fertilizers and irrigation. The growth has been sustained by public investment in rural infrastructure and in research and technology development.

Rapid agricultural growth has taken place against the backdrop of significant structural changes in China's economy. While agriculture accounted for more than 35 percent of the GDP in 1970, it fell to 15 percent in 2004. Rising incomes and urbanization have been among the driving forces for significant changes in the level and pattern of food consumption. The farming sector has diversified production to meet changing food demands. Meat consumption (pork and poultry) shot up and with it the demand for feedgrains (maize and soybeans). Consumption of aquatic products also showed very rapid growth.

As a result of market and trade liberalization, what we witness in general is the gradual shift from land-intensive commodities to high-value labour-intensive commodities such as horticultural crops, livestock and fisheries. Trade policy and exchange rate reforms have given a further boost to agricultural production for export. The ratio of total exports to the GDP increased from 6 percent in 1980 to 36 percent in 2004 and, while agriculture's share of exports declined from 3 to 2.5 percent, the US dollar value of net agricultural exports increased 100-fold over the two decades.

Poverty Reduction

Based on China's official poverty line, poverty has declined from over 33 percent to less than 3 percent of the total rural population, and as indicated earlier most of this occurred in the early reform period. Based on the dollar-a-day poverty line index, the incidence of poverty dropped from 33 to 16 percent from 1990 to 2002. The estimated decline in numbers in this period was from 377 to 203 million. Overall economic growth (as measured by per capita GDP) has been a primary source of rural poverty reduction in China. The TVEs have played an important role in contributing to rural poverty reduction. However, the effect of economic growth on poverty reduction has weakened since the 1980s. Furthermore, agricultural growth, not just economic growth, matters for poverty reduction. The widening urban-rural income gap affects poverty reduction and suggests that in the future growth has to be more broadly based.

Trade liberalization is a source of regional income disparities. The coastal areas benefited from growth in agricultural exports, whereas central China, the largest producer of soybeans and edible oils, was hurt by trade liberalization.

Food Security

One measure of food security is the change in per capita food availability. Between the early 1960s and early reform years daily per capita food availability in China increased from 1 717 kcal to 2 328 kcal. By 2000 it exceeded 3 000 kcal per day, a level nearly comparable to most developed countries. Over time the food security picture has changed. Initially most farm households produced food for their own subsistence. With the passage of time, however, markets have developed and agriculture has become a more commercial enterprise. Farmers face market price risks, but as almost 50 percent of the land area is irrigated, production risks are lower than in most other countries. Diversification of farm household incomes, with at least one family member in non-farm employment, helps to improve food security.

GLOBALIZATION STUDIES IN CHINA

China speaks a fascinating story about globalization and globalization studies, both when it comes to understanding the concept theoretically and how it involves the practice of globalization. On the theoretical plane, in the early half of the 1990s, the word "globalization" was so sensitive politically that scholars feared to mention it in articles and books, while now it has become so fashionable that almost everyone uses it, whether he or she accepts or rejects it. On the practical level, globalization had long been regarded to be synonymous with capitalist development ideologically. More recently, both in China and outside, the country is accepted widely to be one of the biggest winners of globalization in the world.

Chinese scholars scarcely used the concept of globalization before the mid-1990s because it was received ideologically as a synonym for capitalism. Even for those few advocates of globalization, the term was used strictly in its economic sense during the 1990s. In this period, a journal editor would routinely add the adjective "economic" to "globalization" when an author submitted an article on globalization. In 1998, Mr. Jiang Zeming, then President and General Secretary of the Communist Party of China (CPC), spoke for the first time about "economic globalization" as "an objective trend of world economic development." The top leader's recognition of globalization gave a great impetus to scholars and analysts engaged in studies of globalization, making it a hot issue among Chinese intellectuals. A number of essays on globalization have since been published and huge numbers of foreign books and essays on globalization have been translated into Chinese and published in China. I was very lucky to chair the first national conference specifically on globalization held in 1997 in Shengzhen, the most open Special Economic Zone, and to edit the first*Globalization Studies Series* in Chinese. It includes seven books published in 1998. The *Globalization Translation Series*, which I have also been organizing, has published over thirty books, all by the same publishing house — the Chinese Social Sciences and Documentation Publishing House.

At present, Chinese scholars have focused on several important dimensions of globalization: the concept of globalization; types of globalization (besides economic globalization); China's path towards globalization; the implications of globalization for China; and globalization's advantages and disadvantages. Is globalization a blessing or a disaster for China's modernization and development?

In each of these areas, Chinese scholars' views on globalization can be summarized in six paradoxes that they have debated in relation to globalization.

First, is globalization a fact or just a fiction? Some people think that globalization is a fact — that it has an objective existence that deeply impacts human development. They see humankind as entering into a global age. To the contrary, others insist that globalization is simply a fiction promoted by Western scholars and perhaps even represents a conspiracy of new Imperialism. In their view, globalization has to be a myth if only because the diverse human politics, economies, and cultures can never be globalized.

Second, is globalization inherently capitalist or potentially socialist? Many Chinese intellectuals believe that globalization is a necessary result of capitalist productive development and an inherent thrust of capitalism. Globalization represents the extension of capitalist modes of production across the planet and signifies that capitalism has entered a new stage of its development. Therefore, globalization, to be exact, is global capitalism. In contrast, some scholars argue that globalization is ideologically neutral in spite of its origins in advanced capitalist countries. In its nature, globalization is neither capitalist nor socialist. Like the market economy, it can be combined with both capitalism and socialism.

Third, besides economic globalization, are there political or cultural forms of globalization? For many scholars, globalization is nothing but economic integration particularly increased integration on a planetary scale of capital, products, market, technology, production, and communication. They limit globalization strictly to economics and refuse to expand it to other domains of human experience. Many other scholars, however, believe that the concept of globalization extends beyond economics even though it originates in economic processes of integration. A process of political and cultural globalization, they argue, is underway at the same time as economic integration is going on. In their view, globalization has not only economic implications but also political and cultural ones. Thus, globalization is an overall process of social change, including economic, political, and cultural processes.

Fourth, is globalization, on balance, advantageous or harmful for developing countries? Some intellectuals find that developed countries dominate and control the process of globalization with their economic and political power. They suggest that developed, rather than developing countries are the true winners of globalization. Others argue that globalization is not a zero-sum game and all players can be winners. What matters here are the strategies that governments take. China is a good example of a country poised to win a lot from globalization, and thus one to which persons point when they make their case.

Fifth, is globalization nothing more than modernization, Westernization, or Americanization? Many people believe that globalization brings Westernization, and above all, Americanization for China. Such a development is equated with the loss of autonomy. In their eyes, the standards, regimes, and regulations that come to be adopted by countries in response to the processes of globalization are made by Western countries according to their own values and interests. Others disagree.

They think that globalization is quite different from Westernization or Americanization. For these persons, globalization is a fundamental process of modernization in spite of the fact that this process originates in the West and the United States leads it.

Following on this fifth paradox, is there a Chinese model or way towards modernization in the global age? Some say "yes," there is a Chinese model for development with its own special characteristics and some of them even would like to accept the idea of a "Beijing Consensus" raised by American scholar, Joshua Cooper Ramo.

Others, however, reject this argument firmly and argue that there is no specifically Chinese way to modernization, only a capitalist way or following a path towards adopting more of capitalism. For a few of this latter group, the Chinese model for globalization is based on the so-called "Washington Consensus," rather than a "Beijing Consensus."

Given such debates, it is not surprising that intellectuals in China, much as those abroad, divide themselves in two camps. Some are advocates of globalization while others are opponents of it. The former see globalization as a blessing and warmly welcome globalization. The latter resist globalization, viewing it as a disaster. Some Chinese scholars see globalization as the pathway to a Chinese renaissance; China's future, including democracy and economic prosperity, depends largely on its taking advantage of globalization. Other people, however, see globalization to be a trap and regard supporters of globalization as traitors to a modern China.

PRESERVING AUTONOMY UNDER GLOBALIZATION PRESSURES

Many people believe that China is one of the biggest winners from globalization. From 1978 to 2003, the Chinese gross national product increased from 362.4 billion yuan in RMB (US$44.2 billion) to 11,690 billion yuan in RMB (US$1,425.6 billion). In constant RMB (and dollars), it has increased 8.4 times with an average yearly growth rate of over 9 percent. This growth rate is much higher than the 2.5 percent average GNP growth rate of the developed countries, the 5 percent growth rate of developing countries, and the 3 percent average world growth rate during the same period. In this period, China has registered the fastest economic growth in the world. High-speed economic growth has been accompanied by a 22-fold expansion in the scale of foreign trade over the past twenty-two years. At the same time, China successfully protected itself from the shocks of the Asian financial crisis in the 1990s, and has realized its goal of entering the World Trade Organization (WTO) after ten years of assiduous effort.

A primary reason China has become one of the biggest winners from globalization is the policy strategy that the Chinese government has followed in addressing the challenges of globalization. This basic policy has two pillars: actively opening up to the world while straining every nerve to protect the country's autonomy.

The key measures and stances that the Chinese government has adopted in actively joining into the processes of globalization include:

- *An independent globalization strategy.* With a good understanding and anticipation of the processes of globalization, China has adopted an active and independent globalization strategy. China is a country where its politics are highly influenced by ideology; but ideological considerations have been consciously put aside in the pursuit of globalization. While many Chinese scholars were debating on globalization, Chinese leaders made their own judgments about the nature, advantages, and disadvantages of globalization; adopted an active strategy; and took appropriate actions in order to take full advantage of globalization. For example, China made tireless efforts to join the WTO, expanded international cooperation and exchange, actively participated in global governance and global actions to counter international terrorism, established the

Shanghai Cooperation Organization, pushed forward negotiations to eliminate nuclear weapons in the Korean Peninsula, and proposed a strategy of "peaceful development."

- *Leadership development.* China has worked assiduously to improve the qualifications of government officials; to select and promote for leadership positions, knowledge elites who are globalization-oriented; and to train officials in the knowledge economy and problems of globalization. Currently there are 672,531 officials above the county level, and 90 percent of them have academic degrees equal to or above the associate college level, up from 16 percent in 1981. According to the training plan of the central government, 25,000 officials above the rank of county or division will be trained from 2001 to 2005, among these, 2,000 officials at the province and ministry level. This new group of leaders is strongly professionally competent and they are increasingly skilled at conducting international cooperation and exchange activities. In short, these officials are set to become the pivotal force of the Chinese government in dealing with the process of globalization.

- *Adaptive capability and flexibility.* The Chinese government has developed a flexible system and set of mechanisms with strong adaptive capability. Participation in the global game means abiding by global regimes, but global regimes conflict with domestic regimes in a number of areas. How to deal with the relationships and potential conflicts between domestic and international regimes is an issue that the Chinese government has had to face. After careful assessment of the advantages and disadvantages of globalization, Chinese government leaders made a painful but correct choice. They decided to adapt Chinese domestic regimes to international ones, and to revise domestic regimes that are not consistent with international regimes. Consequently, the government bypassed traditional forbidden zones and signed a series of international treaties covering a wide range of issues from political rights, to international security, international trade, and environmental protection. It also revised relevant domestic laws in accordance with related international treaties. In the process of negotiating terms for WTO membership, and subsequent to joining the WTO, the State Council required up to thirty ministries and departments in 2002 to clean up nearly 2,300 relevant laws and regulations. About half of the laws and regulations were eliminated or revised as a result. Local laws and regulations revised or eliminated by various provinces and autonomous regions amount to more than a hundred thousand.

- *Peaceful development.* The Chinese government has been striving for international cooperation and creation of a favorable international environment. China needs a peaceful international environment in order to focus on development, a need that is especially important in an era of globalization. In adapting to the challenges of globalization, the Chinese government proposed an international strategy of "peaceful development." The main elements of this strategy are to insist on the diplomatic principles of independence, self-reliance, and peaceful co-existence; to abide by the guiding ideology of "being peaceful and different"; and to strive for a new notion of security with "mutual trust, mutual benefits, equality, and cooperation." With these as the core principles, the government promotes global democratic governance. It strives to engage in international cooperation more actively in all spheres, and pursues reciprocal benefits in peaceful co-existence and cooperation.

In following this strategic approach, the Chinese government rose above ideological differences and developed bilateral and multilateral relations with various countries and regions in the areas of politics, economy, and culture. Within just five years, from 1998 to 2002, it signed more than 1,056 bilateral and multilateral treaties. At the same time, the Chinese government has encouraged foreign exchange and cooperation activities conducted by local governments, individuals, and civil society groups. In 2002, the number of foreign citizens entering China was close to 13.5 million, while 16.3 million Chinese left China to visit other countries. In the past five years, the number of entries and departures increased more than 10 percent per year on average. As of 2002, 296 Chinese cities had established friendship and partnership relationships with 847 foreign cities.

At the same time as China has participated extensively in globalization, it has taken several important steps to protect its autonomy.

Remaining aware of globalization's negative effects. Generally speaking, the negative effects of globalization for China are three-fold. First, globalization threatens domestic economic security. Foreign corporate control of major company shares and gaining a monopoly on crucial technologies threatens adjustment and the upgrading of the country's industrial structure. Excessive foreign debt may bring potentially enormous risks and increased reliance on foreign capital and trade may weaken China's capacity to protect its economy and its citizens from fluctuations in the world economy.

The large-scale opening of financial markets may also greatly increase financial risks. Second, globalization weakens state sovereignty. One of the basic conditions for participating in globalization is to abide by existing international rules, international treaties, and agreements. Most of these international regimes have been established in accordance with the interests and standards of advanced Western countries. In order to gain the economic benefits brought by globalization, developing countries usually have to make some concessions in administrative jurisdiction, thus weakening their sovereignty. Third, globalization threatens domestic political values and culture, leading to possible loss of control of the social order, and increased risks to domestic governance. With advanced Western countries controlling the course of globalization and constructing global regimes, it is inevitable that they will seek also to export their world views and value systems along with their capital, technology, and products. These world views and value systems may clash with Chinese cultural traditions and political order, creating a potential for social and political instability.

Prevention of foreign capital control in key sectors. On the one hand, China does everything possible to attract foreign investment. Such investment is usually encouraged by favourable policies on taxes, lands, and license permits. On the other hand, foreign investments are greeted with considerable caution when it comes to the most important economic sectors such as energy, communications, finance, education, and mass media.

Controlling the speed of change. The Chinese government has efficiently met its agenda of entering into the world economy. At the same time, it has taken many measures to prevent the country from entering too quickly into the process of globalization, thereby destabilizing political and social order.

Retaining dominance of economic development for core national interests. China has not given up its dominance of economic development for core national interests, even at the cost of slowing down overall economic growth. For example, China has made her own decision on devaluation of Chinese currency regardless of high pressure from the United States and other developed countries.

GLOBALIZATION AND DECENTRALIZATION IN CHINA

As early as the mid 1970s, China's political leaders began to see the opportunities provided by globalization. The remarkable economic progress in East Asia had eroded China's skepticism regarding involvement in the international economy and impressed upon its leadership the need to accelerate its development, especially after 1972 when travel abroad restrictions were eased after China's rapprochement with the U.S. The rapid development of Japan, Taiwan, Hong Kong, and Korea meant that these economies were moving up the product cycle and were beginning to establish international production chains in order to outsource labour intensive production to low cost producers. China with its cheap labour, potentially huge domestic economy, and personal contacts with the overseas Chinese community was an especially attractive location for developing trade and foreign investment. Diplomatic entreaties from the United States promised China access for Chinese exports to the American market.

As early as 1975, Deng Xiaoping, then vice-chairman of the CCP and first vice-premier, began developing a reform strategy that advocated accelerating Chinese industrial development by increasing advanced technologies from abroad and utilizing foreign credits to pay for them. He argued that China should not adopt a closed-door attitude and refuse to learn from the good things of foreign countries. Hua Guofeng's Ten Year Plan initiated in 1978, which proposed to accelerate the development of China's heavy industry through increased petroleum exports, was also a response to the opportunities presented by globalization even though its objective was to strengthen state-owned enterprises (SOE's) rather than reform the economy. However, Hua's plans were doomed when it became clear that China's oil reserves had been overestimated and that local officials had begun to sign a binge of deals that threatened to obligate China to a larger hard currency debt than it could manage.

The promotion of foreign trade has been an important element of China's reforms. Central to China's trade reforms has been the decentralization of the central government's control over foreign trade and foreign exchange in an effort to create more incentives to export. Prior to the reforms, the Ministry of Foreign Trade (renamed the Ministry of Foreign Economic Relations and Trade often referred to by its acronym, MOFERT) monopolized trade through about 10 to 16 foreign trading corporations under its control. Reforms were implemented in 1980 that led to the proliferation of foreign trading corporations, and by 1994 there were 9400 foreign trading corporations. Central government ministries, provinces, municipalities, and a few large SOE's set up these trading corporations. Guangdong alone had 900 trading enterprises by 1987. Changes in the national trade plan also gave subnational governments more autonomy. The scope of the plan shrank from approximately 90 percent of all trade before the reforms to 43 percent at the end of the 80s, and the plan was divided into mandatory and guidance components with local trading corporations falling under the non-binding general targets of the guidance plan instead of the mandatory plan. The trade regime was also decentralized in the sense that SOE's, joint ventures, foreign-owned, collective and private firms were allowed a growing share of China's foreign trade and by 1994 their share grew to more than half.

China's reforms also attempted to promote exports by decentralizing control over foreign exchange during the 1980s. Prior to the reforms, the Ministry of Foreign Trade controlled foreign exchange through its trading corporations. Beginning in 1979, the central government introduced the ?foreign exchange retention system? allowing export-producing enterprises and their superordinate level of government to control a share of the foreign exchange they earned through exports. In 1982, the State Council replaced differential rates for products with rates for different regions with coastal provinces Guangdong and Fujian securing higher rates. In 1985, the state began a two-tier system in which above-plan exports were subject to a preferential retention rate. The value of retained foreign exchange was increased when enterprises with rights to foreign exchange were allowed to trade them in 1980. Foreign exchange markets quickly appeared in Guangzhou and Shanghai even though the first officially sanctioned foreign exchange 'swap center' was established in Shenzhen in 1985. The advantage of these centers for exporters is that they could sell their foreign exchange for rates substantially higher than official rates. By 1988 thirty-nine foreign exchange centers had sprung up with trading valued at more than $6 billion.

During the 1990s, China became by far the largest recipient of foreign direct investment (FDI) in the developing world, receiving 40 percent of developing country FDI in 1997. Chinese FDI in 1997 and 1998 — at approximately $46 billion — accounted for more than 25 percent of all domestic investment and added some 16 million new jobs annually. (World Bank, 1999a, pp. 22, 102; 1997 p. 21) Reforms of FDI regulations have also promoted decentralization and increased the autonomy of subnational governments. They began cautiously with the passage of the Joint Venture Law in 1979. Special economic zones offering tax concessions were opened in Shenzhen, Zhuai and Shantou in Guangdong and Xiamen in Fujian in 1980. Access to foreign investment was gradually extended to different localities and the entire country was open to foreign investment by the end of the 1980s. Subnational governments were gradually devolved authority over FDI. Authority was extended to provinces on different terms. By the end of the 1980s, nine provinces, five cities, and the SEZ's could sanction projects valued at up to $30 million without the central government approval while most interior provinces and cities could sanction projects up to $10 million in value. By the end of 1991, township and village enterprises (TVE's) had attracted 12 percent of total committed FDI.

During the 1990s reforms were implemented to entice foreign investment into infrastructural sectors. The Chinese proposed an investment program requiring $600 billion for a decade beginning in the mid-90s, and it is unlikely that the needed resources can be raised domestically, FDI is especially attractive. The Chinese opened the electric power generation sector to FDI in 1992, and they encouraged build-operate-transfer (BOT) projects in the sector. Foreign investment was also permitted in road, air and rail transportation. Port development and the oil sector also secured major foreign investment projects.

Attracting FDI to industrial and infrastructure sectors were extremely important to subnational governments efforts to promote economic growth. Localities fiercely competed for FDI by tax concessions and other measures to make the investment environment attractive. Measures taken by local governments to protect and promote industry within their jurisdiction has created inefficiencies by truncating the domestic market and supporting sub-optimal scale projects. Localities established — what were in some cases pseudo — joint ventures to gain direct access to the international market and avoid having to accept the dictated by foreign trading corporations which were substantially less than those on the international market. They also used joint ventures to circumvent tariffs and import licences to gain advantage on the domestic market. The preferential treatment accorded to foreign capital has led to the practice of ?roundtripping? whereby enterprises and subnational governments transfer funds offshore — most often to Hong Kong — only to return it in the guise of FDI. According to some estimates, roundtripping may account for 20 percent of all Chinese FDI.

Progress in enacting reforms to attract foreign portfolio investment, while much more limited that the changes in the FDI regime have also showed decentralizing tendencies. Stock exchanges were created at Shanghai in 1990 and Shezhen in 1991 and regulatory authority was devolved to the China Securities and Regulatory Commission in 199?. However, the restriction of foreign investment to a some 72 companies who have issued ?B shares? exclusively for foreigners has limited foreign portfolio inflows, and regulation was lax until the National People's Congress passed the Securities Law in December 1998. Chinese companies have been allowed to access European and American capital markets through global depository receipts and American depository receipts, but the capital raised through this method has been limited.

China has achieved greater access to the international bond market. The China International Trust and Investment Company (CITIC) was chartered to raise funds on international capital markets in 1979. Other international trust and investment companies were established beginning in 1980 by provincial governments in Shandong, Liaoning and Guangdong by major municipalities such as Guangzhou, Xian and Dalian as well as by smaller cities such as Changjiang in Sichuan Province. The Guandong International Trust and Investment Corporation (GITIC) became the China's second largest debt-issuing international trust and investment company. It accumulated approximately $3 billion in assets and $5 billion in liabilities before the government authorized its liquidation in 1999. China raised $4 billion through international bond issues in 1996. The extent of decentralization in the flow of funds from international bonds is indicated by the fact that by 1996 CITIC and along with two other companies accounted for 30 percent of the total.

GLOBALIZATION AND CHINA'S ECONOMIC AND FINANCIAL DEVELOPMENT

To understand China's economic reform and development since 1978 one may conveniently divide the topic into its domestic and international aspects even though the two are closely related. It is the purpose of this essay to examine the international aspects as China has taken part in the process of world economic globalization, a salient feature of world history today. The Chinese leader Deng Xiaoping who initiated and directed economic reform from a planned to a market economy understood the importance of globalization and adopted what he called an "open-door policy" as an essential part of the reform program.

The term globalization refers to the crossing of national boundaries. It means the flow of goods, capital, information/technology and people across national borders. China practiced globalization in the Han dynasty (206BC-220AD) when trade took place between the Han Chinese and neighboring people in the North-west through the Silk Route. During the Tang dynasty (618-901) trade flourished and the Silk Route expanded as Chinese traded with the Romans. However, in the Qing Dynasty and in the period of the PRC up to Deng Xiaoping's open-door policy China tried to close its doors and resisted globalization. I will survey the accomplishments of globalization for China's economic development and clarify some controversial issues concerning globalization.

Foreign Trade

First consider foreign trade or the flow of goods across national borders. Since 1978 China has encouraged free trade and abolished trade restrictions step by step. The government has changed its policy from the administration of foreign trade by the Ministry of Foreign Trade, to giving provincial governments much autonomy in foreign trade and to allowing private enterprises to engage in foreign trade. The total volume of foreign trade or the total volume of exports and imports increased from 20.64 billion US dollars in 1978 to 620.8 billion in 2002, accounting for 65 percent of GDP and was growing at the rate of 35 percent per year. In 2004, the trade volume reached 1.1 trillion US dollars, and had a growth rate of 30 percent. China became the third largest trading country in the world, next to the United States and Germany.

Today exports from China can be found all over the world. In terms of US-China economic relations exports from China have benefited many Americans in providing them with high-quality consumer goods at low prices, but have also generated resentment and resistance by some American manufacturers and workers. Chinese exports to the US may hurt some US industries producing similar products. US workers in these industries may suffer temporarily, but in the long-run the labour market is able to adjust as new industries are developed to hire the displaced workers. In the long run, the aggregate unemployment rate (now at 5 percent) has not been visibly affected by the American imports of foreign goods. Note also that exports from China, in fact about 60 percent of them, are produced by foreign invested enterprises in China and some are American companies.

Outsourcing of jobs such as having someone in Asia read X-ray or answer phones has also created resentment in the United States. From the economic point of view, outsourcing of jobs as illustrated above is the same as import of services from China. The effects are the same as for the import of goods produced in China that I just talked about. Such imports are good for China and for US although some workers may be displaced temporarily. Although this point is valid, Professor Greg Mankiw of Harvard and at the time Chairman of the President's Council of Economic Advisers got into trouble when he made this valid point in a Congressional hearing in 2004 because such a viewpoint can be unpopular for American workers and politicians.

As an importer China provides a large market for foreign manufacturers and has gained economic power as a result. Demand for imports to China propels economic growth of other countries in the world.

China first took a mercantilist stand in the restriction of imports, but after the rapid expansion of Chinese exports, the table has turned as some developed countries including the US are considering the imposition of restrictions on imports from China. The imposition of quotas on textiles from China is an example.

In 2001 China joined the World Trade Organization. Membership in WTO required China to lower its tariffs for manufacturing as well as agricultural products. The lowering of tariffs helped increase competition for Chinese manufacturers and farmers and provide cheaper products for Chinese consumers.

Foreign trade has helped economic growth in China in three aspects. First international specialization that takes place as each country produces the goods for which it has a comparative advantage in producing will enable the country to obtain more goods than by domestic production alone. Second, exports are a part of aggregate demand and an increase in aggregate demand helps increase the country's national output. Thirdly, trade together with foreign investment has brought in modern technology and method of management that has increased productivity in China.

FOREIGN INVESTMENT

Flow of physical capital in the form of foreign direct investment has been good in promoting China's economic growth. Since economic reform started in 1978 China's policy concerning foreign investment has made an 180 degree turn, from treating it as a form of exploitation by foreigners to welcoming it for China's economic development. In the years 2001 to 2003, the amounts of direct foreign investment actually utilized were respectively 49.7, 55.0 and 56.1 billion US dollars. Foreign investment has provided physical and financial capital, technology, and management skill and practice to China. However foreign investment is not a fundamental economic factor in China's rapid growth but only a vehicle propelling that growth. There are three fundamental factors, namely (1) abundance of high-quality human capital that includes skillful and hardworking laborers and resourceful entrepreneurs, (2) sufficiently well functioning market institutions and (3) the position of a late comer that can adopt modern technology from the more developed countries. These three fundamental factors have enabled China to attract foreign capital; otherwise the capital could have been invested elsewhere.

Now China is exporting capital, not only to less developed countries but also to the United States. Chinese investment has helped the economic development of some Asian and African countries. Investment in the United States is illustrated by the attempt in the Spring of 2005 by the Chinese National Offshore Oil Corporation Cnooc to buy Unocal in the United States although the attempt turned out to be unsuccessful. The attempt is a part of the free flow of capital.

From the viewpoint of the United States, export of capital from US to China that takes place when a US factory moves from Cleveland to Shanghai is also considered a case of the outsourcing of jobs as the factory is supposed to go to Shanghai to take advantage of the less expensive and good quality labour in China. This case of outsourcing of jobs is different from simply buying goods or services from China that I talked about earlier since it takes the form of foreign investment. Capital flows to China in this case but not in the previous case that involves only foreign trade. Such an investment is good for the US as it raises US GNP. The reason is that what this piece of capital can produce in China is more than it could be producing in the US;

otherwise the factory would not have moved. Therefore the move increases total output of the US which the economists call gross national product or GNP. The move, however, has a harmful effect on the workers in Cleveland who lose their jobs when such a factory moves. As in the case of competition from imports from China, there will be job loss in selected industries in the short run

But aggregate employment in the US in the long run will not be affected. In the course of globalization there is movement of resources between nations. The movement is good for each nation in the long run but may have harmful effects in the short run for a segment of the population.

The same can be said about the movement of economic resources between different regions of one country. In US history, the movement of textile factories from New England to the South to take advantage of the lower labour cost is good for the country's economic development, both in New England and in the South. In New England some workers were displaced during the move but other industries were developed and people were employed again without leading to an increase in the unemployment rate in the region.

On the negative side, there may be environmental problems associated with new factories built in the course of globalization, but this problem exists for domestically financed factories and for economic development in general. The Chinese government has paid serious attention to environment protection. Economists try to balance the harm from possible damage to the environment with the gain in having more output. In general poorer countries in the course of economic development are willing to accept some environmental degradation in exchange for more output but they should be aware of the damage which may be long-lasting.

Concerning financial investment, the free flow of financial capital is one objective in the development of financial markets. China welcomes foreigner to invest in its stock markets in Shenzhen, Shanghai and Hong Kong, and also desires to invest its capital abroad. Movement of financial capital is one aspect of the free flow of resources to where they yield the highest return so that total output of the world would be larger. In this connection I would like to call your attention to the fact that the working of the free market involving the free flow of resources was well understood by the great Chinese historian Sima Qian of the Han dynasty. In chapter 69 entitled "The biographies of the money markets" of his book *Historical Records* he wrote:

"There must be farmers to produce food, men to extract the wealth of mountains and marshes, artisans to produce these things and merchants to circulate them. There is no need to wait for government orders: each man will play his part, doing his best to get what he desires. So cheap goods will go where they will fetch more, while expensive goods will make men search for cheap ones. When all work willingly at their trade, just as water flows ceaselessly downhill day and night, things will appear unsought and people will produce them without being asked. For clearly this accords with the Way and is in keeping with nature." What he calls nature is what we call the law of economics.

On the negative side of the free flow of financial capital it enables financial crises to take place, including the Asian financial crisis of 1997-8. This crisis did not affect China very much as the Chinese government has had a wise policy of adopting international financial reform at a moderate speed especially in allowing a gradual opening of financial markets and of the capital account in international finance because economic institutions are not ready. But globalization itself is good for the reform of banking and financial institutions in providing foreign competition to push the reform forward. Using foreign competition to speed up economic reform was the main reason for the former Premier Zhu Rongji in leading China to join the WTO in the first place.

The strategy of using foreign competition to speed up economic reform of domestic institutions, however effective, has limitation in promoting the reform of China's banking system and large state-owned enterprises for two reasons. First, while Chinese government officials have been pragmatic in most aspects of economic reform, they have been conservative and slow in allowing foreign banks to enter the domestic market. Second, Chinese banks and state enterprises are state-owned and controlled and operated by bureaucrats who can take advantage of the economic power conferred upon them to benefit themselves. Corruption is a major hindrance to economic reform at the current juncture of China's economic development as I have discussed elsewhere.

The Exchange Rate Issue

An important determinant of foreign trade and foreign investment is the exchange rate. A low value of Chinese RMB makes Chinese exports cheaper and investment in China more attractive if the investment is to produce for export. Many countries in the world including those in the European Union, Japan and Taiwan, have adopted the flexible exchange rate system while China adopted a fixed exchange rate up to July 2005 but the government did change the fixed rate several times in the 1980s and early 1990s relative to the US dollar as its government deemed appropriate. Most recently the Chinese government has adopted a managed floating rate with the government deciding the rate around a small band daily relative to the value of a basket of foreign currencies but the basket is not explicitly specified. There are pros and cons of the fixed and the floating exchange rate systems. A fixed exchange provides an anchor for the government in the conduct of its monetary and fiscal policy. It limits the discretionary power of the government in the exercise of its monetary and fiscal policy that may lead to excessive inflation or deflation. An expansionary monetary or fiscal policy would lead to inflation and lower the value of the currency as compared with a more stable US currency. Thus the fixed exchange rate system might be good for a developing country which has difficulty in disciplining itself in the exercise of its monetary and fiscal policies. The flip side is the power that it gives up and its dependence on the monetary policy of the US if the exchange rate is fixed as in terms of the US dollar. I was one of the several economists who proposed a flexible exchange rate for Taiwan three decades ago. After the Taiwan government adopted it the economy seemed to function well.

Let us consider two questions: First, what exchange rate regime should China adopt? Second, given the current regime of a managed float should the RMB be revalued? Since the Chinese government has already declared its position to adopt a more flexible regime in the long run as the situation permits, I should not comment on the first question. Making recommendations on policy which is already decided is fruitless. Let me just point out that in the adoption of a suitable exchange rate system the Chinese government is practicing its tried and proven method of reform of economic institutions, namely, gradualism and experimentation in order to decide on a good system and when to adopt it.

On the second question many foreign governments including the US government have pressured the Chinese government to raise the value of the RMB for their own benefits. Some US economists including Alan Greenspan have said that the effect of the exchange rate of the RMB on the US economy is rather limited. Concerning the effect on the Chinese economy, I believe that the RMB is still undervalued and revaluation is good for the Chinese economy. We have witnessed the undervaluation of the RMB or the overvaluation of the dollar in terms of the RMB by the excess supply of the dollar in the foreign exchange market in China due to its high price and the resulting accumulation of a large amount of foreign exchange reserves in China in the amount of over 700 billion US dollars. The increase was over 200 billion just in 2004 alone. An undervalued RMB has caused the large export surplus and large inflow of foreign investment and the associated large inflow of foreign exchange reserves. The inflow of foreign exchange has been converted into RMB and has caused a rapid increase in money supply M2 in 2002. The rapid increase in money supply has led to great increases in investment and output in 2003-5 and in prices in 2004-5 (while from 1998 to 2002 China had a very stable or slightly decreasing price level). A more detailed discussion of the effects of money supply on aggregate output and prices can be found in Chow and Shen (2004).

Thus the undervalued RMB was a main cause of an overheated Chinese economy in 2003-4. The Chinese government tried to slow down the overheated economy by the administrative means of controlling the extension of credits by banks and limiting the number of construction projects. If the banks had had no extra money to lend out in the first place, there would have been no need to control the amounts of bank credit and to restrict investment in construction which was financed by such credits. Thus an undervalued RMB is the culprit of the overheated Chinese economy. To solve the potential problem of overheating and inflation in the future the government needs to raise the value of the RMB substantially. Another reason for revaluation of the RMB is that a high valued RMB would enable the Chinese to buy more imports for consumption and economic development rather than accumulating an extremely large amount of foreign reserves that are mostly lying idle or earning a small amount of interest from investing in US Treasury bonds.

TRANSFER OF INFORMATION AND TECHNOLOGY

Together with the flow of goods and capital is the transmission of information and technology. This has benefited China by upgrading its technology. So far China has mainly been an importer of technology but it will soon be an important exporter as it is already an exporter of technology to some less developed countries. In recent years the

Chinese government has spent a large amount on higher education and Chinese universities, especially the top ones, improved rapidly.

As of today, China has already helped many developing countries in Asia and in Africa by investing in these countries, providing them with technology, labour and assisting them in economic development in general. China seems to have done very well in this regard, in view of the fact that it has its own poor regions to develop also. Chinese diplomacy is based on mutual respect, treating a small country as equal and trying to help solve its problems if it is feasible. The effort of the Chinese government in assisting the developing countries and its diplomatic posture as a friendly country are doing as much in increasing China's influence in the world scene as its rising economic power.

Returning to China as an importer of technology, we know that the import of technology from the US to China is good for China, but is it good for the US? A part of the answer is yes. The main reason for capital and technology to move from US to China is to get a higher return to capital. It raises US GNP as I have explained and that is good for the US. In the very long run, however, one can make a case that this transfer of technology might be bad for the US although it is not necessarily so. To make the case, the transfer may enable China to improve its technology in the future to a point when it will overtake the US in the industries in which the US now has monopoly power. To illustrate, when the Japanese took over much of the monopoly power of the US automobile industry in the 1950s and 1960s, the US lost is comparative advantage in producing automobiles. One can argue that the transfer of technology in producing automobiles from the US to Japan was bad for the US.

This above argument that the US may lose economically by transferring technology to China is different from the fear of military threat from China after it acquires the technology. The fear of military threat can justify restricting the transfer of military technology to China.

5

The Fragmentation of the Chinese Domestic Market

The degree of integration of the Chinese domestic market has taken on particular importance since China's entry into the World Trade Organisation (WTO). Indeed, the opening up of the Chinese market to foreign companies can only be effective if free trade is guaranteed domestically. The preparedness of the central authorities to put an end to local protectionist measures has become apparent with the commitment to their WTO partners to ensure free access and free circulation of goods, services and capital. The fear of the Chinese leaders that domestic impediments are a source of friction with their partners would seem to explain the recent steps taken.

The idea of domestic economic integration was promoted at the third plenary session of the sixteenth central committee of the Chinese Communist Party (CCP), devoted to perfecting the socialist market economy, in October 2003 in Peking. Local protectionism appeared as one of the main concerns, while the leaders had the objective of taking the reform process further, providing for more balanced development and maintaining a sustained growth rate in order to absorb the workforce released by the restructurings from agriculture and state-owned enterprises.

A World Bank memorandum of October 2003 is of this view: "A domestic market that is flexible and integrated is vital for the development of Chinese competitiveness and growth, as well as for the structural adjustment of the Chinese economy. A free and integrated domestic market for goods and services, coupled with a free entry and exit for firms, allowing the most productive ones to grow and take advantage of economies of scale, facilitate the spread of technologies, and stimulate improvements in productivity that increase the competitiveness of firms and growth. (...) In the same way, the structural adjustment currently underway is all the more likely to produce sustainable, long-term results if it takes place within an integrated domestic market, one operating in accordance with the laws of the market place".

The fragmentation of the Chinese economy in an increasingly globalised context is also problematic for maintaining macro-economic stability. A limited integration—or even one going backwards—of the Chinese provincial markets suggests a limited capacity on the part of provinces to absorb the asymmetrical shocks. For some authors, significant discontinuities brought about by the provincial borders could even jeopardise national unity.

The degree of integration of the Chinese domestic market. First of all, it aims to identify the causes of local protectionism, before recounting the history of the commercial integration of the provinces over the course of the 1990s, based on intra-provincial exchange data. As Barry Naughton has shown, examining inter-provincial exchanges is the most direct way to study regional integration. This approach also enables an analysis of the importance of domestic trade in China in relation to international trade.

The rise of local protectionism in the late 1980s

Trade between provinces developed considerably after the launch of the reforms in the late 1970s. Ten years later, however, problems related to decentralisation and distortions in the pricing system were impediments to such exchanges. Andrew Wedeman has described these two stages in the development of local protectionism6. First, between 1987 and 1989, there were many inter-regional wars for the supply of resources. The regions producing raw materials blocked and even banned the export of scarce resources. The manufacturing regions, seeing their supply of essential inputs threatened, then launched counter-offensives, unleashing real clashes that were based in a multitude of products ranging from strategic inputs for industry (cotton, silk, tobacco, wool and tea), to foodstuffs (cereals, eggs, pork), and local spice specialities (mint oil, aniseed...)

The wool wars constituted a good example of this. They broke out in the productive provinces, essentially in the north-west (Inner

Mongolia, Gansu, Ningxia, Qinghai and Xinjiang). These provinces adopted a policy of "local production, use and sale" that required a limitation on exports to the rest of the country in order to satisfy the growing demand for local wool transformers. The introduction of production quotas was accompanied by export restrictions (concerning both tariffs and non-tariffs). The same logic was at the root of the silk wars that ensued in 1988 between Sichuan province, the main producer of cocoons, and the coastal provinces that were the users (Guangdong, Jiangsu and Zhejiang). The regions cultivating silk worms went so far as to deploy armed forces and militia on the borders to prevent the coastal provinces, which had the resources to offer better prices, from acquiring cotton. The rice war of 1988 between Guangdong province and the producing province of Hunan, or the cereal war between 1987 and 1989, that saw Fujian province pitted against producing provinces such as Hubei, Zhejiang, Jiangxi, Anhui and Henan, also illustrated the tensions born from the distortions in the pricing system and the divergence of interests between provinces.

A second form of regional protectionism appeared at the end of 1989, one that this time concerned imports from other provinces. Local governments, confronted with stockpiles and budgetary restrictions, due to the recession and the tight monetary policy of then Prime Minister Li Peng, restricted or outlawed the importation of many goods. At the time of the recession of late 1989, the manufacturing coastal provinces flooded the country with their unsold stock. Many inland provinces drew up lists of goods which were banned from being imported and set up "inspection posts" to collect taxes and fines.

The restrictions mainly affected manufactured goods, particularly television sets, household appliances, bicycles, stereos or electrical equipment. Virtually all the provinces, even the most open ones like Guangdong or Peking, had recourse to protectionist measures. Thus, Peking limited imports of wood from Hebei province in 1992. Yet, these sorts of measures were especially adopted by the western provinces anxious to protect local production, such as Hubei, Shaanxi, Sichuan, Qinghai and most especially Xinjiang province.

Local governments implemented their protectionist policies through the use of all sorts of measures: road blocks, the seizing of merchandise, *ad hoc* taxes, administrative charges, biased technical standards, bureaucratic red tape. Outside firms were confronted with enormous difficulties, whether for the purchase of premises, equipment or land, or for obtaining finance. They could become purely and simply victims of the theft of goods or of the vehicles being used to transport them. A prohibition on sales of certain imported goods was commonplace, parallel to the promotion of local production and its distribution through preferential financing arrangements.

The situation came to be of such concern that in November 1990, the State Council and the Central Committee of the CCP had to make repeated calls for the dismantling of the "vertical" and "horizontal" impediments to trade, for regional specialisation and the mobility of factors, advocated by the reforms.

The origins of protectionism

Local protectionism can be explained by two structural factors9. On the one hand, decentralisation, launched in 1980, gave added financial responsibility to the provinces without, however, providing them with more resources. On the other hand, the less developed regions pursued a policy of industrialisation through substitution for imports, in order to offer less money to the coastal provinces.

The generalisation of protectionism has been interpreted as a manifestation of serious shortcomings in the reform programme. Distortions in pricing had existed well before 1978 (and were surely more widespread), but they were compensated for by the central government's budgetary redistribution policy. The latter taxed the industrialised regions and reallocated, via fiscal subsidies, a part of their profits to the provinces producing raw materials. Indeed, in spite of the increases in the purchase price of raw materials, particularly in the agricultural sector, the pricing system in the early days of the reforms gave a clear advantage to industry to the detriment of agriculture, thereby creating a "wedge factor between agricultural and industrial prices". The provinces producing raw materials (agricultural or energy sectors) lost out, suffering both from the depreciation of the prices of the goods that they sold and the high prices of the processed goods that they bought. On the other side, the provinces that specialised in light industry benefited twice over, in that they bought their inputs for a low cost and sold processed goods for a handsome profit. The extraction of a financial surplus in agriculture nationally to guarantee the financing of a rapid process of industrialisation had constituted a key element in the strategy of development prior to the reforms. The system of compulsory delivery (*tonggou*) for strategic goods (cereals, energy...) maintained prices artificially low with respect to industrial goods. Farmers would never have accepted selling their produce to the state if a free market had been allowed11. Prior to 1978 and even until recently, agricultural produce was divided into three categories. The first included cereals, cotton, oilseed, and medicinal herbs. The second covered most of the inputs used by the food industry like meat, eggs, vegetables or fruit. The third category contained remaining agricultural produce, but unlike it, the first two were subject to a quota system, within which the state required that a part of the production be given up to it at a fixed, depreciated price. The irrationality of this pricing system induced a transfer of profits from the regions producing raw materials (in the centre and west of the country) towards the manufacturing provinces on the coast.

The reform of the fiscal system in 1980 put an end to the redistribution to the disadvantaged provinces; and the implementation of the policy of "separation of fiscal centres" amplified the feeling of injustice felt by the land-locked provinces. Decentralisation made each province responsible for the management of its expenditure based on its local revenues. As these came in large part from industrial profits, the provinces became very sensitive to the industry-agriculture relative prices. Whereas the coastal regions still benefited from the wedge effect of prices, the inland provinces that produced raw materials suffered from these distortions, without the central government being able to compensate them by reason of its lower returns.

The fiscally disadvantaged regions therefore used the new powers obtained through decentralisation to launch into policies of industrialisation and turned to protectionism to limit the imports of consumer goods from the coast and facilitate the development of infant industries sheltered from outside competition. As every jurisdiction was keen to develop its industrial base and keep its own resources, all types of industry were to be found in all of the provinces. This meant that factories making fridges, television sets and other household appliances existed practically everywhere, leading to major operations that were often less than optimal, and hence hardly competitive, especially in times of recession. The industrialisation of the provinces flew in the face of the principle of comparative advantage.

The central government was unable to manage the protectionist behaviour of the provinces, something that was magnified both by the centre's preferential policy and the actual motivations of provincial officials: "the provincial governments set up the policy of *geben qiancheng* (everyone runs their own race) or *gexian shentong* (everyone shows their particular achievements), which resulted in a situation of *gezi weizheng* (everyone acts consciously without regard for the general interest)". The absence of any co-ordination between the provincial governments not only brought about a duplication of activities, but also the implementation of local preferential policies and protectionist measures. Clashes between provinces with identical industrial structures became inevitable, as they struggled to get their inputs and gain markets.

Another source of protectionism⁻adding to the pricing distortions and the fiscal reform⁻lay in the flagrant bias of the policy of development in favour of the coastal regions. The central authorities gave priority in terms of investment to the coast and facilitated the rapid development of the east by allowing it to keep a greater part of its income in foreign currency and to create new financial instruments. This favouritism magnified the gap between the east and the west, by increasing the competitiveness of the coastal regions.

Disputes went hand in hand with the poorly controlled macro-economic fluctuations. At times of growth (1985-1988), the coastal industries massively bought the needed inputs, causing an increase in the price of raw materials such that the less efficient producers in the inland regions could no longer pay for their inputs. At the other extreme, during periods of recession (1989-1990), the country's interior saw itself being flooded with manufactured goods from the east. Inter-regional clashes for resources in times of expansion were thus followed by import restrictions in periods of recession.

The disputes were made possible by the absence of any legislation banning the inter-provincial trade barriers. Several laws and regulations were adopted by the State Council between 1980 and 1990, but they were not given any priority status and figured in catch-all texts.

The protectionism of the provincial authorities with regard to goods from the rest of the country was part and parcel of the twin strategy of preserving socio-economic stability and maximising fiscal receipts. The barriers to inter-provincial trade had the goal of limiting the unfavourable social, economic and political consequences of the reforms (retrenchments, bankruptcies of local firms, declining profits)13. Local protectionism emerged as a strong fiscal autonomy of the local authorities and high unemployment, where the public sector provided the lion's share of job opportunities and where labour-intensive industries predominated.

CHALLENGES AND IMPLICATIONS FOR DOMESTIC POLICY REFORM

The challenges facing China and India for sustaining rapid economic growth and meeting the MDGs are similar in nature. First there is the matter of continuing to reduce poverty and hunger and maintain food security. Two other serious issues concern the widening rural-urban income gap and the degradation of the environment. Also of concern is the need to restructure agriculture and markets to meet more diversified consumer and export market food demand, and the need to adopt policies that enable both countries to maintain comparative advantage in commodity production. How these challenges are addressed will determine to a large degree the success in meeting the MDGs, the ability to sustain growth and the role that these economies will play in world markets.

Food Security and Poverty

Two important questions related to achieving the MDGs of poverty and hunger reduction need to be answered. How does the growth in agriculture and in the non-agricultural economy affect poverty alleviation? What can we learn from the experience of China and India?

Ravallion and Chen (2004) for China and Ravallion and Datt (1996) for India conclude that there is a strong link between poverty reduction and increased agricultural productivity. However, Besley *et al.* (2004) argues on the basis of an enormously rich data set and very sophisticated econometrics that agriculture has played a minimal role at best in India's reduction of poverty (Timmer 2005). The China case study provides several interesting results on key factors that have determined the changes in rural poverty in China. Overall economic growth has been a key primary source of rural poverty reduction.

But while economic growth is an essential and necessary condition for nationwide poverty reduction, it is not a sufficient condition. As incomes have grown the impact and effectiveness of general economic growth on poverty reduction has weakened. Fan *et al.* (2002) for China and Fan *et al.* for India (2002) examine the poverty impact of various agricultural investments and subsidies. Their work suggests that there are important multipliers at work and that the impact of these multipliers changes over time. In addressing the question of poverty impact of agriculture *per se* we need to look at the links between the agricultural and non-agricultural economy including rural non-farm employment.

Taking the aforesaid views into consideration, we observe in China that the TVEs provided a strong link between agricultural and non-agricultural economy which undoubtedly accounted for the sharp drop in poverty. Also fostering poverty alleviation has been the egalitarian nature of the reforms under the HRS. By contrast, the links between the agricultural and non-agricultural economy have been less strong in India and have been hampered by a host of regulations which have slowed the development of both agriculture and industry. Overall growth in the GDP is increasing in India while growth in agricultural GDP has been declining which does not speak well for reducing rural poverty.

Based on projections using the GTAP model both country studies conclude that they can meet domestic cereal grain demands without reliance on significant imports. Since the food shortages of the mid-1960s, foodgrain self-sufficiency has been a dominant feature of Indian agricultural policy. China also sets a high priority on foodgrain self-sufficiency.

However, maintaining self-sufficiency in wheat production will almost certainly require improved management of water resources in the Punjab and neighbouring states and in the North China Plain. Foodgrain self-sufficiency at the national level does not ensure food security at the regional or household level. It is a paradox that with more than 260 million people below the official poverty line in 1999-2000, India is one of the leading exporters of rice. Poverty incidence is expected to continue to fall in India from 26.1 percent in 1999-2000, reaching 8 percent in 2015 well beyond the MDG. But achieving this goal would appear to depend on the success of the reforms which target the growth in agriculture to rise from the sluggish 1.5 percent to 4 percent*per annum*.

From the experience of both China and India, the policy implications seem clear. Attention must be given to raising agricultural productivity and incomes in those areas that have thus far not benefited from new technologies or trade liberalization. At the same time emphasis should be on creating jobs in the non-farm sector, whether rural or urban based. For China this will require continuing reform of state-owned enterprises (SOEs) and encouragement of labour-intensive private industry. India's continuing reforms should foster growth in employment in both the manufacturing and service sectors.

The Widening Income Gap

In addition to the rural-urban income gap, especially that between agriculture and new, dynamic industries, there are regional disparities such as between the coastal and the central and western provinces in China or between the Punjab and Haryana and the states of Eastern India. Further within regions there is the disparity between those that have become commercialized, for example through contract farming and those that follow traditional practices. Disparity in India exists between the more commercialized farmers in the Punjab and Haryana as opposed to those in Bihar and Orissa.

The issue here is not necessarily absolute poverty, but what Hayami (2005) describes as relative poverty. The less favourable areas need better education and health services and equal access to social services. Gulati *et al.* (2005) argue to this end that China and India should accelerate growth, improve efficiency and at the same time ensure that growth is both equitable and sustainable. To improve efficiency, India should phase out subsidies and efforts should be focused on developing infrastructure and new technologies. However, for many the path out of poverty lies not in agriculture but in non-farm opportunities. Both countries are experiencing rapid migration from rural to urban areas. But too little attention is paid to facilitating migration of rural workers to urban jobs where investments in the rural economy have a low payoff.

Both China and India are committed to addressing the income gap, but the approaches will be very different. China recently approved a 15 percent increase in the money earmarked for agricultural development, and rural services.

Also China has initiated the "Five Balanced Development Strategies: balanced development between rural and urban, between economic growth and social progress, among regions, between human intervention and environmental conservation, and between internal and external economies." The proposed strategies and reforms are bold but there are many barriers to achieving the lofty goals of the programme.

The UPA Government came to power in India in May 2004 and the National Common Minimum Programme forms the bedrock of economic policy with the highest priority for agriculture and a holistic approach to agriculture and rural development. But India faces a different set of policy and institutional constraints. Rationalizing subsidies and extending reforms that liberalized industry to agriculture through the removal of regulations and restrictions to trade seem to be crucial. India also must address the problem of a high variability in income and livelihood among regions and states.

Environmental Issues

Rapid economic development challenges the ability of China and India to manage resources, sustain agricultural growth rates and meet food security and poverty reduction objectives. In both countries, economic development has taken precedence over protection of the environment. The environmental issues can be summarized under five main headings: air, water, soil, habitat destruction and biodiversity losses. Of particular concern to sustainability of agricultural growth and to food security are problems relating to misuse of land and water resources.

Soil problems — erosion, fertility losses, salinization and desertification are reducing the land area suitable for cultivation. Overuse of fertilizer (China's use of nitrogen is three times the world average) is resulting in both environmental problems and problems related to food and water safety. For example, the high levels of nitrates found in the drinking water in many cities in north China pose a threat to the health of infants. Of immediate concern to both China and India is the growing scarcity and competition for water and declining water quality. The overexploitation of groundwater has contributed to the slowing of growth in grain production in two of Asia's breadbaskets, Northwest India and the North China Plain. This has important implications in particular for the long-term growth in wheat production in these regions.

The Indian National Common Minimum Programme, a politico-economic agenda that guides new government policy decisions, lists among its reform priorities stopping the misuse of water and the unsustainable use of land.

In China and India major schemes are underway both to conserve water and to reallocate water between basins — for example from the Yangtze (north). These are long-range projects. Meanwhile, institutional changes are being tested and implemented with mixed success to improve the efficiency of water use and provide equitable allocation of water among competing uses and users.

This includes programmes and projects designed to transfer operation and management responsibilities to local user groups —

known as irrigation management transfer. Managing the common property resource, groundwater, to avoid overexploitation presents the biggest challenge.

The Restructuring of Agriculture

A conceptual framework plotting the transformation of agriculture against the degree of diversification. As incomes rise, food consumption moves at first toward less diversification. Households give up consumption of inferior sources (maize and root crops) for preferred cereal grains (rice and wheat). This is followed by diversification into horticultural crops and livestock products (including fisheries). This transformation set off by a rise in incomes began in China in the early reform period (1978-1984) and occurred in India largely as a result of the 1991 reforms. The result of these non-agricultural reforms in India was to improve the terms of trade for agriculture and bring forth private investments in horticultural and livestock products. Farms may become more specialized, but agriculture as a whole becomes more diversified to meet changing consumer demands and the potential for exports. Finally, as suggested above, farm household incomes are likely to become more diversified. Countries, regions of countries, and farm households may, of course, be at different stages in this transformation process. The challenge is to provide as wide a scope as possible for participation in the transformation process at the farm level.

Farms in Asia are small (2 ha or less) and in many instances are getting smaller. There is currently a sharp debate among academics as to whether small-scale agriculture can continue to play its historic role. In short, how will agriculture be commercialized? Can small farms have productive cultivation let alone provide the minimum output required to earn a livelihood? Does commercialization of agriculture imply larger farms? Increasing commercial orientation, vertical integration and coordination of the farming sector with large-scale food processors, wholesalers and retailers who have private standards of food quality and safety could affect the viability of small farms.

Evidence from China and India and elsewhere in Asia suggest that small-scale farms will continue to have a role to play. But restructuring of agriculture implies a change in the farm household unit to accommodate changes in domestic and export marketing. While there are economies of scale in distribution and marketing, there are few, if any, economies of scale in the production process. In fact, as demonstrated in China with both family plots under collective agriculture and with smallholdings under the household responsibility system, small-scale farming can be more efficient than large-scale enterprises. At the same time the high degree of fragmentation in farm holdings, particularly in China where the farm may be divided into five or more scattered plots, presents an obstacle to efficient management. Furthermore, there are advantages for farms to work together or to form groups to share services such as extension or tractor provision or for contracting with private sector marketing firms.

The farm size issue has important policy ramifications. The skewed land tenure situation in India suggests that large farms are likely to be more commercially oriented. In China and other parts of Asia there is often a restriction on farm size to maintain an egalitarian policy.

Maintaining Competitive Agriculture

A traditional response to the widening rural-urban income gap has been to subsidize agriculture. Countries have taxed agriculture in the early stages of development and then subsidized agriculture. The transition from tax to subsidy tends to occur when agriculture declines to 15 percent of the GDP. The experience of India shows that continuing the current pattern of subsidies can be costly. They absorb funds that could be more effectively used for measures to enhance agricultural productivity — rural infrastructure and agricultural research. Furthermore, WTO and FTA agreements are putting pressure on developing countries to reduce protection.

China has looked upon this as an opportunity to promote trade liberalization and decrease the highly protected state-owned industries. Trade liberalization has brought about a sharp shift in trade of goods in a manner consistent with comparative advantage. The export of less labour-intensive bulk commodities such as grains has declined while the export of labour-intensive higher valued commodities such as horticultural crops and animal products has risen.

In India there has been trade liberalization since the 1990s. Contingent on domestic reforms, the India study argues that present high levels of bound tariff for agricultural commodities can be further reduced, barring certain sectors identified as sensitive (notably edible oils and dairy products), as India is cost competitive in agricultural products.

The India country study refers to the "spaghetti bowl" of trade agreements that India has with trading partners and the same would hold true for China. Multilateral trade agreements are preferable to discretionary regional agreements although progress in negotiating the latter has been slow.

This fact notwithstanding, it is clear that Asia is moving toward a more liberalized trading environment. This stands in sharp contrast to the developed countries who continue to protect their farm economies. Subsidies to farmers in these countries are extremely large despite promises made in the Uruguay Round to reduce them significantly.

REGIONAL POLICIES SINCE THE EARLY 1990S

Peking's response to regionalism

The central leadership quickly took on board the danger represented by the centrifugal forces of regionalism and clearly criticised the policies of industrialisation through substitution for imports resulting in the proliferation of less than optimal firms. As early as 1990, Li Peng and Zhou Jiahua, the President of the Planning Commission, pointed out the damage wrought by regional protectionism and announced urgent measures to fight against the chaos brought on by regionalism. In actual fact, however, the central authorities had to be content with verbal threats and changes in provincial leadership. It was forced to admit that the emergence of regionalisms, even if it put the country's unity in danger, was inseparable from the process of opening up and the reforms, the extension of which was vital for the political survival of the Party.

The few concrete steps taken by the central authorities to discourage protectionist practices did not manage to get the provincial authorities to see reason. They were targeted at particular cases. Thus, following disputes over the supply of silk cocoons between Zhejiang and Jiangsu provinces, the Zhejiang provincial authorities were criticised, and forced to pay a fine and engage in self-criticism.

Artificially low fixed prices for cereals have hit agricultural regions hard

However, some developments enabled a partial response to be made to the primary causes of the disputes. The impatience of the inland provinces to benefit also from the reforms was finally heard at the start of the 1990s with the calling into question of the priority of coastal development and the model of spreading economic development on which the sixth and seventh five-year plans were based (1981-1985 and 1986-1990). The central authorities were keen to promote regional equity and hence to favour the development of the country's interior in step with that of the coast. The reform of the system of subsidising external trade, initiated in 1991, reduced the measures in favour of the special economic zones and the coastal cities. The subsidies were abolished and there was a harmonisation of the system of hard currency retention. This policy of more equal treatment of the various provinces favoured the take-off of trade directly managed by the inland provinces.

The eighth five-year plan (1991-1995) abandoned the tripartite (coast, centre and west) regionalisation of the seventh plan to draw up priorities in relation to sectors. In fact, it gave priority to agriculture and energy, areas in which the inland provinces specialised. The broadening of the reforms, particularly the decision adopted by the third plenary session of the Central Committee in November 1993 to promote a "balanced regional development", and the reduction in pricing distortions that had been unfavourable to the producers of raw materials, reduced the protectionist motivations of the provinces that had felt wronged.

The ninth five-year plan (1996-2000) continued on this path, by giving priority to the fight against regional disparities on the basis of significant investments in infrastructure, to co-operation between the coastal and inland provinces, and to the promotion of Foreign Direct Investment (FDI) and trade in the west of the country. Since the 1990s, the central authorities have made many calls for co-operation between the provinces and promoted the creation of multi-regional economic co-operation zones. The objectives have been, *inter alia*, the co-ordination of policies of regional development and the development of inter-border links. But it seems that in spite of the many co-operation zones thus created, the actual realisations have been few and far between, in the absence of any preparedness on the part of provincial governments to subsume their own short-term interests under the long-term ones of the region or the country as a whole.

The fiscal reform introduced at the beginning of 1994 enabled a recentralising of a part of the tax revenue and hence a strengthening of Peking's power. But it did not altogether eliminate the possibility for local governments to increase their revenue by taking action in terms of the volume of local sales. The new fiscal system did not sever the link between the government's income derived from taxation and the health of local firms. Thus, it was not a deterrent to protectionist measures since these were capable of safeguarding the tax base. Moreover, the reform of pricing is not complete yet, so local governments still have a tendency to favour investment in light processing industries, to the detriment of the logic of comparative advantage and of long-term national development.

The present situation

The inter-provincial economic "wars" of the kind that took place in the late 1980s have ceased, but the integration of the domestic market is still impeded on account of the twin role played by the local authorities, at once regulators and players in the field of economic activity. Not only do local governments own companies, but they also finance and regulate them, which means that they have complex and sometimes contradictory objectives. A firm's drive for profit in accordance with the laws of the marketplace goes hand in hand with the objective of maximising employment and growth, as well as local revenue derived from taxation. Local governments have control at once over production, distribution, taxation and subsidies... they are therefore in a position to turn to protectionist measures in order to provide for the development of their firms sheltered from external competition.

According to Barry Naughton, several factors have reduced the interest in having recourse to protectionism. An improvement in the transport infrastructure, a reduction in the distortions of the pricing system, as well as a rebalancing of supply and demand for raw materials have weakened the incentive of local governments to intervene in the sphere of economic activity.

Furthermore, interventionist policies have become more difficult with the increasing complexity of the economy. The multiplication of distribution networks has made government intervention less efficacious. Barry Naughton also states that the efforts of Prime Minister Zhu Rongji to reorganise and impose a severe budgetary constraint on the state banking system have weakened the strong connection that existed between the authorities and local banks. The stress placed by the central government on the necessary increase in budgetary revenue has made it more costly and more difficult to maintain the practice of supporting local firms through tax exemptions or hidden subsidies.

Finally, interventions have become less necessary since the national policy of systematic defence of employment was abandoned in 1996.

Yet, local protectionist policies have not disappeared. The methods used include applying more rigorous procedures and technical and qualitative standards to imported goods than to local ones, granting local firms preferential access to the banking system and meting out biased treatment to outside firms when it comes to the settling of disputes through the courts. The international press reports regularly on protectionist practices, a case in point being the support given by the municipal government to Shanghai Volkswagen, a joint venture of Volkswagen and the Shanghai Automotive Industrial Corp., whereby the company's Santana model was approved by the municipality as the car to constitute its fleet of taxis. At the same time, additional costs were imposed on licence plates and sales tax for cars from outside of Shanghai, which increased their final purchase price by an additional 10% on average. In Jiangxi province, supplementary taxes imposed by the provincial authorities amounted to 15%. For Renault's Sanjiang model produced by a joint venture between China Aerospace and Renault, based in Xiaogan in Hubei province the surcharge amounted to 70,000 yuan (US$8,500) per car and was the root cause of the withdrawal of the make from China in the late 1990s.

While present efforts at restructuring (particularly the closing down of firms in the sectors having an overabundance of supply such as in the textile industry, coal-mining and beer manufacturing) are a step in the right direction towards integration, regional specialisation and a search for comparative advantage, their impact is for the time being difficult to quantify. Moreover, while the central government has been confirming its commitment to the rationalisation of production put in place at the end of the 1980s, the industrial policy of the ninth five-year plan made the blunder of favouring yet a further wave of duplication. Indeed, this plan identified a list of key industries characterised by a high-yield capacity, a strong technological content and a potential for spreading economic development. These were, in particular, transportation equipment (cars and motorbikes), electrical appliances, petrochemical goods, machines, metallurgy and construction materials. The central government encouraged the provinces to develop their own plans for investment and production based on local specificities and likely future returns. The logical upshot was the commitment of massive investment by the provinces in most of these sectors. The over-capacity and over-production of these goods brought about ferocious competition and a disastrous fall in prices, particularly for the provinces that had developed these sectors without any consideration for their comparative advantages.

Local protectionism and the impediments to the economic unification of the domestic market remain current, as attested by the many declarations, regulations and studies on these subjects since 2000. At the annual session of the National People's Assembly (NPA) in March 2000, Wang Zhongfu, the Minister for Industry and Commerce, stated that the administrative monopolies, the imposed commercial contracts and the impediments to the market had become "a cancer in the Chinese market". In April 2001, the State Council issued a directive outlawing regional barriers.

This 2001 regulation was published only in Chinese, without appearing in the English-language newspapers normally covering economic policy, a practice out of step with the reporting traditionally given to the other directives. This regulation contained 28 articles and had the aim of establishing a unified, equitable, normal market system, eliminating local protectionist measures and preserving the economic order of the socialist market economy. The above insert sets out the clearly formulated prohibitions and measures announced to deal with cases of abuse of these legal provisions concerning the suspension of functionaries and prison sentences.

A 2003 study of the break-up of the domestic market was carried out by the Development Research Centre of the State Council, involving academics, entrepreneurs and officials in order to assess the importance of impediments to economic activity in the various provinces23. The results clearly show the tobacco, alcoholic beverages and automobile sectors to be the worst affected by dint of their high profitability, strong tax base and monopolistic organisation. Among the main impediments denounced by the respondents are the job discrimination practices in favour of locals, the difficulties encountered by migrants in finding a school for their children, the local bias in the way disputes are dealt with by the courts, and the preferential treatment given to local firms in the public tendering process.

The increasing intensity of commercial activity between 1987 and 1997

While there have been many analyses of what curbs the process of national integration, whether these be natural or cultural impediments or political barriers set up by local governments, studies on the degree of integration of the Chinese domestic market have always run into the problem of the absence of data. Until now, researchers have had to be satisfied with data on transport and the sectorial structure of industrial production. Similarly, they have had to put up with aggregate pricing data or else attempt to make deductions based on trade data. Furthermore, most studies have had a limited impact where conclusions cannot really be generalised in so far as they are limited to a given region of China or a particular period of time. The objective of the final section of this article is to make up for this gap by examining the economic integration of the Chinese provinces based on trade data taken from the input-output (IO) tables drawn up by the provinces between 1987 and 1997.

In each province, goods have three potential origins, namely local (or intra-provincial) production, the importation of goods produced in another province (inter-provincial importation) and international importation. The policy of reform was followed by a rapid increase in the rate of opening up to international trade as well as by the growth in imports. This increase in the imported proportion of consumer goods linked to a weakening of impediments to international trade implied a drop in one or both of the other two sources. In so far as the economic reforms have promoted the integration of the Chinese domestic market in tandem with the opening up internationally, one would expect imports to take the place of locally produced goods more than of supplies from elsewhere in the country. However, a statistical analysis of the data on the trade flows of the provinces between 1987 and 1997 does not confirm this hypothesis.

As Barry Naughton has pointed out, on the basis of the 1987 and 1992 data25, inter-provincial exchanges are very important, whether measured relative to either GDP or to foreign trade. This gives the lie to the picture of a Chinese market made up of a juxtaposition of self-sufficient provinces such as that painted by Audrey Donnithorne in the early 1970s. The export and import rates in relation to the rest of the country amounted on average to 50% of the provincial GDP. In comparison, the average international export and import ratios of national GDP were 16% and 8% respectively over the period 1987-1997. Table 1 enables us to compare the participation in inter-provincial and international trade for the coastal, central and western zones.

Chinese domestic trade appears to be proportionally higher than trade within Western Europe, NAFTA (North American Free Trade Agreement) or ASEAN (Association of Southeast Asian Nations). The intra-zone exchanges reached 18% of the GDP of Western Europe in 1999, 5.6% of the NAFTA GDP in 1998, and 12% of ASEAN in 1998. By way of comparison, the intra-China trade ratio as a percentage of GDP amounted to 38% on average in 1997. Inter-provincial exchanges were hence very important compared to international ones, which could undermine the view of self-sufficient Chinese provinces. Yet between 1992 and 1997, these exchanges were in decline, whereas intra-provincial exchanges progressed.

Between 1987 and 1997, the importance of inter-provincial exchanges showed a marked decline, whereas international exchanges experienced a rapid growth. While the average inter-provincial export rate was eight times higher than the average international export rate in 1987, in 1997 it was no more than 1.5. The same downward trend in the relation between inter-provincial and international trade can be seen for imports. A developing fragmentation of the Chinese domestic market, such as that suggested by Alwyn Young, would thus seem to be confirmed. While inter-provincial trade in China increased in value, it underwent a significant drop as a percentage of GDP between 1987 and 1997, in particular after 1992. Between 1987 and 1997, inter-provincial trade increased less quickly than did the GDP, whereas the rates of international opening more than doubled. While inter-provincial exchanges went up overall in value by 5% between 1987 and 1997, international imports and exports increased by 13% and 25% respectively. A larger part of provincial trade thus occurred with foreign partners.

The main partner of the Chinese provinces in 1997 remained, however, the other provinces, although the situation was very uneven, both in terms of development and level. While the coastal provinces, especially during the 1990s, stood out through a rapid decline in the inter-provincial exchange ratio as a percentage of GDP, in line with a virtually symmetrical growth in their international exchanges, the other provinces experienced a less significant roll-back of their inter-provincial opening up and, in particular, did not benefit from any increase in their rates of opening up internationally. The coastal provinces appeared as the most integrated, not only with the rest of China, but also with the foreign market. In 1997, the average rate of international export by the coastal provinces caught up with the level of the inter-provincial export rate at 37% of GDP. The inland provinces had less significant internal and international exchanges (30% and 5% respectively in 1997). The provinces in the west of the country put an end to the progress of integration, their international exchanges being quite minor (3%) and their inter-provincial rate of opening up only half that of the coast (25%).

The Chinese regions all have one common feature. This concerns the progressive roll back of the inter-provincial opening between 1987 and 1997. The question then is whether this corresponds to an effective reorientation of exchanges linked to internationalisation or whether, on the contrary, it may be interpreted as a movement of disintegration. The drop in internal trade within the coastal and interior zones happened mainly between 1992 and 1997, which would seem to be coherent with the chronology of the reforms and reflect their opening up to international exchanges, which increased in particular after 1992). The dynamic nature of inter-provincial exchanges was subject to dual forces. First, all economic liberalisation should have favoured exchanges between provinces, in comparison with the era of planned exchanges and the policy of self-sufficiency. Next, the policy of international opening up (no longer restricted to the coast, but stepped up and broadened to the provinces as a whole) should have led to an intensification of relations with the outside world that seems to have worked to the detriment of internal (intra- and inter-provincial) trade. A phenomenon of substitution between international and inter-provincial trade certainly seems to have taken hold, particularly since 1992. The predominance of inter-provincial over international trade thus appears to be quite relative and above all temporary. The policy of opening up to world trade by the Chinese provinces is something recent following several decades of a virtually totally closed shop and hence of necessary internal supply. The rebalancing of exchanges is therefore only in its infancy. The Chinese provinces are still heavily protected from the world market, as confirmed by the difficult negotiations on China's entry into the WTO. It will only really be possible to reach a conclusion about the importance of inter-provincial exchanges relative to international exchanges, and hence about the real commercial integration of the Chinese provinces, once there is a broader liberalisation of international exchanges.

Moreover, the view of China as a set of cellular provinces can be excluded only by comparing the part of locally consumed production with that of the production exchanged with the other provinces. Setting inter-provincial trade on the same footing as international trade is not enough. We must compare the scope and development of inter-provincial exchanges with those of intra-provincial ones. Table 2 provides the breakdown of absorption between the three potential sources of goods: international, inter-provincial and intra-provincial. A province's absorption are calculated as the sum of production and imports minus exports. The total imports and exports include trade with the rest of China and internationally. Logically, the inland and western provinces appear to be the most self-sufficient, with 80% of their expenses going on local goods, as against around 20% on products from other parts of the country and a small portion for foreign goods. Conversely, the coastal provinces appear to be the most outward-looking both with regard to the rest of the country and international markets.

Concerning developments over time, a drop in the inter-provincial trade can be observed for the period 1987-1997, in line with an increase in intra-provincial and international trade for the three groups of provinces. Differences appear nonetheless between these groups for the sub-periods 1987-1992 and 1992-1997. In the western provinces, the decline in the share of inter-provincial consumer goods mainly occurred prior to 1992, no doubt in relation to the trade disputes¯their being replaced by local goods. Subsequently, one can notice a relative stabilisation between 1992 and 1997, at a very low level, around 17%-19%. In the coastal provinces, the drop in the share of goods from the rest of the country was also significant prior to 1992, but it continued, by reason this time of the effect of substitution of international imports: the fall back from 27.7% to 22.1% of the share of domestic goods corresponded to an increase from 6.3% to 12.1% of the share of foreign goods, without any change in the share of local goods. In the inland provinces, the drop in the inter-provincial supply also occurred under the twin effect of substitution of international and local goods. It would appear that these provinces, faced with the rapid take-off of the coast, were engaged throughout the 1990s in the active promotion of substitution industries for imports sheltered from competition with the rest of the country in order to develop their economy and support employment and the survival of loss-making public enterprises.

It therefore appears that the drop in intensity of inter-provincial trade is due both to internationalisation and the development of intra-provincial exchanges (greater self-sufficiency of the provinces). This leads one to have doubts about any real integration of the domestic market. Indeed, the promotion of the process of internal opening up by the reforms in parallel with the international opening up was motivated by the search for both static and dynamic gains. These had to result from the intensification of competition, the spread of technological progress and the productive specialisation as a function of comparative advantage.

Prior to the reforms, the policies of inward-looking development led to inefficient and non-competitive production that completely overlooked the questions of comparative advantage, economies of scale and productive specialisation. In this sense, at a provincial level, it is logical that with the opening up to world trade, imported goods be substituted both for locally produced ones (intra-provincial trade) and for goods from other provinces (inter-provincial trade). It can even be expected that substitution will occur more to the detriment of local goods than of goods imported from the other provinces. Indeed, the liberalisation of the economy should promote competition between the provinces. The reduction in the share of national goods to the benefit of local production in the absorption of the Chinese provinces, on consumption, between 1987 and 1997, ran counter to the logic, promoted by the reforms, of regional specialisation in terms of comparative advantage and economies of scale. Concerns about the growing fragmentation of the domestic market cannot but increase.

6

Economic Emergence and Political Change in China

Seeds of economic change have long been embedded in the liberal system that North America and Europe together constructed after the Second World War. Indeed, as more of the world adopted liberal market-oriented strategies, the club of developed countries widened, and the international system evolved as a result. This has not always been a seamless process; shifts in the economic balance of power invariably alter relations among states, and in so doing generate no small degree of friction. China's explosive economic emergence, however, promises the greatest shake-up ever of the reigning post-war economic order. It will invariably alter international relations and, by extension, North American-European relations in profound and perhaps unanticipated ways.

China, however, is hardly a new economic power. Prior to the closing of its borders in 1500, its emperors presided over the world's largest and most sophisticated economy. Although modern Europe moved quickly to catch up and ultimately surpass China over the ensuing centuries, it still generated 32% of the world's wealth in 1820. (Hale and Hale) The forced reopening of its borders at the hands of colonial powers marked the beginning of China's return to the world stage; yet colonialism, anarchy, warlordism, nationalist reaction, world war, occupation, civil war and communist revolution rendered this an exceedingly fitful and terribly painful process. It was only with the 1978 reforms launched by Deng Xiaoping that Communist China began to develop in a more organic fashion. Oddly enough, this reform commenced in the countryside when the state suddenly allowed peasants to adopt market structures in order to encourage production and boost income. Since 1994, however, China's economic revolution has been largely an urban and industrial phenomenon. Growth along the Eastern coast has far outstripped development in the countryside. Between 1978 and 2003, China's per capita GDP grew by 6.1% a year, registering a 337% increase over that period. (Wolf) Large swathes of China's vast hinterland have however been left behind in this process.

China has very quickly moved from a communist ownership model, in which the state possessed virtually all the means of production, to a far more complex system in which private ownership increasingly overshadows state ownership. It has also advanced rapidly up the production scale, moving from very simple assembly to ever more complex manufacturing processes.

The area for autonomous action by the individual in China generally has also been expanding, despite persistent, regrettable and ultimately counter-productive limitations on political freedom. The Chinese people now enjoy unprecedented freedom of movement, information flows are far more developed and open today, and young Chinese possess ever-greater control over their destiny despite the real political constraints they confront. In the words of one western analyst, the Chinese at least enjoy the freedom not to engage in politics. This is hardly the same thing as democracy, but it suggests an important evolution away from the totalitarianism of the Cultural Revolution when the Chinese were compelled to live and breath politics.

Yet, within parameters defined largely by the Communist leadership, China's economic boom is providing an outlet for the country's long pent-up commercial energies and the aspirations of its people for a better life. The possibility of achieving this has certainly diverted some of the political passions that spilled onto Tiananmen Square in 1989, (Hutzler) although repression has done its part as well. China's huge student population certainly has its share of aspirant democrats, but many have simply abandoned politics to focus on their careers. Recent polls suggest that the Chinese are tremendously optimistic about the future; particularly the well educated, who are best positioned to benefit from China's economic expansion and global integration. (Giles)

China's civil society has grown more complex and articulated since 1989 and this too is shaping both the aspirations of its people and the likely manner in which future political change will unfold.

Many people today recognize their growing stake in the preservation of civil order. This does not mean that democratic reform will not come, rather it points toward new modalities for pushing for these changes-strategies in which pressure comes from both within the governing elite and from an ever-more articulated civil society. In the words of the historian Lanxin Xiang, the Chinese have embraced Perestroika (restructuring) but have no desire to push for glasnost (openness). (Meeting with Lanxin Xiang) The great threat to the current order may come not from the kind of students who were targeted during the Tiananmen crackdown, but rather from the millions of disenfranchised Chinese, many living in the country's vast interior, who have not benefited from economic reform and growth. China's elite is aware of this and clearly hopes that by easing conditions in the vast hinterland, the regime will be better positioned to defend the political status quo and the stability needed to generate economic growth. But even this offers only a temporary solution to the longer-term problem of China's lack of democracy.

Several years ago after the high technology stock bubble, American economists were ringing their hands over the question of which country might possibly serve as the engine of a global economic recovery. Europe, it was said, was hopelessly over-regulated and increasingly uncompetitive; the United States was heading down a path of rising government and consumer debt, corporate accounting scandals and investor uncertainties; and Japan's economy remained mired in a deflationary recession. Two bright spots, India and China, it was then claimed, lacked the economic weight for their high growth rates to have any significant spillover impact on global growth. Such forecasts, it seems, were made under the old assumption that the global economy and OECD member countries, with a few important caveats, were more or less the same thing.

That assumption proved false. According to a recent Economist survey, China now accounts for 13% of world output in purchasing power parity terms (second only to America's) and will soon be the world's third largest exporter after the United States and Germany. Its domestic demand has been the single greatest factor in Asia's recent recovery, and it is a major underwriter of American deficit spending through its purchase of US treasury bills. The IMF has suggested that if China proves able to implement much needed banking reform, the country will continue growing over the coming decade at 7-8% per annum, a rate which could push the country's GDP above that of the United States by 2020 in purchasing power parity terms. (The Economist, October 2, 2004.) China is thus crossing a threshold. Its economy can no longer be judged as a mere potentiality. It is now an integral player in the global economy, and its international economic weight has grown extraordinarily consequential. Over the last year, the world economy grew by 5%. The two engines of that growth were an American economy unleashed by loose monetary and fiscal policies, very low savings rates and a high propensity to import, and Chinese producers, who are orchestrating one of the greatest economic expansions in recent memory. Yet, China remains a developing country. This accords it a rather unique place in the world economy, one that is perhaps rendered all the more paradoxical by the fact that this ever more economically liberal society is still administered by a Communist party.

THE LABOUR AND DEVELOPMENT ANGLE

China still has a huge underdeveloped rural economy and its hinterland is the source of China's seemingly limitless labour supply. There are as many as 200 million underemployed Chinese agrarian workers who are effectively positioned to move quickly into manufacturing and service jobs when and where these open up. This mobile work force exercises a strong discipline over the labour market. For the time being, therefore, wages for unskilled workers are likely to remain very low compared to western wages, although in coastal regions China's growth and rising productivity is already leading to broader wage hikes. Wages are sufficiently high to keep workers in their jobs as opposed to returning to rural villages. As salaries rise along the coast, some production is migrating westward, and thus the fruits of economic development are rapidly spreading, although vast swathes of China remain mired in poverty.

China's ever mounting presence in global commercial markets is having important labour market effects. This is pushing down the costs of labour intensive exports the world over in sectors like textiles as well as in standardized consumer electronics goods. China has also bid down the cost of global capital. Its purchase of US treasury bills, for example, has helped keep US interest rates down and may have helped bias investment toward labour-saving capital goods-one possible explanation for America's so-called "jobless recovery".

Chinese demand, however, is driving up commodity prices including steel, oil, cement and certain high technology components.

The effect on Western economies here is complex, because China is helping drive energy bills higher while bolstering the price of a range of Western exports and pushing other prices down. Clothing prices, for example, have fallen 30% in the United States over the last decade, in part because of a surge in highly competitive Chinese exports. This has proven a boon to American consumers but has posed serious problems for American textile industries and workers. The same processes have also been evident in Europe, although Europe's retail markets are somewhat less competitive and price falls have not been passed on to consumers to the same extent as they have in the United States.

Nearly two thirds of the increase in China's exports is from non-Chinese firms with plants in China. This points to yet another benefit from China's economic development now accruing to Western owners of capital. Some might argue that such "outsourcing" is indeed costing jobs in the West. Yet, a dynamic view again would suggest that this is also creating opportunities for western labour to move into even more productive sectors as they move up the production ladder. At the same time, China is clearly posing a problem for those developing countries against which it directly competes. It has changed the terms of trade for many of these countries, often driving down the price of their manufactured export goods while raising the price of imported commodities. The end of quotas in the textile sector on January 1, 2005 is accelerating this competition, and a number of developing country textile exporters are already suffering price shocks as a result of China's competitiveness in this sector. Other developing countries, however, have benefited from China's demand for raw materials and energy. It is increasingly apparent that in order to compete with China, developing countries will have adapt; but some poor and smaller developing country economies will need special and differential treatment from the WTO for a transition period. Nevertheless, Chinese Competition will put pressure on these countries to liberalise their economies. If they move in this direction the effect of China's challenge will be positive for these countries as well as for the world economy as a whole.

THE TRADE IMPLICATIONS OF CHINA'S EMERGENCE

China's economic development has hardly been mono-dimensional. It is not simply a creation of Western capitalists seeking to outsource labour to the lowest bidder; nor is China any longer simply a manufacturing centre of cheap plastic and simple electronic products. Chinese industry has moved rapidly up the production chain and is now producing a very large share of the world's office equipment, DVD players, digital cameras, personal computers as well as clothing and shoes and other simpler manufactured goods.

China's swift development has rerouted global supply chains forged over the last thirty years. It now runs large trade deficits with Eastern Asia while enjoying inexorably expanding trade surpluses with North America and Europe. It has become a trading nation par excellence and currently generates 70% of its national income through foreign trade. China's overall share of world trade has increased from 5% in 2000 to 10% today. (Rossi)

China is also exerting trade pressures on a range of developing and transition countries with which it is directly competing. Mexico and Turkey, for example, are losing market share in textiles to the Chinese without the kind of offsetting compensation that has proven so beneficial to much of Asia. Central and Eastern Europe now find themselves engaged in a global battle to win new investments. Hungary won important investments for basic assembly manufacturing in the mid-1990s; yet some of those plants have subsequently relocated to China. The Hungarians now recognize that in the face of serious Chinese competition, their best option is to move into ever more sophisticated production if they are to flourish in the emerging global division of labour.

The net effect of China's rapid growth on the global economy has been highly positive, despite the inevitable dislocation suffered in certain sectors. Its booming economy is generating wealth worldwide. Those benefits accrue through countless channels. Yet, mercantilists and protectionists falsely argue that rising Chinese imports are invariably a bad thing and are simply sparking plant closures and job losses.

Trade economists counter that this is a misleading and partial economic interpretation of what transpires when a large country undergoes economic take-off and emerges as a major global commercial player. First of all, trading with that low cost producer invariably lowers prices for consumers as well as producers, who, as a result, are able to purchase lower cost capital goods. Price falls, in turn, check inflationary pressures in the importing economy, raise consumer welfare, and lower exporters' production costs. The resulting productivity gains help certain domestic industries win market share both domestically and internationally while rewarding workers employed in those sectors. It must also be noted that non-Chinese companies are currently generating over half of China's export earnings and 60% of import revenue. In 2000 alone, U.S corporate earnings generated in China reached $7.2 billion. (Hale and Hale) Western firms are also selling value added inputs to Chinese producers and are thus benefiting from China's place in the international division of labour. These are the winners in the game.

The losers are both the producers of import competing industries that cannot match the price/quality of imported Chinese goods and workers in those industries. Yet, those domestic import competing firms that manage to compete are likely to emerge even stronger. Most empirical work on the broad effects of expanding trade suggests that the gains of the winners in open trading systems significantly outweigh the losses of those suffering from new competition. In this process, moreover, trading countries are likely to grow more specialized in their production, leading to further productivity gains and wealth generation.

Empirical evidence tends to confirm that precisely such processes are at work in those developed and developing countries with growing trade links to China. The Economist recently estimated that if China continues to develop, and if parts of the developing world respond to its competitive challenge by adopting liberal commercial policies, the developed world could enjoy an additional 1% of growth a year, while the developing world would undergo a substantially larger rate of growth despite the dislocation which some economies would obviously undergo. (The Economist, October 2, 2004) The capacity of a single non-oil exporting developing country to have such a broad global economic impact represents an undeniable revolution in international financial and trading systems. As suggested above, it is an economic shift laden with political, diplomatic and strategic significance. Yet, in order to capture the potential gains, Western governments must ensure their economies are ever more agile and flexible. They should increase their respective capacities to shift both capital and labour into those sectors in which they are most competitive and out of those in which they are least productive.

The McKinsey Global Institute recently examined the fate of western workers who lost jobs because of firms moving production facilities to China or India. According to this study, 70% of such American workers find new work within six months, while in Germany only 40% do. This suggests that labour market rigidities can gravely complicate efforts to adapt to changing international market conditions.

China is also having a strong effect on global demand. While many casual observers see its most substantial economic impact largely in terms of its enormous exports, China is also a large and growing capital and consumer goods market. It is estimated that if current growth and income distribution were sustained until 2020, China would offer the world 100 million consumers with an average income equivalent to the current income average of Western Europe. (The Economist, October 2, 2004.) Already it has almost single-handedly revived the previously flagging economies of East Asia through high demand for a range of manufacturing inputs, high technology components and consumer goods. Australia - like a range of other commodity exporters - is enjoying a veritable economic boom thanks to burgeoning Chinese demand.

China's imports are growing at a very rapid rate - 40% in 2003 alone. Since 2001, it has accounted for one third of the increase in global import volume. China is the world's third largest importer, and in 2004 accounted for 17% of Japan's exports, 16% of the European Union's, 8.5% of the United States', 38.5% of the rest of Asia's, and 20% for the rest of the World. (Rossi) It is now Japan's leading trade partner and the second largest trade partner of the European Union behind only the United States. EU-China Trade doubled between 1999 and 2003. (Eurostat, 14/6/2004, Kihara and Takeuchi) China is also providing an important market for developing countries; 45% of China's $400 billion in annual imports comes from developing countries, and these rose by $55 billion in 2003. It is, in fact, running a significant trade deficit with the developing world. (Kharas) Some optimistic forecasts suggest that if China continues down the reform path it could be the world's largest exporter and importer within ten years.

The US trade with China deficit has reached the enormous sum of $162 billion. (Teather) Yet, imports from China do not explain the explosive growth of the US current account deficit, now at 7% of GDP and rising, partly because China has, in fact, simply replaced other suppliers to the US market. In 1988, for example, only 2% of US shoe imports came from China, while 60% came from Taiwan and South Korea.

Today China has 70% of the US shoe import market, having all but displaced South Korea and Taiwan from the US market, although the Koreans and Taiwanese effectively own many of the Chinese plants selling to the United States. Many of Taiwan's electronics companies have also relocated to the Chinese mainland and are playing a pivotal role in China's electronics exports to the United States. By the end of 2003, China's deficit with Taiwan stood at $31.5 billion; $13.1 billion with South Korea; $7.6 billion with ASEAN; $5 billion with Japan; and $1.3 billion with Australia. (Hale and Hale) A similar trend can be traced in other goods markets including personal computers. While Asian countries are losing market share in the United States to China, they are being compensated by a massive increase in exports to China in higher end and more valuable products.

The Chinese economy is far more open than the Korean or Japanese economies were at similar points in their economic take-off, and the state seems to have rejected the more dirigiste model of development employed by the Japanese. China's general tariff rates have fallen precipitously from 40% in the early 1990s to 10.4% in 2004. (Beattie) It entered the WTO under highly stringent conditions that have helped to open its market even further. In 2004, exports and imports together accounted for nearly 75% of China's total GDP. This is an extraordinarily high share for such a large country, and more than double that of the United States. Part of the reason is that China's domestic non-tradable economy remains very underdeveloped.

China has also implemented exceedingly open investment rules, although foreign investors still complain about serious administrative burdens and creeping non-tariff barriers in areas like financial services and investment rules. Still, foreign investment in China accounts for some 35% of its GDP. (The Economist, October 2, 2004) It is now the world's fifth largest recipient of foreign direct investment (FDI) and is moving quickly up the list. FDI in the first ten months of 2004 reached $54 billion. These funds are fundamentally transforming China's manufacturing and transport infrastructure.

THE TEXTILE BATTLES: A CASE STUDY

In January 2005, the Multi Fibre Arrangement (MFA) expired. That agreement had limited the export of textiles to the developed world for thirty years. It has long been known that once that quota system was dismantled, there would be a sudden shift in global textile production and trade patterns. This has indeed occurred, and China's entry into this newly open market has had an immediate and indeed revolutionary impact. The WTO estimates that China is poised to seize half of the world's market or twice its current share of the textiles market. (Beattie and Harney) Soon after that dramatic market opening, Chinese leaders attempted to calm its increasingly distraught trade partners by unilaterally imposing an export tax on its clothing producers. But this failed to quell the brewing political storm precipitated by China's clothing export surge. Since January 1, Chinese textile imports to the United States jumped by a remarkable 54%. US clothing manufacturers now claim that this influx has resulted in the closure of 19 textile plants with the loss of 26,000 jobs. (Daily Mail, September 2, 2005)

The impact of this market opening has been equally stark in the European Union. China is exporting more clothing there than ever before - about $8bn worth (•6.5bn) in the first half of 2005, almost the same amount as in the whole of 2004. The fall-out in southern Europe, which is directly competing against the Chinese, has been significant. There has been a 30% decline in T-shirt production in Portugal and a 12% fall in Greece since January. Not surprisingly, these countries along with Spain, Italy and France were most vocal in calling for the imposition of textile quotas in Europe. Washington confronted similar domestic pressures from textile industrialists and trade unions. Not surprisingly given the political correlation of forces, both America and Europe reimposed quotas soon after they had been lifted. Quotas, it should be pointed out, are highly damaging to free trade; the economic costs they inflict are often more damaging than straight tariff systems because of the administrative burdens and dead weight losses associated with allotting and managing quota rights.

After a gruelling set of negotiations, the European Union signed a voluntary agreement with China on 11 June 2005, which temporarily reintroduced quotas on a range of textile products. These quantitative restrictions aimed to limit import growth in selected textile categories to between 8% and 12.5% per year until 2008. Yet within a month, Chinese exports had already exceeded the new quotas in most of these categories. European customs officials were blocking further imports and had impounded an estimated 80 million garments at EU ports. European retailers supported by several European governments were outraged and argued that the newly minted deal would make it impossible to fill orders for the rest of the year.

This battle over Chinese textiles has not only pitted manufacturers against retailers and consumers, it has also divided EU governments. Countries with sizeable domestic textile industries, such as Greece, Italy, Spain and France, have pressed hard for further restrictions, while those governments more willing to embrace open trading systems including Denmark, Sweden, the United Kingdom, Germany and the Netherlands - have all spoken out against the quotas. Ministers from the Netherlands, Denmark, Sweden and Finland recently penned an editorial in the Financial Times urging Brussels to re-examine Chinese export quotas that had been introduced "without proper regard for the realities of modern commerce". They suggested that the curbs not apply to goods imported under contracts concluded before the quotas were announced in June. (Karien van Gennip et.al.)

On the other side, Spain's Trade and Industry Minister accused retailers of acting in bad faith by rushing to place orders in the weeks before the new quotas became fully operational. "This crisis has been created by importers who clearly and simply wanted to break the textile agreement," he said. (Parker)

On August 30, EU Trade Commissioner Peter Mandelson shifted gears and warned that failure to loosen the quotas could upset trade relations with Beijing and cause more economic hardship in Europe. "The consequences of not doing so will be severe economic pain for many small retailers and businesses in the member states", he said. The Commissioner warned that consumers will pay higher prices and face clothing shortages unless EU governments release more than 80 million Chinese garments blocked from entering Europe. After another set of difficult negotiations running up to the EU-China Summit, an eleventh hour agreement was struck on September 5. The Commission has agreed to wave through customs half of the impounded garments, while the other half would be deducted from the 2006 quota or attributed to quotas in other categories. At this writing, member governments have not approved the agreement, and the European parliament has already charged that clothing quotas should be extended where necessary because of a playing field allegedly slanted by an "artificially undervalued Chinese currency".

This dispute and the heated rhetoric surrounding it has overshadowed the EU-China summit this September, and in some respects undermined aspirations to forge a strategic partnership between Europe and China. At that Summit, British Prime Minister Tony Blair, who holds the rotating EU presidency, argued that Europe should see China's rapid growth as an opportunity and not a threat. He counselled that while there is a case for managing change, "What there is not a case for is resisting change." Mr. Blair's problem is that several important EU member states seem not to accept this logic.

The United States has imposed its own curbs on Chinese imports by invoking a "safeguard" procedure agreed when China entered the WTO in 2001. Under the safeguard procedure, the United States has asserted its right to impose restrictions on those textile imports allegedly disrupting domestic markets; it can maintain these restrictions until the end of 2008. Its quotas on seven large categories of Chinese clothing imports allow for 7.5% annual growth rate of textile imports. As was the case in Europe, American textile importers have urged the US administration to ease the quotas and allow larger annual increases of Chinese imports, and US retailers want no short-term measures that might trigger shortages. (Alden)

The Administration, however, appears to be leaning towards restraining imports in more than 35 textile categories to levels of roughly 7.5% of annual growth (the level allowed under US safeguard mechanisms) if no deal is reached. This position is supported by American textile producers who want a broad deal that would set restrictive quotas on most large categories of imports until the end of 2008. At this writing, the United States has not struck a deal with China and the US government has also reintroduced quotas on imports of two more categories of Chinese textiles. (McGregor, August 31, 2005)

MONETARY IMPLICATIONS

China's mounting economic weight is also apparent in its ever-greater impact on global money markets. In recent year's China's policy of pegging the Renminbi to the dollar helped ensure stable prices for Chinese exporters selling in the United States and in other markets tied to the US dollar, particularly those in Asia. But it had also provoked controversy in the United States and in Europe. By July 2005, the Chinese had accumulated over $711 billion in foreign exchange reserves - a hoard that was growing by $24 million a day. In the process, the People's Bank of China, like other Asian central banks, was acquiring a significant share of US government securities and particularly US Treasury bills to underwrite a weakening dollar. Asian countries as a whole financed over half of the US budget and current account deficits in 2003 through such operations. Yet American leaders have grown increasingly pointed in their complaints that China's exchange rate policy was undermining American exporters and making it difficult to precipitate a full correction in the balance of payments. The operating assumption was that Renminbi appreciation would spark a precipitous increase in US exports to China. It would also allegedly engender a corresponding decline in US imports as the dollar fell. Meanwhile, Europe claimed that the Renminbi-dollar link was placing the burden of adjustment to a falling dollar squarely on its shoulders. The European Union, like the United States, was calling on the Chinese to allow its currency to appreciate in order to correct these disequilibria.

China recently decided to abandon the hard dollar peg for several reasons. First of all, it was stoking global protectionism, which is in neither China's nor its trading partners' interest. As suggested above, American political leaders and manufacturers in exposed sectors had suggested that the peg was increasingly conferring an unfair competitive advantage upon Chinese goods sold on US markets. By June, a bill tabled by Senator Charles Schumer threatened to slap a 27.5% duty on Chinese goods if it failed to revalue the currency by October. Chinese leaders did not want to respond directly to such threats, but clearly the political climate in Washington conditioned their thinking.

Secondly, the dollar peg was leading China to import easy monetary conditions from the United States. This, in turn, has helped trigger asset bubbles in real estate and other markets and generated inflationary pressures. (Crawford and Young) An exchange rate correction was seen as one way to inject greater macro-economic stability into an economy that may well be growing too fast for its own good.

Finally, Chinese authorities hope to put growth on a more sustainable basis by developing their domestic economy relative to their overly expanded export sector. An appreciation of the currency was seen as one tool for achieving this change.

For all of these reasons, on July 21, China revalued the Renminbi by 2.1% against the dollar and announced its decision to end the hard peg. Henceforward, China will peg to a basket of currencies including the dollar and float within a 0.3 percent range from its new value of 8.11 Renminbi to the dollar. According to Zhou Xiaochuan, Governor of the People's Bank of China, the move to a very restricted managed floating exchange is only the first step. China claims it will eventually embrace a free floating regime. The institutional capacities of the state and the economy today do not appear to be sufficiently robust to manage a free-floating system. Time is needed to build up these capacities. Outstanding non-serviceable bank loans, an absence of exchange rate hedging mechanisms and other systemic weaknesses would leave the economy vulnerable in free floating exchange systems. The Chinese have furnished no timetable for widening the fluctuation band.

The Americans have responded positively to the Chinese decision. US treasury Secretary John Snow said China was "on the right path", and described the move as "extremely positive" while Senator Schumer described it as a "good first step, albeit a baby step". American industrialists have also generally welcomed the decision.

But Renminbi revaluation alone will not be the panacea for American trade deficits. Most monetary economists are very quick to point out that those deficits are largely a function of dissavings - i.e. public deficits and low national savings. In order to bring trade flows into balance over the long run, revaluation needs to be accompanied by higher savings or "expenditure reduction" - as well as so called "expenditure switching" from imported to domestically produced goods. Managing this without triggering a recession is perhaps the greatest economic challenge the United States currently faces. (Bergsten) China's central bankers, in turn, recognise that they will need to lower their savings rate (currently at 45%) and encourage increased household expenditure through more expansive demand management policies. This will help them lower their economy's overwhelming reliance on export markets. Joseph Stiglitz, a Nobel Prize winning American economist argues that, "Unless domestic investment goes down or domestic savings go up, the trade deficit will persist unabated". (Stiglitz) The US trade deficit of $700 billion is nine times the size of China's trade surplus; eliminating the trade surplus with China will therefore not solve a broader problem arising from fundamental macro-economic conditions.

Another reason why a dramatic change is unlikely in the near term is that Chinese exports to the United States derive a high share (70-80%) of value added from imported inputs. A revaluation could, theoretically, even lower the costs of Chinese exports because of falling input prices. (Stiglitz) Secondly, other low-cost producers from developing countries stand prepared to jump into US and European markets, meaning that the overall trade deficit will not be substantially affected other things being equal.

Over the last year, the euro appreciated significantly vis-à-vis both the dollar and the Renminbi. It was thus absorbing a very high share of the burden of adjustment to the dollar depreciation. There have been concerns in European circles that the Americans were gaining market share in Asia as a result of the euros appreciation while relative exchange rates between Asia and the United States had not significantly shifted. For this reason, many European voices were also calling for Renminbi appreciation. At the same time though, European firms were building plants in China both to exploit cost advantages and to insulate themselves from exchange rate movements

The European Commission has also welcomed the Renminbi's revaluation as "a move in the right direction". Peter Mandelson, the EU trade commissioner, said he did not foresee any 'significant' impact on trade between the European Union and China, adding that the revaluation represented a "further step in China assuming greater international responsibility". Jean-Claude Trichet, the head of the European Central Bank (ECB), has argued that the narrow band or "dirty" floating arrangement for the Renminbi would improve the stability of the global financial system and help spread the burden of the dollar's recent fall.

It is not clear, however, whether it will significantly bolster the competitiveness of European products vis-à-vis Chinese products. Indeed, "the effect will be marginal given the vast difference in labour cost and the small initial change in value". Furthermore, "the use of the "basket" might eventually result in a resumption by the People's Bank of China of the purchase of euros so that the balance of its foreign exchange reserves matches the composition of the "basket". "This would obviously tend to push up the value of the euro and thereby reduce the competitive position of euro zone exports". (Herenstein)

WEAKNESSES IN THE CHINESE MODEL

Although the general tenor of all economic forecasts for China is extraordinarily positive, there are a number of weak points. China's long-term political uncertainty remains the most serious concern. Contemporary China is no longer guided by a Marxist ideology, and its authoritarian political class has recognized that economic liberty is the best means of securing prosperity for its people and by extension the Communist party's control of the State. China's citizens consequently enjoy some latitude for autonomous activity, particularly in economic relations, while many of the old Communist strictures have been left to die quietly on the vine. That said, an apparently insecure Communist Party still haunted by the Tiananmen Square massacre, sternly controls national and regional political life. President

Hu Jintao seems increasingly focused on asserting party discipline and cracking down on independent voices in the media and civil society. Political rights are highly restricted, and there are signs of some back pedalling in areas like media openness. (The Economist, August 20 2005) The stasis of Communist Party political hegemony thus stands in marked contrast to the sheer dynamism of China's economy and the vitality of its ever more complex civil society.

On the face of it, the current status quo seems unsustainable, particularly as one party government is associated with all manner of economic inefficiencies including corruption which is a particularly compelling problem in the provinces. Building a prosperous and ultimately more service-oriented economy will invariably require the state to abandon the strict controls it still exercises over information and decision-making and require far greater public accountability. Of course, the ruling party has already ceded much of the economic sphere to private actors. The private sector is playing a more significant role in the management of crucial infrastructure and even health care and education. Yet, uncertainty will remain as long as the government pays insufficient regard to human rights and fails to give a greater political voice to its citizens and an even greater role in social mediation to civil society institutions. In economic terms, insufficient political reform will place limits on Chinese growth and development - something that seems difficult to imagine given the rapid pace of Chinese growth today.

Political reform may become all the more important when one considers the growing wealth gap that China's development has triggered. Unemployment in the cities is estimated at 8% and is far higher in the countryside. The decline of state-owned heavy industries has increased joblessness in recent years. Trying economic conditions in the provinces have bred resentment and fomented spontaneous riots in various regions of the country. Protests against local government officials have arisen as a result of property seizures, corruption, environmental neglect and the low capacity of the state to mediate such disputes in a just fashion and even to engage in basic dialogue. One concern is that the state will resort to repression rather than reform to cope with mounting social pressures. In general terms, Communist authorities do not seem willing to consider these as structural political problems that have much to do with their own party's utter hegemony over national and local political life. In the countryside riot is frequently the only effective means of expressing political grievance. The choice now seems to lie between dialogue and repression. The problem is that many authorities conceptualise dialogue as a breech in the wall of party power and see repression as the safer alternative. But that course will never resolve the underlying problems.

China is also beset by widening regional inequalities that are fostering rural/urban, coastline/interior and East/West divisions. Foreign investors, who place an estimated 86% of their capital in the east, 9.6% in the Centre and only 4.6% in the West, reinforce these divisions. (Hale and Hale) This disparity will continue to stoke mass migration to already crowded and environmentally stressed eastern urban centres and will likely foment new political tensions. In recent years, China's urban areas have absorbed 114 million rural workers with another 300 million expected over the next thirty years. (Pei) This will place unbelievable stress on urban infrastructure, the environment and social institutions.

The Chinese state is seeking to extend the country's development out to these economically stagnant regions. Many rural taxes are to be abolished while the central budget is increasingly covering important local expenses in poor regions, for example, by paying for schoolbooks. Obviously creating economic equality with the Eastern cities is beyond the state's capacity, but officials maintain that the goal is to create equality of opportunity with a particular focus on equality of educational opportunity. (Meeting with Li Jiange) There are currently wide disparities in access to education, health care and social services. Local and regional governments play a key role in providing many of these services; yet, China's inefficient tax system is not highly effective at redistributing income. The government, however, is now working to improve tax collection methods. It recently introduced a system whereby every retail receipt is also a lottery ticket - a means to encourage clients to ask for a receipt and thereby bring the grey economy into the official economy. The People's Bank of China is also dedicating about 70% of its resources to the Western provinces to foster development in the region, and every government Ministry must also dedicate resources and expertise to respond to development challenges in the more impoverished parts of the country. (Meeting at the People's Bank of China)

China's still large state sector also poses problems. The recent collapse of China Aviation Oil Corporation Ltd. due to ill-advised positions taken in derivative markets has raised questions about governance of state owned firms. These firms were once seen as safe one-way bets for foreign investors and Chinese banks because of state backing. It is now evident that substantial risks were involved.

China's banks hold loans to a range of public and private firms with highly questionable balance sheets, and many loans simply cannot be serviced. Meanwhile, smaller private sector firms confront capital shortages because funding tends to go to politically connected large public and private companies. China has made important progress in improving the banking situation, but has further to go. It is tapping into western know-how to gain insights on best practices, proper audit regulation and skills development. The key question today is whether these banks are sufficiently robust to survive a generalized economic slow-down.

The blistering pace of investment driven growth in China is challenging those responsible for macro-economic policy in China to prevent the economy from overheating. This has been no easy task, and this past year China's Central Bank raised interest rates to prevent the boom from turning to bust. Investment growth is proving difficult to control in this huge and effectively decentralised country. There are, for example, countless u,, nderground investment networks that simply evade regulation. China's central bank has so far done an admirable job in difficult circumstances. Bank officials acknowledge that many of China's outstanding investments are not highly efficient, and this is partly a function of the state's still powerful role in the economy. They recognize that privatisation should render capital allocation more efficient.

Resource pricing poses a related problem. State controlled prices for scarce resources like water and energy have exacerbated shortages and discovered environmentally friendly policies. Yet, moving to market pricing will be politically difficult and the state has acted with caution on this front. (Meeting at the People's Bank of China)

Even China's economic growth is posing problems. China's manufacturing capacity has expanded so precipitously that returns on investment there have been falling. Already in 2003 China's automobile plants could produce 2.8 million cars; yet only 1.8 million were sold. (Hale and Hale) This situation would again become highly problematic were the Chinese or the world economy to slow down. (Hale and Hale) A crisis in any of China's over-invested sectors - steel, cars, property - would have ripple effects across the economy, weakening its already vulnerable banking sector, and likely precipitating a serious credit contraction. This is a scenario that concerns Chinese officials who have been anxious to slow growth. But their capacity to do so is suspect, in part, because regional governments are often pushing in the opposite direction.

Intellectual property rights raise another serious concern and international pressure is mounting on China and several other Asian states to fight piracy. It is estimated, for example, that 92% of software units sold in China are illegal copies. (Baucus) Some progress has been made on this front, and government law now largely reflects western standards.

The problem today lies in legal implementation, particularly at the local and regional levels. It will persist until the Chinese no longer see piracy as being in their own interest. Some would argue that during China's initial economic take-off, piracy was something of a development catalyst. It is increasingly seen as a liability, particularly as China is expected to develop ever more intellectual property of its own and will want to protect it both domestically and internationally.

China's economy is also distorted by the many incentives local and national governments extend to foreign investors. Chinese officials are taking steps to correct this problem as well and want local governments to curtail the subsidies accorded to foreign investors. The central government has promised eventually to harmonize tax rates on foreign corporations with those paid by local producers, but there is not yet a timetable for doing so. (McGregor)

Like a number of Western countries, China also confronts a demographic crisis. Its one child policy was perhaps too successful in stemming rapid population increases. Now it must develop financial instruments to brace the country for the demographic shock of sustaining a quarter of the population over 65 by 2030. Western investors are already helping to lay the groundwork for this financial architecture through a range of joint ventures with Chinese counterparts. Continued growth will generate the finances needed to underwrite any sustainable pension schemes.

CHINA - THE ENVIRONMENT AND OIL MARKETS

China confronts a range of environmental problems. These include the absence of legal transparency, environmental problems exacerbated by a lack of environmental protections and resources, a systematic failure to engage in proper environmental costing and regional authorities' resistance to implementing new environmental laws. China is increasingly a consumer society but it lacks the infrastructure to manage industrial and consumer waste. This is a ticking environmental time bomb.

China is the world's second largest producer of CO2 gases, and while it has signed the Kyoto Protocol, its obligations are minimal and it has until 2012 to comply with Kyoto's strictures. (Sub-Committee visit to London, March 2005) The Chinese hope that large domestic coal reserves, nuclear power, imported oil and gas and the eventual deployment of additional renewable energy sources including hydro-electric power will help the country meet its exploding energy needs. (Meeting with Zhang Yesui) But there will be environmental costs involved. As Chinese wealth grows, consumers will invariably demand more cars. Last year, car sales in China rose by an astounding 50% at a time when many cities in China are suffering from energy shortages. To take one example of the dilemma China is facing, factories were temporarily closed near Beijing recently because there was not sufficient power to run both hotel air conditioning and factories. (Sub-Committee Visit to London) How China manages the energy burdens associated with rapidly rising consumption will have a range of global implications both for the environment and for global energy supplies.

China is no longer a "price taker" in global commodities markets; its growing demand for a range of critical commodities is having an ever-larger effect on global demand and supply conditions as well as on prices. This has been a boon to commodity producers, particularly in the developing world, and it has been the driving force in ever-tighter global oil markets.

Today, China is the world's second largest consumer of oil after the United States. It alone has generated nearly two fifths of the growth in global oil consumption since 2000. Its demand increased by 15% in 2003 alone.

World energy prices have soared over the last year for a range of reasons including uncertainty in the Middle East, Venezuela and Nigeria and refinery capacity problems; yet, China's burgeoning demand poses the central dilemma. The International Energy Agency projects that China's net oil imports will rise from 1.7 million barrels of oil a day in 2001 to 9.8 million by 2030. It will have to boost its export levels to ever-higher levels to generate the foreign exchange it needs to cover the cost of a commodity that will grow dearer as a result of its own demand. It is not surprising that the US Energy Department has revised its long-term forecast of oil prices to $50/barrel largely because of China's huge and expanding appetite for energy. In the current climate of very high prices and the energy price shock arising from Hurricane Katrina, that figure seems very low.

China is also an important energy producer, and is still able to meet 75% of its energy needs through domestic production of oil, gas, coal, nuclear and hydroelectric power. (European Policy Centre Conference, remarks by Ambassador Ma Zhengang). But its oil fields are now declining, and it will have to tap further into world markets to make up the difference. China, like other developing countries, needs more energy to produce a unit of output than developed countries and so further oil price hikes could pose a genuine threat to its growth prospects unless its own energy efficiency improves. So far, relatively lax monetary conditions and asset bubbles in the US and China have prevented high energy prices from slowing growth; that may be about to change. (The Economist, August 27, 2005)

China's energy needs are also conditioning its long-term geo-political and military strategies. Because China lacks a blue sea navy capable of projecting power beyond its coastline, it depends on the United States to defend the sea lines of communication that ensure the safe passage of petroleum. While the Chinese do not see this as an immediate problem, it is nonetheless recognized as a long-term strategic vulnerability and one that is certainly inspiring its own naval build-up. (Mederios and Fravel) For its part, the United States seems prepared to use its own influence and power to check a rising power like China in order preserve its predominant global position and its own considerable influence in Asia. (Mearsheimer) In those terms, the possibility for future frictions seems inevitable.

China has also embarked upon a global energy investment spree, and some analysts suggest it is paying too dearly for these assets. China's long-term interest in gaining access to oil and gas supplies to drive its economy lies behind these purchases. China has now become a "Premier Division" player in the Central Asian "great game". It is exploiting America's deteriorating relationship with the Venezuelan leader Hugo Chavez to sign several deals with Latin America's largest energy producer, and is very active in African energy development. American officials have criticized China for its activity in several of these repressive countries, but of course, China's foray into democratic America's energy sector was blocked in Washington. ("Beijing's Great Game: Don't expect China to be ethical on oil - until the US is," Financial Times, August 24 2005) Indeed, strong pressure from the United States Congress dissuaded the Chinese firm CNOOC from purchasing the American energy concern Unocal after it made an offer for $18.5 billion. (Peltz) Like most Western countries, China recognizes that global oil endowments are a function of geography and not political virtue, and they will act accordingly. This is one of the reasons why they have been very hesitant to criticize Iran and other more nefarious oil producers in the United Nations Security Council while even extolling the "virtues" of regimes in Uzbekistan and Zimbabwe. Analysts also suggest that China's lack of co-operation in the UN Security Council on the Darfur question is strongly conditioned by the oil deals it has struck with the Sudanese government. Its close relations with Iran are also driven by its energy strategy.

THE GEOPOLITICS OF CHINA'S EMERGENCE AND ITS TRANSATLANTIC IMPLICATIONS

China's economic emergence is laden with geo-strategic implications, many of which cannot but recast crucial elements of the transatlantic relationship. It is not yet a truly global power, certainly not in the way the United States is. China is, however, a major power in East Asia and its reach is extending. It is, of course, a nuclear state possessing inter-continental missiles; it has a very large military establishment in possession of ever more sophisticated weaponry, it is a permanent member of the UN Security Council; and its global economic weight is increasing by leaps and bounds. One would therefore be utterly remiss to look at China simply in static terms. It is an ascendant if somewhat contradictory world power, and its growing presence on the global stage is altering the strategic and economic map. At the same time though, China has dramatically abandoned the revolutionary ideology which once inspired its foreign policy.

It is increasingly understood as a status quo power, with a deepening interest in sustaining a global and regional economically liberal order that its leaders now embrace as the key to national prosperity, internal stability and continued party hegemony. It has also altered its foreign policy at least tactically. Where China once considered the developing world as its greatest foreign policy priority, now its relations with the United States, Japan and Europe receive pride of place, followed by its regional neighbours, and then by the developing world. (European Policy Centre Conference, Remarks by Xinning Song) China's recent accession to the WTO and its clearly expressed goals within that body reinforce the view that it has become more of a status quo power dedicated to the preservation of an open trading order. This approach has eased China's relations with developed countries, most of which enjoy improved and fruitful economic relations with China. Yet tensions persist over issues like human rights, China's military ambition, Taiwan, Burma and arms sales. Although Taiwan is certainly the region's most likely strategic flash point, there are other dangerous regional security challenges including North Korea's attempts to manufacture nuclear weapons and China's alarmingly poor relations with Japan. Accommodating an ever more powerful and wealthy China was invariably going to pose challenges to the world's other great powers. (Schwarz)

Since 2003, China has hosted four rounds of the six-party talks among Japan, North Korea, Russia, South Korea, and the United States. It considers itself to be a mediator between North Korea and the United States in negotiations over the burgeoning North Korean nuclear programme. China crafted the framework for the negotiations. The United States has commended China for its broad efforts to facilitate the six-party talks, but has criticized China for not using all its influence to convince North Korea to commit to Complete, Verifiable, Irreversible, Dismantlement (CVID). China provides North Korea with approximately 40% of its food and 90% of its oil and is North Korea's sole formal military ally. Prior to the recent agreement, some US officials and experts had speculated that China prefers to keep this nuclear issue unresolved because it counterbalances US policy in the Taiwan straits. China has a strong interest in preserving stability in North Korea, which it views as a buffer state, and it resisted threatened use of sanctions or force to resolve the North Korean problem. The United States has now applauded China's role as mediator in the six-party talks, which appear to have resulted in an arrangement that will end North Korea's nuclear programme.

The level of hostility between Japan and China has risen in recent months, in part because Japanese Prime Minister Junichiro Koizumi has paid several visits to the Yasukuni shrine where war criminals, who were responsible for terrible atrocities in China during the Second World War, are buried. Japanese owned businesses in Shanghai were attacked earlier this year after the introduction of a history textbook in some Japanese schools that glossed over Japanese atrocities during World War II. Mr Koizumi, however, recently apologized for the wartime invasion and declined to visit the shrine this year. (People's

Daily Online, August 15, 2005) The creation of a bilateral panel of historians to review the legacy of the occupation could also help ease tensions. But difficulties in the relationship persist. Japanese recent endorsement of the American view that China's Taiwan policy represents the greatest threat to regional stability at a recent "two plus two" bilateral security meeting raised alarm bells in Beijing. (Briefing by Lanxin Xiang) Tension is also arising out of the fact that Chinese economic power is threatening to eclipse that of Japan. Managing this shifting relationship is proving difficult. Finding ways to accommodate the new China while delineating what cannot be given up in the process poses a genuine intellectual and political challenge for the entire western community. (Brzezinski)

Perhaps the most apparent manifestation of how China's evolution might alter US-European relations has been the recent transatlantic tension over a European push to lift its long-standing arms embargo imposed after the military crackdown on demonstrators in Tiananmen Square. In December 2004 EU leaders announced their intention to replace that embargo with an export code of conduct. This would include provisions on arms brokering and technology transfers and supposedly would trigger no increase in quantity or quality of weapons sold to China. But it would also be non-binding, and as such might not constrain members eager to sell more sophisticated systems to the Chinese. (Financial Times, January 22, 2005.) Over the past year, American officials communicated to their European counterparts that lifting the embargo would seriously complicate transatlantic defence trade and cooperation. American leaders strongly oppose any move by Europe that might help tip the delicate balance in the Taiwan Straits. European advocates of lifting the embargo maintain that they have no intention of doing so; but this has hardly quelled US concerns.

American officials and many in Europe strongly oppose lifting the embargo for a range of strategic and political reasons including the fragile military balance in East Asia, the possibility that Western weapons might be used by China in a possible confrontation with China, and the fact that China's political system remains fundamentally undemocratic and unaccountable. Washington is committed to helping Taiwan defend itself in the event of a Chinese invasion; but it is engaged in a delicate balancing game. The Americans have helped arm Taiwan to the point where its self-defence capability is credible, but not sufficiently to tempt it to declare full independence. US officials welcome dialogue and negotiation as the best means of preventing a military conflict. The Americans do not generally share the view of those in Taipei who would abandon the single China ideal, although they are committed to deterring a Chinese military intervention.

American policy should be understood in terms of a classic balance of power politics. Historically great powers have never welcomed the rise of new powers and often work to impede that rise. (Mearsheimer) Several Chinese analysts, including Lanxing Xiang, have suggested, however, that there are risks involved in pursuing this course as well. Xiang uses an historical analogy to point out that Britain's tough policies toward an authoritarian Wilhelmine Germany helped make conflict between the two powers a preordained conclusion. Xiang worries that a policy of aggressive containment toward China might have the same effect, contributing to a climate of suspicion and tension and adding to the risk of miscalculation. (Lanxin Xiang, "Survival", Autumn 2001.)

American officials are somewhat divided on all of this. Those focused on commercial matters have a different view than those responsible for managing strategic-military issues. The US navy, for example, foresees a future Chinese "blue water" naval challenge (Kaplan) although the Chinese currently express an ambition to develop naval assets that would only advance their navy from a posture of coastal defence to a posture that would allow its fleet to exercise some suasion power in the China Sea. At this point, the building of a genuine "blue water" navy is beyond the means of the Chinese, who recognize that they are prepared neither to match American naval power nor to challenge America's overall geopolitical superiority. (Jisi) The US navy will therefore exercise ultimate control of the sea-lanes that are vital to Chinese commercial and energy needs for some time to come. (Mallet, Financial Times) China's growing energy concerns certainly inform its evolving strategic orientation, but so too does its focus on the Taiwan question. The recent Chinese-Russian military exercises included an amphibious assault of the kind that could one day be used in Taiwan. That exercise was coupled with a joint Russian-Chinese demand that the United States abandon bases in Central Asia - something that certainly raised the level of concern in Washington.

China's National People's Congress recently adopted a law that explicitly states that a Taiwanese declaration of independence could be met with a Chinese military response. Chinese officials who met members of this Committee in Beijing insisted that this law has been misinterpreted in the West and that Americans and Europeans do not seem to understand how central Taiwan is to Chinese identity. The Taiwanese government's flirtation with independence has raised a red flag in China.

According to the Vice-Chairman of the Foreign Affairs Committee of the National People's Congress, Wang Yingfan, and a number of Chinese foreign policy experts, no Chinese leader could ever concede to the establishment of a separate Taiwanese nation; to do so would be seen by the Chinese people as an act of treason. Ambassador Yingfan asserted to this Committee that China "would pay any price" to preserve what it sees as its territorial integrity and admitted that the law does imply the existence of a military option. (Meeting with Wang Yingfan, July 2005) Ambassador Yingfan suggested that the new law expresses China's desire to resolve the Taiwan question in a peaceful manner, while calling for the tightening of already substantial links between the island and the mainland. The law has certainly not been seen in such a benign light either in the United States or in Europe.

Indeed, the newly promulgated law on Taiwan certainly provoked second thoughts in Europe about revoking the arms embargo.

For example, four parliamentary Committees in the British House of Commons - Defence, Foreign Affairs, International Development, and Trade and Industry - expressed strong reservations last spring about lifting the embargo without first clarifying how the European Council will ensure that this does not result in any qualitative or quantitative increase in arms sales to China. The Committees were alarmed by the ongoing human rights problem in China and felt that to lift the embargo would send the wrong political signals to Beijing. They also expressed concern that lifting the embargo could poison armaments cooperation and broader diplomatic relations with the United States. (House of Commons Report.)

Indeed, if not properly managed, trans-Atlantic fall-outs on China policy, like the recent spat over arms sales to China, could collectively weaken the recent efforts of some European and American leaders to deepen trans-Atlantic defence industrial cooperation. It is worth noting that the mood in the US Congress in recent years has not been particularly receptive to open trans-Atlantic defence markets. Secretary of Defence Donald Rumsfeld and other officials have actually fought some of the more restrictive bills coming from Capitol Hill. There is a sense now that were the European Union to end the embargo without stringent controls, the Department of Defence could no longer defend the very notion of a transatlantic defence market in the halls of Congress.

While the United States has long enjoyed a privileged relationship with the Chinese both because of its extensive economic links to that country and because it too is a key power in the Pacific, Europe's relationship with China has expanded rather dramatically. In 2004, Europe passed the United States as China's largest trade partner. (Kynge) Some in Europe now suggest that Europe and China share common views on a range of questions like the central role of the UN Security Council in dealing with international crises and in the desirability of a multi-polar as opposed to a unilateral global order.

The Chinese themselves have picked up on this and have recognized the potential economic and strategic value of developing stronger ties to Europe. There is indeed a certain symmetry in Chinese and EU global ambitions.

They are both powerful regional actors playing important, if not hegemonic, global roles. They see each other as potential partners with a common need to bolster their respective global influence and prosperity. This symmetry is certainly one of the sub-texts in the battle over the arms embargo, and it likely presages the rise of other transatlantic tensions that will involve China.

The European Union defines its relationship with China as a "strategic partnership", a status it accords to its most important partners including the United States, Canada, Russia and India. (European Policy Centre Conference, Remarks by Dirk Sterckx) At the recent EU-China summit, both sides reaffirmed their commitment to building an effective multilateral order.

Not surprisingly, some European and North American Atlanticists see this thinking as a direct challenge to the primacy of the NATO alliance. This is one reason why it may be an opportune moment to develop a nascent NATO-China dialogue.

There have already been informal diplomatic contacts in Brussels; the Chinese have participated in several NATO seminars and were invited to observe a NATO exercise. Several NATO officials have also visited Beijing in recent months. Given China's participation in a number of peacekeeping activities, there is clearly ample room for dialogue. Zhang Yesui, China's Vice Foreign Minister recently told a NATO PA delegation that his government is closely following NATO's transformation and that his country warmly welcomes NATO's role in peacekeeping. He also indicated that NATO's presence in Afghanistan has contributed to regional stability. Yet China and Russia have also called for the closing of American bases in Central Asia, so its position is nuanced if not somewhat contradictory. The public's view of NATO is equally ambiguous; the bombing of the Chinese Embassy by US planes operating in a NATO mission over Belgrade provoked a strong nationalist outcry in China and this event, according to Mr. Yesui, is not entirely forgotten

Notwithstanding the improving European-Chinese relationship, there are also tensions between the two. These include China's policy toward Burma, its relationship with Taiwan and human rights issues in general. Europe's central bankers had expressed displeasure with China's foreign exchange policy of tying the Renminbi to the falling dollar and so welcomed the recent decision to allow the Renminbi to appreciate. At the same time, a range of groups worry that Europe's less traditional manufacturing competitive sectors could be overwhelmed by Chinese imports. In recent months, trade tensions with China have risen with Brussels and Washington alike seeking to limit Chinese imports and investments in sensitive sectors like textiles.

The Chinese see the EU model of regional integration as a way to build a more stable and prosperous East Asia. (Perlez) China is currently not a member of The Association of South Eastern Asian Nations (ASEAN), but it has struck up an important dialogue with that regional body through what has become known as the "ASEAN plus Three" process in which both Japan and South Korea are also engaged.

Recently China and ASEAN agreed to negotiate an ambitious trade liberalization agreement, and China has negotiated bilateral deals with a number of ASEAN countries. Intra-Asian trade is growing explosively, placing six regional players into the ranks of the world's ten fastest growing economies. (Baucus) China's new tactic of extending its influence through trade policy and cooperative multilateralism, rather than by simply brandishing its military muscle, points to its growing international maturity and sophistication. It has learned to extend its influence through win-win and not just confrontational approaches, and this is opening new doors. (Xiang "Survival" Summer 2004) Yet China has hardly forgotten the importance of military power; and it is embarked on a major military modernization effort. Moreover, it is not reluctant to brandish this power when it feels key national security interests are at stake.

CONCLUSIONS

Europe and North America share a range of common aspirations with regard to China. Working together on those common interests and maintaining a constructive dialogue on matters where diverging interests are in play makes eminent sense and will help eliminate "bolt from the blue" surprises. The Secretary General of the OECD, Donald Johnson, recently asked member governments to consider deepening OECD cooperation with China. On the face of it, this seems like sound advice. Finding ways to construct a sustained economic dialogue with China is vital to both North America and Europe and it makes sense for Europe and North America to "sing off the same page" on the most important issues shaping China's relations with the West insofar as this is possible. In other words, the China card should be played jointly.

The Prime Minister of China, Wen Jiabao has clearly set his sights on building an East Asian Free Trade Area which could have elements of exclusivity. Both the European Union and the United States are likely to find the notion of an exclusive East Asian trading club disadvantageous both in economic and strategic terms. The best means to keep Asia open is to ensure that the multilateral trade talks under the auspices of the WTO are deepened.

The Asia Pacific Economic Cooperation (APEC) was initially seen as a way to help keep Asia an open trading region. But this is no longer sufficient. Both Europe and the United States should strive to ensure that global trade talks move forward, precisely to avoid fracturing the global trade system. They need to stress to China that the creation of a new Asian regional bloc will limit rather than advance its own economic development if it is a system that is not equally open to the multilateral trading order.

Of course, America and Europe will, in turn, need to ensure that China enjoys access to their markets even when this poses short-term difficulties. The recent fiasco precipitated by the imposition of ill-conceived quotas on Chinese textile imports in the United States and the European Union only hints at the costs to Western economies of blocking Chinese imports.

Many political leaders have not woken up to the fact that China has become a crucial link in the global economy; it supplies a range of goods that cannot be had elsewhere, or at least at comparable prices. Arbitrarily shutting off its access to global markets therefore is akin to shooting oneself in the foot. Equally, the West needs to be open to China's outward investment. The rapid integration of China into the global economy will help ensure that its rise is pacific and not bellicose. (Financial Times, June 25/26, 2005) An energy dialogue with China is also imperative given its escalating demand at a time when prices are soaring. This will mitigate the risk both of an energy and a security crisis stemming out of disagreements over energy,

The European Union and the United States also need to devise a common arms export policy to China with a shared list of forbidden systems and components. But this can only be done effectively if premised on a broadly shared strategic vision. Obviously this will entail some combination of accommodation and resistance, as is often the case when established powers adjust to the rise of newly ascendant powers. One of those principles should be that the West will not welcome and will indeed oppose any effort to resolve the Taiwan question through force.

Yet it should simultaneously encourage further dialogue and accommodation between Taiwan and the mainland. Accordingly, the European Union should not undertake policies that might weaken the US deterrent to a Chinese invasion of Taiwan - a highly delicate American posture that is based on the presence of a US carrier battle group in and around the Taiwan Straits. Equally, the West does not want to foreordain the rise of an aggressive China by imposing a kind of draconian containment policy that might drive a cornered China to bellicosity. This will involve a highly complex and subtle balancing game and constant dialogue across the board will be essential. China has recently indicated that it will eventually sign the Convention on the Protection of Human Rights. This is an important gesture, but far greater change is needed despite the progress that has been made. The Chinese are now relatively free to avoid politics in a country where once they were forced to live and breathe the dictates of the Politburo. But China's political evolution cannot stop there. Stability in China will not be ensured until a more open and democratic political order is built in which citizens have access to decision making processes. The West needs to encourage this transformation, recognizing both that democratic transitions do not always unfold over night, particularly in societies lacking those traditions, and that the forms these transitions take are never the same.

Western support for democratic reform in China must therefore remain one pillar of its approach to China. Such support can be expressed in myriad forms. Education is perhaps one of the most profound vehicles for doing so. China's new elite is increasingly familiar with Western economic and political life, and many have brought what they have learned to bear on their society.

There are more Chinese currently studying English in China than British subjects living in the United Kingdom! Openness to Chinese participation in Western intellectual life is simply a win-win proposition. Western institutions including NGOs, corporations, banks and the media should broaden efforts to share information and know-how with their Chinese counterparts.

This, in turn, will extend to the Chinese people the rich fruit of democratic societies dedicated to open enquiry. Links to China's 2,236 universities and colleges, which are educating some 17 million students, should also be upgraded. These rapidly improving institutions are increasingly centres for free enquiry and a natural bridge between Western and Chinese thinkers.

The Chinese economy is beset with a range of inefficiencies, particularly in its public sector, and these problems could have global economic consequences. The Chinese need technical assistance in a range of policy areas to cope with these inefficiencies. They also want to advance transparency and a rules based administration. The West has the expertise and increasingly the incentive to help China make progress in these areas, which, at the end of the day, are also fundamental to building a more democratic order. China's new openness thus presents both a daunting challenge and a compelling opportunity. Western governments must be very clear-eyed about the risks while seizing the opportunities to engage China where this makes sense.

As has been suggested above, it would be misguided to see the Chinese challenge in strictly military terms. Its greatest long-term challenges may, in fact, be economic and political. The former challenge is a healthy one and could be a catalyst both for positive economic change in the West and political change in China itself. The West needs to look again at a range of policies that weaken its own long-term competitiveness including rising debt burdens, low savings and investment rates, market rigidities, and education systems which are not preparing young people for a rapidly changing world. Only in this way will it be positioned to derive benefits from China's economic emergence. The biggest error would be to react through protectionist measures.

This would only entrench bad practices and inflict enormous economic costs on Western economies and the global economic system as a whole. Moreover, China's economic development will inevitably foster political change in that society despite the protestations from the regime that the two are unrelated, or even worse, that China's current growth is somehow a vindication of its ideology.

It is rather a vindication of sound economic practices that have nothing to do with Marxism. That paradox will ultimately induce change. The challenge for the West will be to implement policies that encourage a positive evolution while discouraging reaction and turmoil.

7

Financial and Banking System of China

Most of China's financial institutions are state owned and governed. The chief instruments of financial and fiscal control are the People's Bank of China (PBC) and the Ministry of Finance, both under the authority of the State Council. The People's Bank of China replaced the Central Bank of China in 1950 and gradually took over private banks. It fulfills many of the functions of other central and commercial banks. It issues the currency, controls circulation, and plays an important role in disbursing budgetary expenditures. Additionally, it administers the accounts, payments, and receipts of government organizations and other bodies, which enables it to exert thorough supervision over their financial and general performances in consideration to the government's economic plans. The PBC is also responsible for international trade and other overseas transactions. Remittances by overseas Chinese are managed by the Bank of China (BOC), which has a number of branch offices in several countries.

Other financial institutions that are crucial, include the China Development Bank (CDB), which funds economic development and directs foreign investment; the Agricultural Bank of China (ABC), which provides for the agricultural sector; the China Construction Bank (CCB), which is responsible for capitalizing a portion of overall investment and for providing capital funds for certain industrial and construction enterprises; and the Industrial and Commercial Bank of China (ICBC), which conducts ordinary commercial transactions and acts as a savings bank for the public.

China's economic reforms greatly increased the economic role of the banking system. In theory any enterprises or individuals can go to the banks to obtain loans outside the state plan, in practice 75% of state bank loans go to State Owned Enterprises. (SOEs) Even though nearly all investment capital was previously provided on a grant basis according to the state plan, policy has since the start of the reform shifted to a loan basis through the various state-directed financial institutions.

It is estimated that, as of 2011, 14 trillion Yuan in loans were outstanding to local governments. Much of that total is believed by outside observers to be nonperforming. Increasing amounts of funds are made available through the banks for economic and commercial purposes.

Foreign sources of capital have also increased. China has received loans from the World Bank and several United Nations programs, as well as from countries (particularly Japan) and, to a lesser extent, commercial banks. Hong Kong has been a major conduit of this investment, as well as a source itself. On 23 February 2012, the PBC evinced its inclination to liberalise its capital markets when it circulated a telling ten-year timetable. Following on the heels of this development, Shenzhen banks were able to launch cross-border yuan remittances for individuals, a significant shift in the PBC's capital control strictures since Chinese nationals had been previously barred from transferring their yuan to overseas account.

With two stock exchanges (Shanghai Stock Exchange and Shenzhen Stock Exchange), mainland China's stock market had a market value of $4.48 trillion as of November 2014, which makes it the second largest stock market in the world.

In August 2013 creation of an as yet unnamed high-level body to gather and analyze financial information and trends was announced by the central government. The central bank would participate as would people from other organizations engaged in financial matters. It would not have direct regulatory authority, but would attempt to function at the highest professional level in order to provide appropriate guidance to regulators with respect to matters such as shadow banking which are potential sources of instability. An article published in International Review of Economics & Finance in 2010 by Mete Feridun (University of Greenwich Business School) and his colleagues provide empirical evidence that financial development fosters economic growth in China.

Stock markets

As of 2014 and the first quarter of 2015 the financial industry had been providing about 1.5% of China's 7% annual growth rate.

Despite slowing of the economy, as of June 2015 the Chinese stock index, the CSI 300 Index, which is based on 300 stocks traded in the Shanghai and Shenzhen stock exchanges, had risen nearly 150% over the past 12 months. In an effort to forestall damage from collapse of a possible economic bubble fueled by margin trading the central government raised requirements for margin lending. Economic damage from a crash in 2007-2008 was limited due to margin lending being highly restricted. In early July, after a fall in the markets of nearly 30% from their June 12 highs, there were efforts by blue-chip, often state-owned, firms, the Chinese securities industry, and the central government to stabilize the market by buying back stock and increasing purchases of the stock of established firms; however, much of the volatility has been in smaller, less-established firms that had been heavily invested in by unsophisticated, often working class, investors who had purchased stock based solely on its rapid increase in valuation. 80% of Chinese stocks are owned by individual investors, many novices. As of July 10, 2015 efforts by the China Securities Finance Corporation, CFS, a firm created by China's commodities and stock exchanges to finance trades, had apparently stabilized the market. Major Chinese securities firms were required by the China Securities Regulatory Commission to buy, and hold, a substantial amount of securities affected by the downturn. Using funds supplied by the central bank and commercial banks the China Securities Finance Corporation purchased enough stocks to halt the slide acquiring as much as 5% of the stock in some firms. Lines of credit were extended by CFS to 21 securities firms, some of which also purchased up to 5% of some companies stocks. Some of the small cap stocks acquired may be overvalued.

Chinese stocks fell about 10% during the last week of July 2015 with record breaking losses on Monday.

Currency system

The renminbi ("people's currency") is the currency of China, denominated as the yuan, subdivided into 10 jiao or 100 fen. The renminbi is issued by the People's Bank of China, the monetary authority of China. The ISO 4217 abbreviation is CNY, although also commonly abbreviated as "RMB". As of 2005 the yuan was generally considered by outside observers to be undervalued by about 30-40%. However the IMF stated that the yuan is now correctly valued.

The renminbi is held in a floating exchange-rate system managed primarily against the US dollar. On 21 July 2005, China revalued its currency by 2.1% against the US dollar and, since then has moved to an exchange rate system that references a basket of currencies and has allowed the renminbi to fluctuate at a daily rate of up to half a percent.

The rate of exchange (Chinese yuan per US$1) on 31 July 2008, was RMB 6.846, in mid-2007 was RMB 7.45, while in early 2006 was RMB 8.07:US $1=8.2793 yuan (January 2000), 8.2783 (1999), 8.2790 (1998), 8.2898 (1997), 8.3142 (1996), 8.3514 (1995).

There is a complex relationship between China's balance of trade, inflation, measured by the consumer price index and the value of its currency. Despite allowing the value of the yuan to "float", China's central bank has decisive ability to control its value with relationship to other currencies.

Inflation in 2007, reflecting sharply rising prices for meat and fuel, is probably related to the worldwide rise in commodities used as animal feed or as fuel. Thus rapid rises in the value of the yuan permitted in December 2007 are possibly related to efforts to mitigate inflation by permitting the renminbi to be worth more. An article published in International Review of Economics & Finance in 2010 by Mete Feridun (University of Greenwich Business School) and his colleagues provide empirical evidence that financial development fosters economic growth in China.

During the week of August 10, 2015, against the background of a slowing Chinese economy and appreciation of the U.S. dollar, the People's Bank of China devalued the renminbi by about 5%. The devaluation was accomplished by pegging the official rate to closing market rates. A market-based "representative" exchange rate against the U.S. dollar is one of the requirements for designation of a currency as one with Special Drawing Rights (SDR) by the International Monetary Fund (IMF), one of China's goals. Since the late-2000s, China has sought to internationalize the renminbi. As of 2013, the RMB is the 8th most widely traded currency in the world. In November 2015 in advance of G-20 and IMF meetings, IMF director Christine Lagarde announced her support for adding the yuan to the SDR currency basket. The announcement gave 'green-light' to official approval at the November 30 IMF meeting.

TAXATION IN CHINA

Taxes provide the most important revenue source for the Government of the People's Republic of China. As the most important source of fiscal revenue, tax is a key component of macro-economic policy, and greatly affects China's economic and social development. With the changes made since the 1994 tax reform, China has preliminarily set up a streamlined tax system geared to the socialist market economy.

China's tax revenue came to 11.05 trillion yuan (1.8 trillion U.S. dollars) in 2013, up 9.8 percent on 2012. The 2017 the World Bank "Doing Business" rankings estimated that China's total tax rate for corporations was 68% a percentage of profits through direct and indirect tax. As a percentage of GDP, according to the State Administration of Taxation, overall tax revenues were 30% in China.

The government agency in charge of tax policy is the Ministry of Finance. For tax collection, State Administration of Taxation.

As part of US$586 billion economic stimulus package of November 2008, the government planned to reform the VAT, stating the plan could cut corporation taxes by 120 billion yuan.

Types of taxes

Under the current tax system in China, there are 26 types of taxes, which, according to their nature and function, can be divided into the following 8 categories:

- Turnover taxes. This includes three kinds of taxes, namely, Value-Added Tax, Consumption Tax and Business Tax. The levy of these taxes are normally based on the volume of turnover or sales of the taxpayers in the manufacturing, circulation or service sectors.

- Income taxes. This includes Enterprise Income Tax (effective prior to 2008, applicable to such domestic enterprises as state-owned enterprises, collectively owned enterprises, private enterprises, joint operation enterprises and joint equity enterprises) and Individual Income Tax. These taxes are levied on the basis of the profits gained by producers or dealers, or the income earned by individuals. Please note that the new Enterprise Income Tax Law of the People's Republic of China has replaced the above two enterprise taxes as of 1 January 2008.

- Resource taxes. This consists of Resource Tax and Urban and Township Land Use Tax. These taxes are applicable to the exploiters engaged in natural resource exploitation or to the users of urban and township land. These taxes reflect the chargeable use of state-owned natural resources, and aim to adjust the different profits derived by taxpayers who have access to different availability of natural resources.

- Taxes for special purposes. These taxes are City Maintenance and Construction Tax, Farmland Occupation Tax, Fixed Asset Investment Orientation Regulation Tax, Land Appreciation Tax, and Vehicle Acquisition Tax. These taxes are levied on specific items for special regulative purposes.

- Property taxes. This encompasses House Property Tax, Urban Real Estate Tax, and Inheritance Tax (not yet levied).

- Behavioural taxes. This includes Vehicle and Vessel Usage Tax, Vehicle and Vessel Usage License Plate Tax, Stamp Tax, Deed Tax, Securities Exchange Tax (not yet levied), Slaughter Tax and Banquet Tax. These taxes are levied on specified behaviour.

- Agricultural taxes. Taxes belonging to this category are Agriculture Tax (including Agricultural Specialty Tax) and Animal Husbandry Tax which are levied on the enterprises, units and/or individuals receiving income from agriculture and animal husbandry activities.

- Customs duties. Customs duties are imposed on the goods and articles imported into and exported out of the territory of the People's Republic of China, including Excise Tax.

Tax legislation

State organs that have the authority to formulate tax laws or tax policy include the National People's Congress and its Standing Committee, the State Council, the Ministry of Finance, the State Administration of Taxation, the Tariff and Classification Committee of the State Council, and the General Administration of Customs.

Tax laws are enacted by the National People's Congress, e.g., the Individual Income Tax Law of the People's Republic of China; or enacted by the Standing Committee of the National People's Congress, e.g., the Tax Collection and Administration Law of the People's Republic of China.

The administrative regulations and rules concerning taxation are formulated by the State Council, e.g., the Detailed Rules for the

Implementation of the Tax Collection and Administration Law of the People' s Republic of China, the Detailed Regulations for the Implementation of the Individual Income Tax Law of the People's Republic of China, the Provisional Regulations of the People's Republic of China on Value Added Tax.

The departmental rules concerning taxation are formulated by the Ministry of Finance, the State Administration of Taxation, the Tariff and Classification Committee of the State Council, and the General Administration of Customs, e.g., the Detailed Rules for the Implementation of the Provisional Regulations of the People's Republic of China on Value Added Tax, the Provisional Measures for Voluntary Reporting of the Individual Income Tax.

The formulation of tax laws follow four steps: drafting, examination, voting and promulgation. The four steps for the formulation of tax administrative regulations and rules are: planning, drafting, verification and promulgation. The four steps mentioned above take place in accordance with laws, regulations and rules.

Besides, the laws of China stipulates that within the framework of the national tax laws and regulations, some local tax regulations and rules may be formulated by the People's Congress at the provincial level and its Standing Committee, the People's Congress of minority nationality autonomous prefectures and the People's Government at provincial level.

Foreign investment taxation

There are 14 kinds of taxes currently applicable to the enterprises with foreign investment, foreign enterprises and/or foreigners, namely: Value Added Tax, Consumption Tax, Business Tax, Income Tax on Enterprises with Foreign Investment and Foreign Enterprises, Individual Income Tax, Resource Tax, Land Appreciation Tax, Urban Real Estate Tax, Vehicle and Vessel Usage License Plate Tax, Stamp Tax, Deed Tax, Slaughter Tax, Agriculture Tax, and Customs Duties.

Hong Kong, Macau and Taiwan and overseas Chinese and the enterprises with their investment are taxed in reference to the taxation on foreigners, enterprises with foreign investment and/or foreign enterprises. In an effort to encourage inward flow of funds, technology and information, China provides numerous preferential treatments in foreign taxation, and has successively concluded tax treaties with 60 countries (by July 1999): Japan, the USA, France, UK, Belgium, Germany, Malaysia, Norway, Denmark, Singapore, Finland, Canada,

Sweden, New Zealand, Thailand, Italy, the Netherlands, Poland, Australia, Bulgaria, Pakistan, Kuwait, Switzerland, Cyprus, Spain, Romania, Austria, Brazil, Mongolia, Hungary, Malta, the UAE, Luxembourg, South Korea, Russia, Papua New Guinea, India, Mauritius, Croatia, Belarus, Slovenia, Israel, Vietnam, Turkey, Ukraine, Armenia, Jamaica, Iceland, Lithuania, Latvia, Uzbekistan, Bangladesh, Yugoslavia, Sudan, Macedonia, Egypt, Portugal, Estonia, and Laos, 51 of which have been in force.

Urban and Township Land Use Tax

Taxpayers

The taxpayers of Urban and Township Land Use Tax include all enterprises, units, individual household businesses and other individuals (excluding enterprises with foreign investment, foreign enterprises and foreigners).

Tax payable per unit

The tax payable per unit is differentiated with different ranges for different regions, i.e., the annual amount of tax payable per square meter is: 0.5-10 yuan for large cities, 0.4-8 yuan for medium-size cities, 0.3-6 yuan for small cities, or 0.2-4 yuan for mining districts. Upon approval, the tax payable per unit for poor area may be lowered or that for developed area may be raised to some extent.

Computation

The amount of tax payable is computed on the basis of the actual size of the land occupied by the taxpayers and by applying the specified applicable tax payable per unit. The formula is:

Tax payable = Size of land occupied ×Tax payable per unit

Major exemptions

Tax exemptions may be given on land occupied by governmental organs, people's organizations and military units for their own use; land occupied by units for their own use which are financed by the institutional allocation of funds from financial departments of the State; land occupied by religious temples, parks and historic scenic spots for their own use; land for public use occupied by Municipal Administration, squares and green land; land directly utilized for production in the fields of agriculture, forestry, animal husbandry and fishery industries; land used for water reservation and protection; and land occupied for energy and transportation development upon approval of the State.

City Maintenance and Construction Tax

Taxpayers

The enterprises of any nature, units, individual household businesses and other individuals (excluding enterprises with foreign investment, foreign enterprises and foreigners) who are obliged to pay Value Added Tax, consumption Tax and/or Business Tax are the taxpayers of City Maintenance and Construction Tax.

Tax rates and computation of tax payable

Differential rates are adopted: 7% rate for city area, 5% rate for county and township area and 1% rate for other area. The tax is based on the actual amount of VAT, Consumption Tax and/or Business Tax paid by the taxpayers, and paid together with the three taxes mentioned above. The formula for calculating the amount of the tax payable:

Tax payable = Tax base × tax rate Applicable

Fixed Assets Investment Orientation Regulation Tax

Taxpayers

This tax is imposed on enterprises, units, individual household businesses and other individuals who invest into fixed assets within the territory of the People's Republic of China (excluding enterprises with foreign investment, foreign enterprises and foreigners).

Computation of tax payable

This tax is based on the total investment actually put into fixed assets. For renewal and transformation projects, the tax is imposed on the investment of the completed part of the construction project. The formula for calculating the tax payable is:

Tax payable - Amount of investment completed or amount of investment in construction project × Applicable rate

Urban Real Estate Tax

Taxpayers

At present, this tax is only applied to enterprises with foreign investment, foreign enterprises and foreigners, and levied on house property only. Taxpayers are owners, mortgagees custodians and/or users of house property.

Tax base, tax rates and computation of tax payable

Two different rates are applied to two different bases: one rate of 1. 2% is applied to the value of house property, and the other rate of 18% is applied to the rental income from the property. The formula for calculating House Property Tax payable is:

Tax payable = Tax base ×Applicable rate

Major exemptions and reductions

Newly constructed buildings shall be exempt from the tax for three years commencing from the month in which the construction is completed. Renovated buildings for which the renovation expenses exceed one half of the expenses of the new construction of such buildings shall be exempt from the tax for two years commencing from the month in which the renovation is completed. Other house property may be granted tax exemption or reduction for special reasons by the People's Government at provincial level or above.

Vehicle and Vessel Usage License Plate Tax

Taxpayers

At this moment, this tax is only applied to the enterprises with foreign investment, foreign enterprises, and foreigners. The users of the taxable vehicles and vessels are taxpayers of this tax.

Tax amount per unit

The tax amount per unit is different for vehicles and vessels:

a. Tax amount per unit for vehicles: 15-80 yuan per passenger vehicle per quarter; 4-15 yuan per net tonnage per quarter for cargo vehicles; 5-20 yuan per motorcycle per quarter. 0.3-8 yuan per non-motored vehicle per quarter.

b. Tax amount per unit for vessels: 0.3- 1.1 yuan per net tonnage per quarter for motorized vessels; 0.15-0.35 yuan per non-motorized vessel.

Computation

The tax base for vehicles is the quantity or the net tonnage of taxable vehicles The tax base for vessels is the net-tonnage or the deadweight tonnage of the taxable vessels. The formula for computing the tax payable is:

a. Tax payable = Quantity (or net-tonnage) of taxable vehicles × Applicable tax amount per unit b. Tax payable = Net-tonnage (or deadweight tonnage) of taxable vessels × Applicable tax amount per unit

Exemptions

a. Tax exemptions may be given on the vehicles used by Embassies and Consulates in China; the vehicles used by diplomatic representatives, consuls, administrative and technical staffs and their spouses and non-grown-up children living together with them.

b. Tax exemptions may be given as stipulated in some provinces and municipalities on the fire vehicles, ambulances, water sprinkling vehicles and similar vehicles of enterprises with foreign investment and foreign enterprises.

CHINESE FINANCIAL SYSTEM

China's financial system has recently begun to expand rapidly as monetary policy becomes integral to its overall economic policy. As a result, banks are becoming more important to China's economy by providing increasingly more finance to enterprises for investment, seeking deposits from the public to mop up excess liquidity, and lending money to the government.

As part of US$586 billion economic stimulus package of November 2008, the government is planning to remove loan quotas and ceilings for all lenders, and increase bank credit for priority projects, including rural areas, small businesses, technology companies, iron and cement companies.

Financial reform

For the past few decades, the People's Bank of China has exercised the functions and powers of a central bank, as well as handling industrial and commercial credits and savings business; it was neither the central bank in the true sense, nor a commercial entity conforming to the law of the market economy. But since reform and opening-up began in 1978, China has carried out a series of significant reforms in its banking system, and strengthened its opening to the outside world. Consequently, the finance industry has made steady development. At the end of 2004, the balance of domestic and foreign currency savings deposits stood at 25,318.8 billion yuan and the balance of home and foreign currency loans came to 18,856.6 billion yuan. Now China has basically formed a financial system under the regulation, control and supervision of the central bank, with its state banks as the mainstay, featuring the separation of policy-related finance and commercial finance, the cooperation of various financial institutions with mutually complementary functions.

In 1984, the People's Bank of China stopped handling credit and savings business, and began formally to exercise central bank functions and powers by conducting macro-control and supervision over the nation's banking system. In 1994, the Industrial and Commercial Bank of China, the Bank of China, the Agricultural Bank of China and the China Construction Bank were transformed into state-owned commercial banks; and three policy-related banks were founded, namely, the Agricultural Development Bank of China, the China Development Bank and the China Import and Export Bank. In 1995, the Commercial Bank Law was promulgated, creating the conditions for forming the commercial bank system and organizational structure, and providing a legal basis for changing the specialized state banks to state-owned commercial banks.

Since 1996, the financial organizational system has gradually been improved; the wholly state-owned commercial banks have been transformed into modern financial enterprises handling currencies; over 120 shareholding medium and small-sized commercial banks have been set up or reorganized; and securities and insurance financial institutions have been further standardized and developed. April 2003 saw the formal establishment of the China Banking Regulatory Commission (CBRC). Since then, a financial regulatory system has been formed in which CBRC, China Securities Regulatory Commission (CSRC) and China Insurance Regulatory Commission (CIRC) work in coordination, each body having its own clearly defined responsibilities.

In January 2004, the State Council decided that the Bank of China and the China Construction Bank would start the experiment of transforming the shareholding system. The main tasks are to establish a standardized corporate governance and an internal system of rights and responsibilities in accordance with the requirements for modern commercial banks; to restructure the financial system, speed up the disposal of non-performing assets and to reinforce minimum capital requirement to build up first-class modern financial enterprises. Now, six shareholding commercial banks and urban commercial banks in China have begun to accept overseas investors as shareholders.

Opening up of the financial industry

Over the past 20-odd years,[when?] China's financial institutions in the Special Economic Zone, coastal open cities and inland central cities have approved a range of wholly foreign-owned and Chinese-foreign joint venture financial institutions. Every year since 2002, China has increased the number of cities where foreign banks are allowed to handle RMB business, and within five years such banks will be allowed to handle RMB business in any city. At the end of 2004, the total assets of foreign financial institutions in China reached over US$47 billion; foreign banks were allowed to handle RMB business in 16 areas, and 62 foreign banks from 19 countries and regions set up 191 business institutions in China, of which 116 were approved to handle RMB business. There were 211 foreign bank branches in China.

The CSRC has approved the establishment of 13 Sino-foreign equity joint venture fund management companies, and started to formally handle the application of establishment of joint venture fund management companies with a maximum 49 percent foreign share; the CIRC declared that: from December 11, 2004 on, foreign insurance companies could handle health insurance, group insurance, life insurance and annuity insurance businesses; regional restrictions on establishing wholly foreign-funded insurance institutions were canceled and the proportion of the foreign share in joint venture insurance agencies was allowed to reach 51 percent.

Foreign banks have expanded their China-related business scope. In November 2003, the CBRC started to implement new policies, e.g., permitting foreign banks to provide RMB services to all kinds of Chinese enterprises in areas with open RMB business (previously, these banks' RMB services were restricted to foreign-funded enterprises, foreigners and people from Hong Kong, Macao and Taiwan in cities with open RMB business). The new policy also encourages qualified international strategic investors to join the restructuring and reforming of China's banking and financial institutions on a voluntary and commercial basis.

Meanwhile, all China's commercial banks have set up branches overseas, and started an international credit business. The Bank of China ranks first in the number and scale of overseas outlets. In 1980, China resumed membership of the World Bank, and returned to the

International Monetary Fund. In 1984, China started business contacts with the Bank for International Settlements. In 1985, China formally joined the African Development Bank and in 1986 formally became a member of the Asian Development Bank.

Advisory body

In August 2013 creation of an as yet unnamed high-level body to gather and analyze financial information and trends was announced by the central government. The central bank would participate as would people from other organizations engaged in financial matters. It would not have direct regulatory authority, but would attempt to function at the highest professional level in order to provide appropriate guidance to regulators with respect to matters such as shadow banking which are potential sources of instability.

Economic reform

The ongoing development of China's financial system will play a critical role in the country's effort to narrow social disparities and pursue balanced growth. Reforming the financial system would increase the rate of GDP growth and help spread China's new wealth more evenly. If the reforms directed additional funds to private companies – China's new growth engine – the economy would generate significantly higher returns for the same level of investment and GDP would rise. Such a shift will stimulate mass job creation in the strongest areas of China's economy and increase tax revenues to finance social programs.

After more than a quarter century of reform and opening to the outside world, by 2005 China's economy had become the second largest in the world after the United States when measured on a purchasing power parity (PPP) basis. The government has a goal of quadrupling the gross domestic product (GDP) by 2020 and more than doubling the per capita GDP. Central planning has been curtailed, and widespread market mechanisms and a reduced government role have prevailed since 1978. The government fosters a dual economic structure that has evolved from a socialist, centrally planned economy to a socialist market economic system, or a "socialist market economy with Chinese characteristics". Industry is marked by increasing technological advancements and productivity. People's communes were eliminated by 1984 – after more than 25 years – and the system of township-collective-household production was introduced to the agricultural sector. Private ownership of production assets is legal, although some nonagricultural and industrial facilities are still state-owned and centrally planned. Restraints on international trade were relaxed when China acceded to the World Trade Organization in 2001. Joint ventures are encouraged, especially in the coastal Special Economic Zones and open coastal cities. A sign of the affluence that the reformed economy has brought to China might be seen in the number of its millionaires (measured in U.S. dollars): a reported 236,000 millionaires in 2004, an increase of 12 percent over two years earlier.

Chinese officials cite two major trends that have an effect on China's market economy and future development: world multipolarization and regional integration. In relation to these trends, they foresee the roles of China and the United States in world affairs and with one another as very important. Despite successes, China's leaders face a variety of challenges to the nation's future economic development. They have to maintain a high growth rate, deal effectively with the rural workforce, improve the financial system, continue to reform the state-owned enterprises, foster the productive private sector, establish a social security system, improve scientific and educational development, promote better international cooperation, and some believe, change the role of the government in the economic system. Despite constraints the international market has placed on China, it nevertheless became the world's third largest trading nation in 2004 after only the United States and Germany.

The Fifth Plenum of the Sixteenth CPC Central Committee took place in October 2005. The Fifth Plenum approved the new Eleventh Five-Year Plan (2006–10), which emphasizes a shift from extensive to intensive growth in order to meet demands for improved economic returns; the conservation of resources to include a 20% reduction in energy consumption by 2010; and an effort to raise profitability. Better coordination of urban and rural development and of development between nearby provincial regions also is emphasized in the new plan.

Government finances and budget

China's government debt is less than 25% of gross domestic product (about 22.10% in 2006).

China has a budget deficit of around 1.5% of GDP. China projected a budget deficit of 295 billion yuan in 2006, down 1.7% from 2005. The overall budget deficit in 2004 was approximately US$26 billion, an amount equivalent to about 1.5% of GDP. In 2007, economic planners expect China's already small budget deficit to shrink again. According to economists, this has afforded China to spend more on public services such as education and healthcare.

The government budget for 2004 was US$330.6 billion in revenue and US$356.8 billion in expenditures. 95.5% of revenue was from taxes and tariffs, 54.9% of which was collected by the central government and 45% by local government. The expenditures were for culture, education, science, and health care (18%); capital construction (12%); administration (14%); national defense (7.7%); agriculture, forestry, and water conservancy (5.9%); subsidies to compensate for price increases (2.7%); pensions and social welfare provisions (1.9%); promotion of innovation, science, and technology (4.3%); operating expenses of industry, transport, and commerce (1.2%); geological prospecting (0.4%), and other (31.9%).

Taxation

Before the reform and opening, China exercised a single taxation system. Because taxation had no connection with the economic activities of enterprises, this system lacked vitality. In 1981, the Chinese government began to collect income tax from Sino-foreign joint ventures and solely foreign-funded enterprises, taking the first step in taxation system reform.

From 1983 to 1984, the reform consisting of the replacement of profits by taxes was carried out in domestic enterprises, and a foreign-related taxation system was set up. As a result, instead of a single tax category, a compound taxation system in which turnover and income taxes were the mainstay and other tax categories were in coordination with it was initially in place and promoted the control of finances and the economy. In 1994, the reform of the taxation system was deepened, and a complete structural adjustment of the taxation system was made by taking the market economy as the norm. In 1996, China lowered the rate of customs duties and export drawback, and exercised import supervision.

Inflation

China's annual rate of inflation averaged 6% per year during the 1990–2002 period. Although consumer prices declined by 0.8% in 2002, they increased by 1.2% in 2003. China's estimated inflation rate in 2006 was 1.8%.

Banking sector

China's banking system is highly regulated with six major banks, each having specific tasks and duties. The People's Bank of China is the largest bank in China and acts as the Treasury. It also issues currency, monitors money supply, regulates monetary organizations and formulates monetary policy for the State Council. The Bank of China manages foreign exchange transactions and manages foreign exchange reserves. The China Development Bank distributes foreign capital from a variety of sources, and the China International Trust and Investment Corporation (CITIC) was previously a financial organization that smoothed the inflow of foreign funds, but is now a full bank, allowing to compete for foreign investment funds with the Bank of China. The China Construction Bank lends funds for capital construction projects from the state budget, and finally the Agricultural Bank of China functions as a lending and deposit taking institution for the agricultural sector.

Banking reform

Financial reform in China's banking sector include the introduction of leasing and insurance, and operational boundaries are being slowly eroded to promote competition for customers who are now permitted to choose banks as well as hold accounts in more than one bank.

Banking reform was initiated in China in 1994, and the Commercial Banking Law took effect in July 1995. The aims of these actions were to strengthen the role of the central bank — the People's Bank of China — and to allow private banks to be established. The People's Bank of China was established in 1948. It issues China's currency and implements the nation's monetary policies. China's oldest bank, founded in 1908, is the Bank of Communications Limited, a commercial enterprise located in Shanghai. China's second oldest bank was established in 1912 as the Bank of China. Since 2004 it has become a shareholding company known as the Bank of China Limited and handles foreign exchange and international financial settlements. The Agricultural Bank of China, founded in 1951, is mainly involved in rural financing and the provision of services to agricultural, industrial, commercial, and transportation enterprises in rural areas. Other major banks include the China Construction Bank; established in 1954 as the People's Construction Bank of China, it has been a state-owned commercial bank since 1994 and maintains some 15,400 business outlets inside and outside China, including six overseas branches and two overseas representative offices. The China Construction Bank was restructured in 2003 into a shareholding bank called the China Construction Bank Corporation, with the state holding the controlling shares.

CITIC was founded in 1979 to assist economic and technological cooperation, finance, banking, investment, and trade. The Industrial and Commercial Bank of China was founded in 1984 to handle industrial and commercial credits and international business. The Agricultural Development Bank of China, Export and Import Bank of China, and State Development Bank all were founded in 1994. China's first private commercial national bank, the China Minsheng Banking Corporation, was opened in 1996. Commercial banks are supervised by the China Banking Regulatory Commission, which was established in 2003. In 2005 the commission announced the launching of a new Postal Savings Bank to replace the old system and its more than 36,000 outdated outlets nationwide.

E-commerce

In the online realm, China's e-commerce industry has grown more slowly than the Europe and the US, with a significant period of development occurring from around 2009 onwards. According to Credit Suisse, the total value of online transactions in China grew from an insignificant size in 2008 to around RMB 4 trillion (US$660 billion) in 2012. Alipay has the biggest market share in China with 300 million users and control of just under half of China's online payment market in February 2014, while Tenpay's share is around 20 percent, and China UnionPay's share is slightly greater than 10 percent.

Foreign banks

Since the inception of the "open door policy", a number of foreign banks have been permitted to open their doors in major cities in China. However, these are largely representative branches, with only a few being permitted to carry out branch functions in Shanghai and Shenzhen. Their participation in China's financial system has been limited, but as China starts to borrow more from abroad, their role may become greater in the future.

When first permitted in the mid-1980s, foreign banks were restricted to designated cities and could deal only with transactions by foreign companies in China. After those restrictions were loosened following China's accession to the World Trade Organization in 2001, some foreign banks have been allowed to provide services to local residents and businesses. In 2004 there were some 70 foreign banks with more than 150 branches in China. In 2007 a limited number of foreign banks were allowed to issue debit cards in China (and Bank of East Asia was allowed to issue a credit card). This made banking with a foreign bank more convenient, as money in accounts could be accessed at ATMs like customers of local banks could. In 2009 this number grew to six, but only two of these are not tied to Hong Kong.

Stock exchanges

There are stock exchanges in Shanghai (the third largest in the world), and Shenzhen and futures exchanges in Shanghai, Dalian, and Zhengzhou. They are regulated by the China Securities Regulatory Commission.

Stock market

In 1990 and 1991, China set up stock exchanges in Shanghai and Shenzhen. In the past decade, the Chinese stock market has completed a journey that took many countries over a century to cover; China's stock market today has capital approaching 3,705.6 billion yuan, 1,377 listed companies and 72.16 million investors.

The Chinese stock market has promoted the reform of government-owned corporations and the change of their systems, and enabled a stable transition between the two systems. On the strength of the stock market in the past decade, many large state-owned enterprises have realized system change.

The change also has stimulated medium and small-sized state-owned enterprises to adopt the shareholding system, thus solving the most important issue - the system problem - during the transition from planned to a market economy. As for ordinary citizens, bank deposit is not the only way to put their money, the stock market has become one of the most important channels for investment.

Methods of stock trading are constantly being improved. Today, a network system for securities exchange and account settlement has been formed, with the Shanghai and Shenzhen exchanges as the powerhouse, radiating to all parts of the country. In 2004, China issued 123 kinds of A share, and 23 rights issues, collecting a total of 83.6 billion yuan; and 28 kinds of B and H shares, collecting a total of 67.5 billion yuan.

Development

As China's economy becomes more integrated with the rest of the world its financial system will become more in line with international practices. China has also learnt from Hong Kong's financial system, with the help of the Hong Kong Monetary Authority.

Trade balance

China had a favorable balance of trade of US$32 billion in 2004 and US$38.7 billion in 2003. These amounts reflect the general course of a favorable trade balance during the previous eight years. In 1996 China's trade balance was US$12.2 billion, peaking at US$43.4 billion in 1998 but declining to US$24.1 billion by 2000 before starting its new increase.

Balance of payments

China's current account balance in 2004 was nearly US$68.7 billion. Added to this total was US$54.9 billion in foreign direct investment (exceeding that invested in the United States). When other investments, assets, and liabilities are brought into the calculation, the overall balance of payments was US$206.1 billion in 2004, compared with US$75.2 billion in 2002 and US$116.5 billion in 2003.

External debt

According to United Nations statistics for 2001, China's external and public, or publicly guaranteed, long-term debt had reached US$91.7 billion. China's debt had grown steadily during the 1990s, peaked at US$112.8 billion in 1997, and then declined annually thereafter. By 2004 China had US$618.5 billion in its international reserve account, 98.6 percent of which was from foreign exchange, not including the Bank of China's foreign exchange holdings.

The Financial Economic Journal article: "Law, finance, and economic growth in China" by Allen and Qian (2005), critically and creatively evaluates through comparisons and inferences on China' alternative institutional arrangement, governing systems, law, and formal financial system,. It also assesses the relationship between China's economic growth and other countries' financial development systems. such as the Stock Market. Contemporary studies cited on China's legal and fiscal systems establishments indicate signs of underdevelopment despite the rapid economic growth compared to other countries. (Liang & Teng, 2006). For instance, the Chinese private sector grow is less inclusive equated to other Listed and State sector thereby demanding transformation to eliminate deficiencies. Comparatively, the Chinese State and listed sectors indicate successful development based on alternative mechanisms employed to build institutional relationships and reputation for other economies. Consequently, exposure of the key factors connecting the Chinese formal systems, financial, law, and economic growth lead to an understanding of how the nonstandard mechanisms impacts on promoting optimal growth and development for China and other countries (Allen, Qian & Qian, 2005).

Broadly, the article employs scholarly evidence to explore China's legal, financial and growth sectors visualizing the Status of Chinese economic based on GPD and growth to contrast the issue against the emerging economies rather than the developed ones. Allen, Qian, and Qian, explore the Chinese firms' financial sources based on aggregated evidence as well as cross-cross country evidence on annual growth rates, Purchase Power Parity, and population density. They also access evidence on both Listed and Private Sector to demonstrate different types of the corporate governance, stocks, ownership structures, financing, valuation, and dividends. Survey and anecdotal evidence, for example, were used by the author to provide background information on the successful regions evaluated as a justification of the findings and results obtained.

Agreeing with the Article Argument: Analyses on the authors' argument in the article indicate delivery of facts, figures, and substantiation from an informed and expert position, which make it worth agreeing with the authors' arguments. The article covers the visualization of China' as an alternative institutional arrangement, with different governing systems, law, and formal financial system. These areas form China's economic growth and relate well with its development targets and agenda. They are also factual through the use of figures and numbers and can be measured scientifically, socially and politically given the current chine's position as an emerging economy and as an influence in the world economy. The second reason for agreeing with the article is a result of the examinations provided in the three major economic sectors that include the state and government controlled companies and enterprises, the publicly traded and exchange sector called listed and the private sector, which is under private ownership. In reviewing the imbalance of the three sectors, and the support for private sector, the article is keen on using measures that include banking systems' domination and the ongoing privatization process. It samples more than 1000 firms, listed and traded on the Shanghai Stock Exchange (SHSE) and Shenzhen Stock Exchange (SZSE) with an indication of concentrated equity on State for firms converted from the State Sector and founder families for the private firms (Allen, Qian & Qian, 2005). As demonstrated from the research by Liang and Teng (2006), the status of the Chinese economy, which is also the position of the article, make it among the most impactful in the world. The country's growth domestic Product (GDP) in 2002 stood at U.S $1,237 ahead of Canada and Spain but now is at $11,391.620 only behind the United States (China GDP, 1960-2016). The feat is remarkable given that China's rapid growth only started in 1979. Other comparisons in the article indicate the same effect of fast Chinese growth. On the legal system, China classifies as an English-origin, which is true given the protection offered to investments and the upholding of creditor and shareholder rights. These attributes, also proclaimed by Liang and Teng, (2006) contribute to strengthening the financial system allowing venture in various finance and capital markets and line with the country's equity versus the population. The mitigation measures outlined in the article such as the formation of the state-owned asset management companies assigned to cash recovery on the bad loans and improving loan structures. Based on an outright reliability of the authors' point of view the' findings and results, I find them accurate and reliable to generalize or use for future studies. One way for this is the referencing from credible sources such as financial, law and politic journals, empirical perspectives, case studies and renowned authors among others further justifying the article's standpoint. For instance, the authors employ both survey and anecdotal evidence to obtain the background information about the most successful regions or sectors in China.

Evaluating the authors' argument persuasiveness based on the consistency of point made for the authors' key inferences and assumptions. The general assumption made by the authors while exploring the topic of research is that the economic status, legal systems and financial system of a country affect the overall economic growth and development. The brief description of the authors' variables and sources, strong inferences and conclusion serves as the best tool and build up in building the authors' arguments. For this reason, I concur with the authors' arguments on the topic of study about China's financial, legal and economic growth.

Reflection on the Economic and Financial in China: Statistically, an economic and financial study of China's financial, law, institutions and economic growth in shows that China serves as a counter example in analyzing weak financial and legal systems despite fastest growing economies Liang & Teng, 2006). The economic and financial phenomenon as learned in previous literature tends to support market-based systems where openness and the role of the state play an important part in the country's financial system development. From a deregulation and financial liberalization point of view, relational, financial systems are regarded as a better approach for long-term Chinese economic development compared to a market-based system (Bruton & Ahlstrom, 2003). In this regard, the Chinese economic growths evolve as the financial systems progress with the financial globalization changes and the alterations of the Chinese power relationships (Bruton & Ahlstrom, 2003).,Also, the economic politics affects financial systems directly. The economic and financial systems constitute financial institutions and market arrangements that channel the country's savings for corporate governance and productive uses. Though, as asserted by (Lee, 2015), the positive correlation between economic and financial development result to better monitoring and allocation of financial resources where financial systems are either categorized as bank-based or market-based. Therefore, similar financial market development and banks influence on the economic outcome. Chinese lower economic performance compared to the developed economies is as a result of inadequate financial and legal systems based on its inefficiency market-based system (Lee, 2015). This is an indication of a high moral hazard that exposes the government policies to economic fragility and financial crisis.

While no financial system is complete, each of the Chinese market and bank-based financial systems has its benefits and disadvantagesMarket-based financial systems are considered stronger and better compared to bank market systems as they can generate adequate data about different firms' performance as well as reflecting on all the fundamentals requirements in a real financial sector (Lee, 2015). The components of the stock market are use essential in the effective financial motoring process atas they can visualize market stock prices and potential bad economic performances (Bruton & Ahlstrom, 2003). Therefore, maximizing the stock market values by firms has a positive implication of improving the economic growth and performance. However, financial market success gives a better reason for corporate groups to allocate resources to their affiliate firms. This reason, China uses bank loans and self-fundraising commercial channels as financial channels to finance Chinese, companies consequently determining the stock market bottom line through price speculations that lead to high transaction costs (Lee, 2015). Evaluation of the Chinese bank-based systems benefits and their particular limitations demonstrate that the existing financial debts help in solving cash flow misreporting as it exerts economic disciplinary effect.

Alternative governance and financial mechanism serve as a turning point in supporting the growth and development of the Chinese private sector through reputation and relationship that enable firms to overcome asymmetric data problems that inhibit contract enforcement and coalitions. Cultural and religious factors also play a significant role in investors' protection, institutional development and legal origin in venturing capital industry growth and development. (Bruton & Ahlstrom, 2003).

To add to these factors, the Chinese economic situation has high social trusts that serve as an alternative mechanism for the development of substantial financial incentives to increase economic participation. Product and input market competitions work successfully in the country by creating a relatively strong comparative advantage for organization thriving and survival. Moreover, the existence of low entry barriers promotes high levels of market competitions allowing companies to grow and develop economically.

The financial, legal, and economic environment control and ownership separation protect shareholders in countries with dominant ownership structures. such as China. At the same time, input suppliers cooperation by forming market compliances and coalitions ensures the optimal outcome of financing and legal systems. (Bruton n& Ahlstrom, 2003).

However, profit sharing among the firms enables firms' growth, reputations, and contractual agreement. As a transitional economy, China and its firms have to adjust both their financial and legal systems to strengthen their economic growth and development. The result will be a diversified commercial work for the transitional economy that is likely to work regardless of the socialistic Adopt drastic economic reforms such the Chinese economy may not work due to the Confucius's influence that essential changes in society should be gradual and fully implemented only after they prove correct, thus reinforcing the existing financial and legal systems Through analyzing different governance systems and their economic support, much can be learned from the Chinese Communist Party based on its autocratic nature, but with the ability to support and promote financial and legal systems for economic growth especially for Private Sector. The government plays a significant role in financial, legal and economic growth reform process especially for transitional and socialist economies. (Liang & Teng, 2006). As socialist governments experience limited support for economic grow progression, much can be observed from democratic economies and richer countries in supporting financial and legal systems. (Liang & Teng, 2006).

For instance, the government officials play a vital role in implementing alternative governing mechanisms and institutional arrangements for the development of financial and legal systems and should be consulted for efficient implementation of an alternative mechanism for economic development.

They also help incorporate the three pillars of financial and legal system constructions entailing information systems, legal environment, and market support system. The Chinese legal environment allows normal market operations as information systems address asymmetric constructs based on information credibility and authoritativeness (Bruton &Ahlstrom, 2003). Finally, market support systems allow investors in alternative mechanisms to improve their experiences and expertise.

Suggestions for Future Reforms Economic Financial Phenomenon in China: The future financial and economic reforms should be directed towards the liberalization of financial and economic matters as globalization takes effect in many countries. Future studies need to encourage China's successful Private Sector transformation to better alternative methods in the state deficiency and listed sectors As suggested by Lee (2015), it is imperative that future explorations on financial opening, liberalization and globalization conducted to visualize proficient financial adjustments that include changes in financial systems, handling a crisis, and alterations in the legal functions. It is equally important to implement better legislative policies that strengthen the pillars of financial and juridical systems construction such as education, information systems, money control, the legal environment, and support market systems. As a populous nation, there is a need to have reforms in areas including social welfare, housing, insurance, employment policies and the state-owned enterprises, which affect the financial system. These will be achieved through initiating favorable determinant areas that include taxation, foreign investment policy, exit policy, power to make decisions, and decentralization thereby ensuring credibility and disclosure of vital information connect economic growth, finance, and legal systems. It is expected that the reforms will be pragmatic due to the obvious basis of experimentation of rather than the use of ideology in China, but adopting a more rapid and privatized system that leases operation of the state-owned assets (Lee, 2015). Consequently, the move will promote efficiency for the enterprises and allow or encourage the development of other non-state and foreign sectors that highly account for China's economic growth.

Currency and foreign exchange control

China's currency is the renminbi (RMB, "people's currency") or yuan. The interbank exchange rate on August 1, 2006, was US$1 = RMB7.98. The RMB is made up of 100 fen or 10 jiao. Coins are issued in denominations of one, two, and five fen; one and five jiao, and one RMB. Banknotes are issued in denominations of one, two, and five jiao; and one, two, five, 10, 50, and 100 RMB.

The Renminbi is issued and controlled solely by the People's Bank of China. RMB exchange rates are decided by the People's Bank of China and issued by the State Administration of Foreign Exchange, the latter exercising the functions and powers of exchange control.

In 1994, China reformed the foreign exchange system, combined the RMB exchange rates, adopted the bank exchange settlement system and set up a unified inter-bank foreign exchange market. On this basis, China included the foreign exchange business of the foreign-invested enterprises in the bank's exchange settlement system in 1996.

On December 1, 1996, China formally accepted Article 8 of the Agreement on International Currencies and Funds, and realized RMB convertibility under the current account ahead of schedule. Meanwhile, China has been active in promoting bilateral currency exchange between ASEAN and China, Japan and the Republic of Korea (10+3).

At the end of 2004, China's foreign exchange reserves reached US$609.9 billion and its share in the International Monetary Fund has risen from 11th to 8th place. The variety of financial businesses has been increasing steadily, and China has opened an array of new businesses to become integrated into the various aspects of modern international financial business, such as consumer credit, securities investment funds and insurance-linked investments.

Fiscal year

The exact parameters of China's fiscal year is not entirely clear, as online sources indicate differing time frames. It is stated that the fiscal years follows the calendar year, beginning January 1 and ending December 31, while other Chinese companies have followed different standards. For example, Tianyin Pharmaceutical Inc. released its second quarter financial results ended December 31, 2013, in accordance with the July 1-to-June 30 fiscal year, while China HGS Real Estate Inc. ended its last fiscal year on September 30, 2013.

Insurance

China's insurance industry started to recover in 1980, after a 20-year standstill. In 1981, the People's Insurance Company of China was transformed from a government department into a specialized company, with branches or sub-branches in every part of China. 1988 witnessed the founding of the Ping An Insurance (Group) Company of China and the China Pacific Insurance, both mainly active in the coastal areas. In 1996, the People's Insurance Company of China made a big step forward in transforming its administration and operational mode, in setting up a modern enterprise system, and integrating with the international market.

The Insurance Law of 1985 and the founding of the China Insurance Regulatory Commission in 1988 provided the legal basis and specific rules for the operation of the insurance market. In 1980, China only had one insurance company; by 2004 there were 62, with a total revenue of premiums of 431.8 billion yuan, of which 100.4 billion were paid as compensation and payment.

BANKING IN CHINA

During the 1990s and 2000s, China's banking system underwent significant changes: banks are now functioning more like western banks than before. Nevertheless, China's banking industry has remained in the government's hands even though banks have gained more autonomy. WTO has accepted China. The central bank of China is the People's Bank of China.

The "big four" state-owned commercial banks are the Bank of China, the China Construction Bank, the Industrial and Commercial Bank of China and the Agricultural Bank of China, all of which are among the largest banks in the world.

History

Chinese financial institutions were conducting all major banking functions, including the acceptance of deposits, the making of loans, issuing notes, money exchange, and long-distance remittance of money by the Song Dynasty (960-1279). In 1024, the first paper currency was issued by the state in Sichuan. The two major types of indigenous Chinese financial institutions, piaohao and qianzhuang, more often cooperated than competed in China's financial market.

Due to structural weaknesses of traditional Chinese law, Chinese financial institutions focused primarily on commercial banking based on close familial and personal relationships, and their working capital was primarily based on the float from short-term money transfers rather than long-term demand deposits.

The modern concepts of consumer banking and fractional reserve banking never developed among traditional Chinese banks and were introduced to China by European bankers in the 19th century.

Piaohao

An early Chinese banking institution was called the piaohao, also known as Shanxi banks because they were owned primarily by natives of Shanxi.

The first piaohao originated from the Xiyuecheng Dye Company of Pingyao. To deal with the transfer of large amounts of cash from one branch to another, the company introduced drafts, cashable in the company's many branches around China. Although this new method was originally designed for business transactions within the Xiyuecheng Company, it became so popular that in 1823 the owner gave up the dye business altogether and reorganised the company as a special remittance firm, Rishengchang Piaohao. In the next thirty years, eleven piaohao were established in Shanxi province, in the counties of Qixian, Taigu, and Pingyao. By the end of the nineteenth century, thirty-two piaohao with 475 branches were in business covering most of China.

All piaohao were organised as single proprietaries or partnerships, where the owners carried unlimited liability. They concentrated on interprovincial remittances, and later on conducting government services. From the time of the Taiping Rebellion, when transportation routes between the capital and the provinces were cut off, piaohao began involved with the delivery of government tax revenue. Piaohao grew by taking on a role in advancing funds and arranging foreign loans for provincial governments, issuing notes, and running regional treasuries.

Qianzhuang

Independent of the nationwide network of piaohao there were a large number of small native banks, generally called qianzhuang. These institutions first appeared in the Yangzi Delta region, in Shanghai, Ningbo, and Shaoxing. The first qianzhuang can be traced to at least the mid-eighteenth century. In 1776, several of these banks in Shanghai organised themselves into a guild under the name of qianye gongsuo. In contrast to piaohao, most qianzhuang were local and functioned as commercial banks by conducting local money exchange, issuing cash notes, exchanging bills and notes, and discounting for the local business community.

Qianzhuang maintained close relationships with Chinese merchants, and grew with the expansion of China's foreign trade. When Western banks first entered China, they issued "chop loans" (caipiao) to the qianzhuang, who would then lend this money to Chinese merchants who used it to purchase goods from foreign firms. It is estimated that there were around 10,000 qianzhuang in China in the early 1890s.

Entry of foreign banks

British and other European banks entered China around the middle of the nineteenth century to service the growing number of Western trade firms. The Chinese coined the term yinhang, meaning "silver institution", for the English word "bank". The first foreign bank in China was the Bombay-based British Oriental Bank, which opened branches in Hong Kong, Guangzhou and Shanghai in the 1840s. Other British banks followed suit and set up their branches in China one after another. The British enjoyed a virtual monopoly on modern banking for forty years. The Hong Kong and Shanghai Banking Corporation, now HSBC, established in 1865 in Hong Kong, later became the largest foreign bank in China.

In the early 1890s, Germany's Deutsch-Asiatische Bank, Japan's Yokohama Specie Bank, France's Banque de l'Indochine, and Russia's Russo-Asiatic Bank opened branches in China and challenged British ascendancy in China's financial market. By the end of the nineteenth century there were nine foreign banks with forty-five branches in China's treaty ports.

At the time due to unfair treaties, foreign banks enjoyed extraterritorial rights. They also enjoyed complete control over China's international remittance and foreign trade financing. Being unregulated by the Chinese government, they were free to issue banknotes for circulation, accept deposits from Chinese citizens, and make loans to the qianzhuang.

Government banks

After the launch of the Self-strengthening movement, the Qing government began initiating large industrial projects which required large amounts of capital. Though the existing domestic financial institutions provided sufficient credit and transfer facilities to support domestic trade and worked well with small-scale enterprises, they could not meet China's new financial demands. China turned to foreign banks for large scale and long term finance. Following a series of military defeats, the Qing government was forced to borrow from foreign banks and syndicates to finance its indemnity payments to foreign powers.

A number of proposals were made by a modern Chinese banking institution from the 1860s onwards. Li Hongzhang, one of the leaders of the self-strengthening movement, made serious efforts to create a foreign-Chinese joint bank in 1885 and again in 1887.

The Imperial Bank of China, China's first modern bank, opened for business in 1897. The bank was organised as a joint-stock firm. It adopted the internal regulations of HSBC, and its senior managers were foreign professionals. After the proclamation of the Republic of China, the bank changed its English name to the Commercial Bank of China in 1912. The name more accurately translated its Chinese name and removed any link to the Qing Dynasty.

In 1905, China's first central bank was established as the Bank of the Board of Revenue. Three years later, its name was changed to the Great Qing Government Bank. Intended as a replacement for all existing banknotes, the Da Qing Bank's note was granted exclusive privilege to be used in all public and private fund transfers, including tax payments and debt settlements. Da Qing Bank was also given exclusive privilege to run the state treasury. The Board of Revenue that controlled most of the central government's revenue transferred most of its tax remittance through the bank and its branches. The government entrusted the bank with the transfer of the Salt Surplus Tax, diplomatic expenditures, the management of foreign loans, the payment of foreign indemnities, and the deposit and transfer of the customs tax in many treaty ports.

Following the Xinhai Revolution of 1911, Daqing Bank was renamed the Bank of China. This bank continues to exist today.

Another government bank, the Bank of Communications, was organised in 1908 by the Ministry of Posts and Communications to raise money for the redemption of the Beijing-Hankou Railway from Belgian contractors. The bank's aim was to unify funding for steamship lines, railways, as well as telegraph and postal facilities.

Private banks

The first private bank dates to 1897, courtesy of the entrepreneurship of Shen Xuanhui. Three private banks appeared in the late Qing period, all created by private entrepreneurs without state funding. The Xincheng Bank was established in Shanghai in 1906, followed by the National Commercial Bank in Hangzhou the following year, and the Ningbo Commercial and Savings Bank in 1908. In that year, the Regulations of Banking Registration was issued by the Ministry of Revenue, which continued to have effect well after the fall of the Qing dynasty.

A lion's share of the profitable official remittance business was taken by the Daqing Bank from the piaohao. The piaohao all but disappeared following the Xinhai Revolution in 1911.

The same period saw the increasing power of private interests in modern Chinese banking and the concentration of banking capital. In Shanghai, the so-called "southern three banks" were established. They were the Shanghai Commercial and Savings Bank, the National Commercial Bank, and the Zhejiang Industrial Bank. Four other banks, known as the "northern four banks" emerged later. They were the Yien Yieh Commercial Bank, the Kincheng Banking Corporation, the Continental Bank, and the China & South Sea Bank. The first three were initiated by current and retired officials of the Beijing government, whilst the last was created by an overseas Chinese.

Note suspension incident

In 1916 the Republican government in Beijing ordered the suspension of paper note conversion to silver. With the backing of the Mixed Court, the Shanghai Branch of the Bank of China successfully resisted the order.

The Bank of China's bylaws were revised in 1917 to restrict government intervention.

Golden Age of Chinese banking

The decade from the Northern Expedition to the Second Sino-Japanese War in 1937 has been described as a "golden decade" for China's modernisation as well as for its banking industry. Modern Chinese banks extended their business in scope, making syndicated industrial loans and offering loans to rural areas.

The Nationalist government created the Central Bank of China in 1928, with Song Ziwen as its first president. The Bank of China was reorganised as a bank specialising in the management of foreign exchange while the Bank of Communications focused on developing industry.

The Bureau of Financial Supervision was set up under the Ministry of Finance, to supervise financial affairs.

Confronted with imminent war with Japan, the Chinese government took control of over 70 percent of the assets of modern Chinese banks through the notorious banking coup.

After 1949

Main article: Banking in the People's Republic of China The history of the Chinese banking system has been somewhat checkered. Nationalization and consolidation of the country's banks received the highest priority in the earliest years of the People's Republic, and banking was the first sector to be completely socialized. In the period of recovery after the Chinese civil war (1949–52), the People's Bank of China moved very effectively to halt raging inflation and bring the nation's finances under central control. Over the course of time, the banking organization was modified repeatedly to suit changing conditions and new policies.

The banking system was centralized early on under the Ministry of Finance, which exercised firm control over all financial services, credit, and the money supply. During the 1980s the banking system was expanded and diversified to meet the needs of the reform program, and the scale of banking activity rose sharply. New budgetary procedures required state enterprises to remit to the state only a tax on income and to seek investment funds in the form of bank loans. Between 1979 and 1985, the volume of deposits nearly tripled and the value of bank loans rose by 260 percent. By 1987 the banking system included the People's Bank of China, Agricultural Bank of China, Bank of China (which handled foreign exchange matters), China Investment Bank, China Industrial and Commercial Bank, People's Construction Bank, Communications Bank, People's Insurance Company of China, rural credit cooperatives, and urban credit cooperatives.

The People's Bank of China was the central bank and the foundation of the banking system. Although the bank overlapped in function with the Ministry of Finance and lost many of its responsibilities during the Cultural Revolution, in the 1970s it was restored to its leading position. As the central bank, the People's Bank of China had sole responsibility for issuing currency and controlling the money supply. It also served as the government treasury, the main source of credit for economic units, the clearing center for financial transactions, the holder of enterprise deposits, the national savings bank, and a ubiquitous monitor of economic activities.

Another financial institution, the Bank of China, handled all dealings in foreign exchange. It was responsible for allocating the country's foreign exchange reserves, arranging foreign loans, setting exchange rates for China's currency, issuing letters of credit, and generally carrying out all financial transactions with foreign firms and individuals. The Bank of China had offices in Beijing and other cities engaged in foreign trade and maintained overseas offices in major international financial centers, including Hong Kong, London, New York City, Singapore, and Luxembourg.

The Agricultural Bank was created in the 1950s to facilitate financial operations in the rural areas. The Agricultural Bank provided financial support to agricultural units. It issued loans, handled state appropriations for agriculture, directed the operations of the rural credit cooperatives, and carried out overall supervision of rural financial affairs. The Agricultural Bank was headquartered in Beijing and had a network of branches throughout the country. It flourished in the late 1950s and mid-1960s but languished thereafter until the late 1970s, when the functions and autonomy of the Agricultural Bank were increased substantially to help promote higher agricultural production. In the 1980s it was restructured again and given greater authority in order to support the growth and diversification of agriculture under the responsibility system.

The People's Construction Bank managed state appropriations and loans for capital construction. It checked the activities of loan recipients to ensure that the funds were used for their designated construction purpose. Money was disbursed in stages as a project progressed. The reform policy shifted the main source of investment funding from the government budget to bank loans and increased the responsibility and activities of the People's Construction Bank.

Rural credit cooperatives were small, collectively owned savings and lending organizations that were the main source of small-scale financial services at the local level in the countryside. They handled deposits and short-term loans for individual farm families, villages, and cooperative organizations. Subject to the direction of the Agricultural Bank, they followed uniform state banking policies but acted as independent units for accounting purposes. In 1985 rural credit cooperatives held total deposits of ¥72.5 billion.

Urban credit cooperatives were a relatively new addition to the banking system in the mid-1980s, when they first began widespread operations. As commercial opportunities grew in the reform period, the thousands of individual and collective enterprises that sprang up in urban areas created a need for small-scale financial services that the formal banks were not prepared to meet. Bank officials therefore encouraged the expansion of urban credit cooperatives as a valuable addition to the banking system. In 1986 there were more than 1,100 urban credit cooperatives, which held a total of ¥3.7 billion in deposits and made loans worth ¥1.9 billion.

In the mid-1980s the banking system still lacked some of the services and characteristics that were considered basic in most countries. Interbank relations were very limited, and interbank borrowing and lending was virtually unknown. Checking accounts were used by very few individuals, and bank credit cards did not exist. In 1986 initial steps were taken in some of these areas. Interbank borrowing and lending networks were created among twenty-seven cities along the Yangtze River and among fourteen cities in north China. Interregional financial networks were created to link banks in eleven leading cities all over China, including Shenyang, Guangzhou, Wuhan, Chongqing, and Xi'an and also to link the branches of the Agricultural Bank. The first Chinese credit card, the Great Wall Card, was introduced in June 1986 to be used for foreign exchange transactions. Another financial innovation in 1986 was the opening of China's first stock exchanges since 1949. Small stock exchanges began operations somewhat tentatively in Shenyang, Liaoning Province, in August 1986 and in Shanghai in September 1986.

Throughout the history of the People's Republic, the banking system has exerted close control over financial transactions and the money supply. All government departments, publicly and collectively owned economic units, and social, political, military, and educational organizations were required to hold their financial balances as bank deposits. They were also instructed to keep on hand only enough cash to meet daily expenses; all major financial transactions were to be conducted through banks. Payment for goods and services exchanged by economic units was accomplished by debiting the account of the purchasing unit and crediting that of the selling unit by the appropriate amount. This practice effectively helped to minimize the need for currency.

Since 1949 China's leaders have urged the Chinese people to build up personal savings accounts to reduce the demand for consumer goods and increase the amount of capital available for investment. Small branch offices of savings banks were conveniently located throughout the urban areas. In the countryside savings were deposited with the rural credit cooperatives, which could be found in most towns and villages. In 1986 savings deposits for the entire country totaled over ¥223.7 billion.

Supervisory bodies

The People's Bank of China (PBOC) is China's central bank, which formulates and implements monetary policy. The PBOC maintains the banking sector's payment, clearing and settlement systems, and manages official foreign exchange and gold reserves. It oversees the State Administration of Foreign Exchange (SAFE) for setting foreign-exchange policies.

According to the 1995 Central Bank law, PBOC has full autonomy in applying the monetary instruments, including setting interest rate for commercial banks and trading in government bonds. The State Council maintains oversight of PBOC policies.

China Banking Regulatory Commission (CBRC) was officially launched on April 28, 2003, to take over the supervisory role of the PBOC. The goal of the landmark reform is to improve the efficiency of bank supervision and to help the PBOC to further focus on the macro economy and currency policy.

According to the official Announcement by CBRC posted on its website, the CBRC is responsible for "the regulation and supervision of banks, asset management companies, trust and investment companies as well as other deposit-taking financial institutions. Its mission is to maintain a safe and sound banking system in China."

Domestic key players

State-owned commercial banks – The Big Four

In 1995, the Chinese Government introduced the Commercial Bank Law to commercialize the operations of the four state-owned banks, the Bank of China (BOC), the China Construction Bank (CCB), the Agricultural Bank of China (ABC), and the Industrial and Commercial Bank of China (ICBC).

The Industrial & Commercial Bank of China (ICBC) is the largest bank in China by total assets, total employees and total customers. ICBC differentiates itself from the other State Owned Commercial Banks by being second in foreign exchange business and 1st in RMB clearing business. It used to be the major supplier of funds to China's urban areas and manufacturing sector.

The Bank of China (BOC) specializes in foreign-exchange transactions and trade finance. In 2002, BOC Hong Kong (Holdings) was successfully listed on the Hong Kong Stock Exchange. The USD2.8 billion offering was over-subscribed by 7.5 times. The deal was a significant move in the reform of China's banking industry.

The China Construction Bank (CCB) specializes in medium to long-term credit for long term specialized projects, such as infrastructure projects and urban housing development.

The Agriculture Bank of China (ABC) specializes in providing financing to China's agricultural sector and offers wholesale and retail banking services to farmers, township and village enterprises (TVEs) and other rural institutions.

Policy banks

Three new "policy" banks, the Agricultural Development Bank of China (ADBC), China Development Bank (CDB), and the Export-Import Bank of China (Chexim), were established in 1994 to take over the government-directed spending functions of the four state-owned commercial banks. These banks are responsible for financing economic and trade development and state-invested projects.

ADBC provides funds for agricultural development projects in rural areas; the CDB specializes in infrastructure financing, and Chexim specializes in trade financing.

Foreign Sponsored State Banks

Due to massive debt problems facing the Chinese economy, the PCB introduced the Foreign Country Sponsored State Banks in late 2016. This type of financial institution is formed when a bank from a different country is allowed to set up retail commercial operations in a joint venture with the PCB. The idea is that foreign players with a large appetite for risk will be incentivized to start operations in China, and the PCB will retain supervision of the bank and possibly remove leverage from the Chinese banking system. Central banks from Egypt and Switzerland are the first banks to be approved for operations, and they will begin those operations as soon as February 2017.

City commercial banks

The third significant group in Chinese banking market is the city commercial banks. Many of them were founded on the basis of urban credit cooperatives. The first one was Shenzhen City Commercial Bank in 1995. In 1998, PBOC announced that all urban cooperative banks change their name to city commercial bank. And there are 69 city commercial banks set up from 1995 to 1998. In 2005 there were 112 city commercial banks in all of China. This number has increased through additional transformations to 140 in 2009. Most city commercial banks have strong ties to their local government and are majority or wholly state owned. Since 2005 some city commercial banks diversify their shareholders, inviting Chinese and international private companies to take minority shares, merging and cross-shareholding. Some of the banks have listed their shares. The city commercial banks market orientation is towards supporting the regional economy, but also towards financing local infrastructure and other government projects. Since 2008 a strong trend has emerged for city commercial banks to extend business beyond their home region. They are also often the main shareholder behind village and township banks (VTB). Some have founded so called small loans units to serve smaller business clients better. Taizhou City Commercial Bank, Bank of Beijing, Bank of Tianjin and Bank of Ningbo are examples for city commercial banks.

Trust and investment corporations

In the midst of the reforms of the 1980s, the government established some new investment banks that engaged in various forms of merchant and investment banking activities. However, many of the 240 or so international trust and investment corporations (ITICs) established by government agencies and provincial authorities experienced severe liquidity problems after the bankruptcy of the Guangdong International Trust and Investment Corporation (GITIC) in late 1998. The largest surviving ITIC is China International Trust and Investment Corporation (CITIC), which has a banking subsidiary known as China CITIC Bank.

County banks

A County Bank is a kind of financial institution with the purpose of boosting rural economic development, which has developed in China since 2005.

Reforms in the banking industry

Years of government-directed lending has presented Chinese banks with large amounts of non-performing loans. According to the Central Bank's report, non-performing loans account for 21.4% to 26.1% of total lending of China's four big banks in 2002. In 1999, four asset management companies (AMC) were established to transfer the non-performing assets from the banks. The AMCs plan to repackage the non-performing loans into viable assets and sell them off to the investors.

PBOC has encouraged banks to diversify their portfolios by increasing their services to the private sector and individual consumers. In July 2000, a personal credit rating system was launched in Shanghai to be used to assess consumer credit risk and set ratings standards. This is an important move in developing China's consumer credit industry, and increase bank loans to individuals.

The central government has allowed several small banks to raise capital through bonds or stock issues. Followed the listing of Shenzhen Development Bank and Pudong Development Bank, China Minsheng Bank, then the only private bank in China, was listed on the Shanghai Stock Exchange (A-Share) in December 2000. More Chinese banks are expected to list in the next two years in order to raise capital.

The reform of the banking system has been accompanied by PBOC's decision to decontrol interest rates. Market-based interest rate reform is intended to establish the pricing mechanism of the deposit and lending rates based on market supply and demand. The central bank would continue to adjust and guide the interest rate development, which allows the market mechanism to play a dominant role in financial resource allocation. The sequence of the reform is to liberalize the interest rate of foreign currency before that of domestic currency, lending before deposit, large amount and long term before small amount and short term.

As a first step, the PBOC liberalized the interest rates for foreign currency loans and large deposits (US$3 million and over) in September 2000. Rate for deposits below US$3 million remain subject to PBOC control. In March 2002, the PBOC unified foreign currency interest rate policies for Chinese and foreign financial institutions in China. Small foreign exchange deposits of Chinese residents with foreign banks in China were included in the PBOC interest rate administration of small foreign exchange deposits, so that domestic and foreign financial institutions are treated fairly with regard to the interest rate policy of foreign exchange deposits.

As interest rate liberalization progressed, the PPOC liberalized, simplified or abandoned 114 categories of interest rates initially under control since 1996. At present, 34 categories of interest rates remain subject to PBOC control. The full liberalization of interest rates on other deposit accounts, including checking and saving accounts, is expected to take much longer. On the lending side, market-determined interest rates on loans will first be introduced in rural areas and then followed by rate liberalization in cities.

Deposit insurance

According to a confidential informant privy to the agenda at the closed meeting, creating a system of deposit insurance was expected to be discussed at the annual Central Economic Work Conference in December, 2012; studying deposit insurance was included in the 5 year plan for 2011–2015. The government's practice, in the absence of formal provisions for deposit insurance or bank failure, has been to reimburse all depositors, large or small, at small banks and rural cooperatives which fail; this is done to avoid the social unrest which might accompany a bank run. Large banks which might have failed without government support have been propped up. Introduction of deposit insurance is part of a projected general reform of the banking system which would wean banks from their close relationship to state-owned enterprises; banks strongly prefer to lend to state-owned enterprises because payment is seen to be guaranteed. Loans to private firms and individuals are seen as risky; consequently, the private sector is starved for credit.

If deposit insurance premiums were based on volume of deposits China's Big Four banks, which would not be permitted to fail in any event, would pay hefty premiums thus subsidizing smaller banks. If adopted, it is anticipated that drafting of regulations and introduction of a system of deposit insurance would take at least a year. In order to attract depositors some banks in China have introduced deposit accounts which use deposited funds to make riskier loans and offer higher interest. Introduction of a scheme of deposit insurance which guarantees only standard low-interest accounts might serve to clarify the situation, explicitly excluding such trust funds from deposit guarantees.

Credit and Debit cards

By the end of the first quarter of 2009, about 1,888,374,100 (1.89 billion) bank cards had been issued in China. Of these cards, 1,737,901,000 (1.74 billion) or 92% were debit cards, while the rest (150,473,100, or 150.5 million) were credit cards. In 2010 China had over 2.4 billion bankcards in circulation growing approximately 16% from the end of 2009. At the end of 2008, China had approximately 1.84 million POS machines and 167,500 ATMs. About 1.18 million merchants in China accept banking cards.

At the end of 2008, there were 196 issuers in China that issue China UnionPay-branded cards. These issuers include the 'big four' banks (Industrial and Commercial Bank of China, the Bank of China, China Construction Bank, and the Agricultural Bank of China), as well as fast-growing second tier banks and city commercial banks, and even some foreign banks with local operations.

Most of China's state-owned commercial banks now issue dual-currency cards, allowing cardholders to purchase goods within China in RMB and overseas in US dollars (Visa/MasterCard/AmEx/JCB), Euros (Visa/MasterCard), Australian dollars (MasterCard), or Japanese yen (JCB). However, only Bank of China provides yen and Australian dollar-denominated credit cards.

According to a 2003 research study by VISA, the average per transaction purchase with a card was USD 253. Consumers used their credit cards mainly to purchase houses, vehicles, and home appliances, as well as to pay utility bills.

One major issue is the lack of a national credit bureau to provide credit information for banks to evaluate individual loan applicants. In 2002, the Shanghai Information Office and the People's Bank of

China Shanghai branch established the first personal credit data organization involving 15 commercial banks. The Chinese Government, aiming to promote a nationwide credit system, has also set up a credit system research group. At present, large cities, such as Beijing, Guangzhou, Shenzhen, Chongqing, and Chengdu, are calling for a reliable credit data system. The PBOC is currently evaluating the feasibility of establishing a nationwide credit bureau.

Other obstacles include lack of merchant acceptance and a weak infrastructure for card processing. At present, only 2% of merchants in China are equipped to handle card transactions, although in some major cities like Shanghai the percentage is over 30%. China UnionPay was established to set up a national processing network connecting merchants and banks. China UnionPay has set up bankcard network service centers in 18 cities in addition to a national bankcard information switch center.

Products and services in the credit card system that the Chinese government wants to develop are credit card-related hardware, including POS and ATMs, credit card-related software for banks and merchants; and Credit and risk management training programs.

Foreign banks

China's entry into the WTO is expected to create opportunities for foreign banks. As a milestone move to honor its WTO commitments, China released the *Rules for Implementing the Regulations Governing Foreign Financial Institutions in the People's Republic of China* in January 2002. The rules provide detailed regulations for implementing the administration of the establishment, registration, scope of business, qualification, supervision, dissolution and liquidation of foreign financial institutions. They also stipulate that foreign bank branches conducting full aspects of foreign-currency business and full aspects of RMB business to all categories of clients are required to have operating capital of at least 600 million RMB (USD\$72.3 million), of which at least 400 million RMB (US\$48.2 million) must be held in RMB and at least 200 million RMB (US\$24.1 million) in freely convertible currency.

Client restriction on foreign currency business was lifted immediately after China's entry into the WTO on December 11, 2001. Since then, foreign financial institutions have been permitted to provide foreign currency services to Chinese enterprises and individuals, and have been permitted to provide local currency business to all Chinese clients by the end of 2006. In 2007 five non-mainland banks were allowed to issue bank cards in China, with Bank of East Asia also allowed to issue UnionPay credit cards in the mainland (United Overseas Bank and Sumitomo Mitsui Financial Group have only issued cards in their home countries; they are not yet allowed to issue cards within the mainland). In May 2009 Woori Bank became the first Korean bank allowed to issue UnionPay debit cards (it issues UnionPay credit cards in Korea only).

Furthermore, when China entered the WTO, geographic restrictions placed on RMB-denominated business was phased out in four major cities—Shanghai, Shenzhen, Tianjin and Dalian. Then, on December 1, 2002, foreign-funded banks were allowed to commence RMB-denominated business in Guangzhou, Zhuhai, Qingdao, Nanjing and Wuhan.

Electronic banking

In 1994, China started the "Golden Card Project," enabling cards issued by banks to be used all over the country through a network. The establishment of the China Association of Banks rapidly promoted the inter-bank card network and by the end of 2004, the inter-region-inter-bank network had reached 600 cities, including all prefecture-level cities and more than 300 economically developed county-level cities.

FOREIGN-EXCHANGE RESERVES OF CHINA

The foreign-exchange reserves of China are the government of China's holdings of cash, bank deposits, bonds, and other financial assets denominated in currencies other than China's national currency (renminbi). In October 2016 China's foreign exchange reserves totaled US$3.12 trillion, the lowest total since 2011, but remained higher than the foreign exchange reserves of any other nation.

The management of foreign-exchange reserves is governed by the State Administration of Foreign Exchange (SAFE) and the People's Bank of China. The composition of foreign-exchange reserves is a state secret in China.

Size

The nation's foreign exchange reserves are held by China's central bank. The total sum of the reserves is regularly announced by the central bank. At the end of September 2015, the foreign-exchange reserves of China were US$3.51 trillion, while, at the end of January 2016, they stood at US$3.23 trillion. They are the highest among foreign-exchange holdings of nations in the world, ostensibly more than triple the size of next country on the list.

Composition

The exact composition of the foreign-exchange reserves of China is a state secret. Foreign analysts agree that about two-thirds of Chinese foreign-exchange reserves are held in U.S. Dollars, approximately one-fifth in Euros, and almost all the rest in Japanese Yen and British pounds.

Most of China's foreign-exchange reserves are held in U.S. dollar-denominated financial assets such as U.S. Treasury securities. Since 2008, when it overtook Japan in this respect, China is the largest foreign owner of U.S. Treasury securities, accounting for about 22 percent of all U.S. Treasuries held by non-Americans.

Concerns over Chinese holdings of U.S. Debt

Many American and other economic analysts have expressed concerns on account of the People's Republic of China's "extensive" holdings of United States government debt, as part of their reserves.

The National Defense Authorization Act of the fiscal year 2012 included a provision requiring the Secretary of Defense to conduct a "national security risk assessment of U.S. federal debt held by China." The Department issued its report in July 2012, stating that "attempting to use U.S. Treasury securities as a coercive tool would have limited effect and likely would do more harm to China than to the United States. As the threat is not credible and the effect would be limited even if carried out, it does not offer China deterrence options, whether in the diplomatic, military, or economic realms, and this would remain true both in peacetime and in scenarios of crisis or war."

The 112th United States Congress introduced legislation whose aim was the assessment of the implications of China's ownership of U.S. debt. The 2013 Report claimed that "[a] potentially serious short-term problem would emerge if China decided to *suddenly* reduce their liquid U.S. financial assets significantly" [emphasis in the original text], noting also that Federal Reserve System Chairman Ben Bernanke had, in 2007, stated that "because foreign holdings of U.S. Treasury securities represent only a small part of total U.S. credit market debt outstanding, U.S. credit markets should be able to absorb without great difficulty any shift of foreign allocations." A significant number of economists and analysts dismiss any and all concerns over foreign holdings of United States government debt denominated in U.S. Dollars, including China's holdings.

However, other economists have also argued that it is only China and Japan's willingness to hold US dollars that prevent a shock to the global economy. Therefore, it is arguable that as the Chinese economy gradually shifts from an export based economy into a service economy, their need to hold US dollars in order to strengthen the renminbi will diminish.

HEDGE FUND INDUSTR Y IN CHINA

Hedge funds started in China in the early 1990s, and has so far undergone four stages: infancy, formation, rapid expansion, and adjustment and standardization.

Categories

Currently hedge funds in China fall into two categories. One is those companies backed up by the government, including brokers managing pooled property, trust and investment companies' trust and investment projects, and investment companies managing their own capital. The other is private hedge funds. Under the name of "Investment Consulting Company" or "Investment Management Company", they provide management for pooled property.

Economic growth trend

Against the background of China's fast growing economy, the number of hedge fund investors is increasing rapidly in the country, and the total amount of their wealth is increasing in step. By the end of June 2008, China's residents had RMB 19,460bn ($2,820bn) in bank deposits, of which 80% was in the name of 20% of the population. With such a huge amount of cash assets in hand, the wealthy's strong investment demand has provided hedge funds in China with a sufficient supply of capital. In addition, China's companies also have a huge sum of spare cash, which is also a primary source of capital for hedge funds.

Share of GDP

Data showed that hedge funds account for 0.6% of the GDP in the USA, 0.35% in Europe, 0.2% in Asia, while only 0.1% in China.

It is expected that China's GDP would quadruple in 10 years time and hedge funds would be about 0.4% of the country's GDP. In this case, China's hedge funds would expand 12-fold, and place China second in the world for hedge fund investments.

Bank deposits

Year Residential Bank Deposits in China (billion RMB)
- 2003 10,360
- 2004 11,960
- 2005 14,110
- 2006 16,160
- 2007 17,250
- 2008H1 19,460

8

China's Silk Road Economic Belt

Investment and trade cooperation is a major task in building the Belt and Road. We should strive to improve investment and trade facilitation, and remove investment and trade barriers for the creation of a sound business environment within the region and in all related countries. We will discuss with countries and regions along the Belt and Road on opening free trade areas so as to unleash the potential for expanded cooperation.

Countries along the Belt and Road should enhance customs cooperation such as information exchange, mutual recognition of regulations, and mutual assistance in law enforcement; improve bilateral and multilateral cooperation in the fields of inspection and quarantine, certification and accreditation, standard measurement, and statistical information; and work to ensure that the WTO Trade Facilitation Agreement takes effect and is implemented.

We should improve the customs clearance facilities of border ports, establish a "single-window" in border ports, reduce customs clearance costs, and improve customs clearance capability.

We should increase cooperation in supply chain safety and convenience, improve the coordination of cross-border supervision procedures, promote online checking of inspection and quarantine certificates, and facilitate mutual recognition of Authorized Economic Operators. We should lower non-tariff barriers, jointly improve the transparency of technical trade measures, and enhance trade liberalization and facilitation.

We should expand trading areas, improve trade structure, explore new growth areas of trade, and promote trade balance. We should make innovations in our forms of trade, and develop cross-border e-commerce and other modern business models. A service trade support system should be set up to consolidate and expand conventional trade, and efforts to develop modern service trade should be strengthened. We should integrate investment and trade, and promote trade through investment.

We should speed up investment facilitation, eliminate investment barriers, and push forward negotiations on bilateral investment protection agreements and double taxation avoidance agreements to protect the lawful rights and interests of investors.

We should expand mutual investment areas, deepen cooperation in agriculture, forestry, animal husbandry and fisheries, agricultural machinery manufacturing and farm produce processing, and promote cooperation in marine-product farming, deep-sea fishing, aquatic product processing, seawater desalination, marine biopharmacy, ocean engineering technology, environmental protection industries, marine tourism and other fields.

We should increase cooperation in the exploration and development of coal, oil, gas, metal minerals and other conventional energy sources; advance cooperation in hydropower, nuclear power, wind power, solar power and other clean, renewable energy sources; and promote cooperation in the processing and conversion of energy and resources at or near places where they are exploited, so as to create an integrated industrial chain of energy and resource cooperation. We should enhance cooperation in deep-processing technology, equipment and engineering services in the fields of energy and resources.

We should push forward cooperation in emerging industries. In accordance with the principles of mutual complementarity and mutual benefit, we should promote in-depth cooperation with other countries along the Belt and Road in new-generation information technology, biotechnology, new energy technology, new materials and other emerging industries, and establish entrepreneurial and investment cooperation mechanisms.

We should improve the division of labor and distribution of industrial chains by encouraging the entire industrial chain and related industries to develop in concert; establish R&D, production and marketing systems; and improve industrial supporting capacity and the overall competitiveness of regional industries. We should increase the openness of our service industry to each other to accelerate the development of regional service industries. We should explore a new mode of investment cooperation, working together to build all forms of industrial parks such as overseas economic and trade cooperation zones and cross-border economic cooperation zones, and promote industrial cluster development.

We should promote ecological progress in conducting investment and trade, increase cooperation in conserving eco-environment, protecting biodiversity, and tackling climate change, and join hands to make the Silk Road an environment-friendly one.

We welcome companies from all countries to invest in China, and encourage Chinese enterprises to participate in infrastructure construction in other countries along the Belt and Road, and make industrial investments there. We support localized operation and management of Chinese companies to boost the local economy, increase local employment, improve local livelihood, and take social responsibilities in protecting local biodiversity and eco-environment.

Financial integration

Financial integration is an important underpinning for implementing the Belt and Road Initiative. We should deepen financial cooperation, and make more efforts in building a currency stability system, investment and financing system and credit information system in Asia.

We should expand the scope and scale of bilateral currency swap and settlement with other countries along the Belt and Road, open and develop the bond market in Asia, make joint efforts to establish the Asian Infrastructure Investment Bank and BRICS New Development Bank, conduct negotiation among related parties on establishing Shanghai Cooperation Organization (SCO) financing institution, and set up and put into operation the Silk Road Fund as early as possible.

We should strengthen practical cooperation of China-ASEAN Interbank Association and SCO Interbank Association, and carry out multilateral financial cooperation in the form of syndicated loans and bank credit. We will support the efforts of governments of the countries along the Belt and Road and their companies and financial institutions with good credit-rating to issue Renminbi bonds in China. Qualified Chinese financial institutions and companies are encouraged to issue bonds in both Renminbi and foreign currencies outside China, and use the funds thus collected in countries along the Belt and Road. We should strengthen financial regulation cooperation, encourage the signing of MOUs on cooperation in bilateral financial regulation, and establish an efficient regulation coordination mechanism in the region.

We should improve the system of risk response and crisis management, build a regional financial risk early-warning system, and create an exchange and cooperation mechanism of addressing cross-border risks and crisis.

.We should increase cross-border exchange and cooperation between credit investigation regulators, credit investigation institutions and credit rating institutions. We should give full play to the role of the Silk Road Fund and that of sovereign wealth funds of countries along the Belt and Road, and encourage commercial equity investment funds and private funds to participate in the construction of key projects of the Initiative.

BELT AND ROAD INITIA TIVE

The Belt and Road Initiative alludes to the Silk Road Economic Belt and 21st Century Maritime Silk Road, a noteworthy improvement system dispatched by the Chinese government with the expectation of advancing financial co-operation among nations along the proposed Belt and Road courses.

The Initiative has been intended to improve the methodical free stream of financial variables and the effective allotment of assets. It is additionally proposed to further market combination and make a provincial financial co-operation structure of advantage to all.

The National Development and Reform Commission (NDRC) issued its Vision and Actions on Jointly Building the Silk Road Economic Belt and 21st Century Maritime Silk Road on 28 March 2015. This delineated the system, key territories of co-operation and co-operation instruments with respect to the Belt and Road Initiative.

Conceptual Framework

The Belt and Road Initiative aims to connect Asia, Europe and Africa along five routes. The Silk Road Economic Belt focusses on: (1) linking China to Europe through Central Asia and Russia; (2) connecting China with the Middle East through Central Asia; and (3) bringing together China and Southeast Asia, South Asia and the Indian Ocean. The 21st Century Maritime Silk Road, meanwhile, focusses on using

Chinese coastal ports to: (4) link China with Europe through the South China Sea and Indian Ocean; and (5) connect China with the South Pacific Ocean through the South China Sea.

Focussing on the above five routes, the Belt and Road will take advantage of international transport routes as well as core cities and key ports to further strengthen collaboration and build six international economic co-operation corridors. These have been identified as the New Eurasia Land Bridge, China-Mongolia-Russia, China-Central Asia-West Asia, China-Indochina Peninsula, China-Pakistan, and Bangladesh-China-India-Myanmar.

The New Eurasia Land Bridge Economic Corridor

The New Eurasia Land Bridge, also known as the Second Eurasia Land Bridge, is an international railway line running from Lianyungang in China's Jiangsu province through Alashankou in Xinjiang to Rotterdam in Holland.

The China section of the line comprises the Lanzhou-Lianyungang Railway and the Lanzhou-Xinjiang Railway and stretches through eastern, central and western China. After exiting Chinese territory, the new land bridge passes through Kazakhstan, Russia, Belarus and Poland, reaching a number of coastal ports in Europe.

Capitalising on the New Eurasia Land Bridge, China has opened an international freight rail route linking Chongqing to Duisburg (Germany); a direct freight train running between Wuhan and Mìlník and Pardubice (Czech Republic); a freight rail route from Chengdu to Lodz (Poland); and a freight rail route from Zhengzhou to Hamburg (Germany). All these new rail routes offer rail-to-rail freight transport, as well as the convenience of "one declaration, one inspection, one cargo release" for any cargo transported.

The China-Mongolia-Russia Economic Corridor

Linked by land, China, Mongolia and Russia have long established various economic ties and co-operation by way of frontier trade and cross-border co-operation. In September 2014, when the three country's heads of state met for the first time at the Shanghai Co-operation Organisation (SCO) Dushanbe Summit, agreement was reached on forging tripartite co-operation on the basis of China-Russia, China-Mongolia and Russia-Mongolia bilateral ties. At the same meeting, the principles, directions and key areas of trilateral co-operation were defined. The three heads of state also agreed to bring together the building of China's Silk Road Economic Belt, the renovation of Russia's Eurasia Land Bridge and the proposed development of Mongolia's Steppe Road.

This commitment will strengthen rail and highway connectivity and construction, advance customs clearance and transport facilitation, promote cross-national co-operation in transportation, and help establish the China-Russia-Mongolia Economic Corridor. In July 2015, the three leaders held a second meeting in the Russian city of Ufa. This second summit saw the official adoption of the *Mid-term Roadmap for Development of Trilateral Co-operation between China, Russia and Mongolia.*

China-Central Asia-West Asia Economic Corridor

The China-Central Asia-West Asia Economic Corridor runs from Xinjiang in China and exits the country via Alashankou to join the railway networks of Central Asia and West Asia before reaching the Mediterranean coast and the Arabian Peninsula. The corridor mainly covers five countries in Central Asia (Kazakhstan, Kyrgyzstan, Tajikistan, Uzbekistan and Turkmenistan) as well as Iran and Turkey in West Asia.

At the third China-Central Asia Co-operation Forum, held in Shandong in June 2015, a commitment to "jointly building the Silk Road Economic Belt" was incorporated into a joint declaration signed by China and the five Central Asian countries. Prior to that, China had signed bilateral agreements on the building of the Silk Road Economic Belt with Tajikistan, Kazakhstan and Kyrgyzstan. China had also concluded a co-operation document with Uzbekistan on the building of the Silk Road Economic Belt.

This was aimed at further deepening and expanding mutually beneficial co-operation in such areas as trade, investment, finance, transport and communication. The national development strategies of the five Central Asian countries – including Kazakhstan's "Road to Brightness", Tajikistan's "Energy, Transport and Food" (a three-pronged strategy aimed at revitalising the country), and Turkmenistan's "Strong and Happy Era" – all share common ground with the establishment of the Silk Road Economic Belt.

China-Indochina Peninsula Economic Corridor

During the Fifth Leaders Meeting on Greater Mekong Sub-regional Economic Co-operation, held in Bangkok in December 2014, Chinese Premier Li Keqiang put forward three suggestions with regard to deepening the relations between China and the five countries in the Indochina Peninsula. The suggestions included: (1) jointly planning and building an extensive transportation network, as well as number of industrial co-operation projects; (2) creating a new mode of co-operation for fundraising; and (3) promoting sustainable and co-ordinated socio-economic development.

Currently, the countries along the Greater Mekong River are engaged in building nine cross-national highways, connecting east and west and linking north to south. A number of these construction projects have already been completed. Guangxi, for example, has already finished work on an expressway leading to the Friendship Gate and the port of Dongxing at the China-Vietnam border. The province has also opened an international rail line, running from Nanning to Hanoi, as well as introducing air routes to several major Southeast Asian cities.

China-Pakistan Economic Corridor

The concept of the China-Pakistan Economic Corridor was first raised by Premier Li Keqiang during his visit to Pakistan in May 2013. At the time, the objective was to build an economic corridor running from Kashgar, Xinjiang, in the north, to Pakistan's Gwadar Port in the south.

At present, the two governments have mapped out a provisional long-term plan for building highways, railways, oil and natural gas pipelines and optic fibre networks stretching from Kashgar to Gwadar Port. According to a joint declaration issued by China and Pakistan in Islamabad in April 2015, the two countries will proactively advance key co-operation projects, including phase II of the upgrade and renovation of the Karakoram Highway (the Thakot-Havelian section), an expressway at the east bay of Gwadar Port, a new international airport, an expressway from Karachi to Lahore (the Multan-Sukkur section), the Lahore rail transport orange line, the Haier-Ruba economic zone, and the China-Pakistan cross-national optic fibre network.

Bangladesh-China-India-Myanmar Economic Corridor

In a series of meetings during Premier Li Keqiang's visit to India in May 2013, China and India jointly proposed the building of the Bangladesh-China-India-Myanmar Economic Corridor. In December 2013, the Bangladesh-China-India-Myanmar Economic Corridor Joint Working Group convened its first meeting in Kunming. Official representatives from the four countries conducted in-depth discussions with regard to the development prospects, priority areas of co-operation and co-operation mechanisms for the economic corridor. They also reached extensive consensus on co-operation in such areas as transportation infrastructure, investment and commercial circulation, and people-to-people connectivity.

The four parties signed meeting minutes and agreed the Bangladesh-China-India-Myanmar Economic Corridor joint study programme, establishing a mechanism for promoting co-operation among the four governments.

Key Areas of Co-operation

The five major goals of the Belt and Road Initiative are: policy co-ordination, facilities connectivity, unimpeded trade, financial integration, and people-to-people bonds.

In terms of specifics, policy co-ordination means that countries along the belt and road will, via consultation on an equal footing, jointly formulate development plans and measures for advancing cross-national or regional co-operation; resolve problems arising from co-operation through consultation; and jointly provide policy support to practical co-operation and large-scale project implementation.

Facilities connectivity refers to prioritising areas of construction as part of the Belt and Road strategy. Efforts will be made to give priority to removing barriers in the missing sections and bottleneck areas of core international transportation passages, advancing the construction of port infrastructure facilities, and clearing land-water intermodal transport passages. The connectivity of infrastructure facilities, including railways, highways, air routes, telecommunications, oil and natural gas pipelines and ports, will also be promoted. This will form part of a move to establish an infrastructure network connecting various Asian sub-regions with other parts of Asia, Europe and Africa.

In order to facilitate unimpeded trade, steps will be taken to resolve investment and trade facilitation issues, reduce investment and trade barriers, lower trade and investment costs, as well as to promote regional economic integration. Efforts will also be made to broaden the scope of trade, propel trade development through investment, and strengthen co-operation in the industry chain with all related countries.

With regard to financial integration, action will be taken to enhance co-ordination in monetary policy, expand the scope of local currency settlement and currency exchange in trade and investment between countries along the route, deepen multilateral and bilateral financial co-operation, set up regional development financial institutions, strengthen co-operation in monitoring financial risks, and enhance the ability of managing financial risks through regional arrangements.

In terms of people-to-people bonds, efforts will be made to promote exchanges and dialogues between different cultures, strengthen friendly interactions between the people of various countries, and heighten mutual understanding and traditional friendships. This will all form the basis for the advancement of regional co-operation.

Co-operation Mechanisms

The Belt and Road Initiative upholds the principles of jointly developing the programme through consultation with all interested parties. Existing bilateral and multilateral co-operation mechanisms will be utilised to promote the integration of the development strategies of the countries along the route.

Steps will be taken to advance the signing of co-operation memorandums of understanding or co-operation plans for the establishment of a number of bilateral co-operation demonstration projects. Efforts will also be made to set up a sound bilateral joint work mechanism, and to devise an implementation plan and action roadmap for advancing the Belt and Road strategy.

The Silk Road Fund

The US$40 billion Silk Road Fund has been established to finance the Belt and Road Initiative. It will invest mainly in infrastructure and resources, as well as in industrial and financial cooperation. The Fund was set up as a limited liability company in December 2014 with its founding shareholders including China's State Administration of Foreign Exchange, the China Investment Corp, the Export-Import Bank of China and the China Development Bank.

The Fund will comply with market rules and the international order of finance, and welcome participation from domestic and overseas investors, such as the China-Africa Development Fund and the Asian Infrastructure Investment Bank.

The Asian Infrastructure Investment Bank (AIIB)

The AIIB, a new multilateral development bank (MDB), has been set up with a view to complementing and cooperating with the existing MDBs in order to address infrastructure needs in Asia. AIIB will focus on the development of infrastructure and other productive sectors in Asia, including energy and power, transportation and telecommunications, rural infrastructure and agriculture development, water supply and sanitation, environmental protection, urban development and logistics.

As of December 2015, all of the 57 Prospective Founding Members of AIIB had signed the Articles of Agreement. The initial signatories were Australia, Austria, Azerbaijan, Bangladesh, Brazil, Brunei Darussalam, Cambodia, China, Denmark, Egypt, Finland, France, Georgia, Germany, Iceland, India, Indonesia, Iran, Israel, Italy, Jordan, Kazakhstan, Republic of Korea, Kyrgyz Republic, Kuwait, Lao PDR, Luxembourg, Malaysia, Maldives, Malta, Mongolia, Myanmar, Nepal, Netherlands, New Zealand, Norway, Oman, Pakistan, Philippines, Poland, Portugal, Qatar, Russia, Saudi Arabia, Singapore, South Africa, Spain, Sri Lanka, Sweden, Switzerland, Tajikistan, Thailand, Turkey, the United Arab Emirates, the United Kingdom, Uzbekistan, and Vietnam.

The AIIB Articles of Agreement entered into force on 25 December 2015. On 16 January 2016, the Board of Governors held its inaugural meeting, declaring the Bank open for business and electing Mr. Jin Liqun as President for an initial five-year term.

CHINA'S ONE BELT ONE ROAD INITIA TIVE

President Xi Jinping propelled China's "One Belt, One Road" (OBOR) activity in 2013 with the expressed expect to interface significant Eurasian economies through framework, exchange and venture. The activity was later indicated to contain two worldwide exchange associations: The area based "Silk Road Economic Belt" and oceangoing "Sea Silk Road."

The "Belt" is a system of overland street and rail courses, oil and characteristic gas pipelines, and other framework extends that will extend from Xi'an in focal China through Central Asia and at last reach similarly as Moscow, Rotterdam, and Venice. As opposed to one course, belt passages are set to keep running along the real Eurasian Land Bridges, through China-Mongolia-Russia, China-Central and

West Asia, China-Indochina Peninsula, China-Pakistan, Bangladesh-China-India-Myanmar.

The "Street" is its sea comparable: a system of arranged ports and other beach front framework extends that dab the guide from South and Southeast Asia to East Africa and the northern Mediterranean Sea. At this stage, the idea, extension and nature of the activity are still liquid and the state of OBOR is liable to develop after some time. Since it was propelled by President Xi, the activity is prone to be unmistakable in China's abroad venture all through his term in office.

How big is it? OBOR can be big, indeed. In its largest definition, OBOR would include 65 countries, 4.4 billion people and about 40 percent of global GDP. China is backing the plan with considerable resources, setting up a New Silk Road Fund of $40 billion to promote private investment along OBOR. The New Silk Road Fund is sponsored by China's foreign exchange reserves, as well as government investment and lending arms.

In addition, the Asia Infrastructure Investment Bank is widely expected to support the initiative with a considerable share of its $100 billion in lending, and the China Development Bank reportedly said it would invest almost $900 billion into more than 900 projects involving 60 countries to bolster the initiative. The Economist magazine reported that $1 trillion in "government money" would be spent on the initiative.

More than infrastructure

The vision document for OBOR goes well beyond infrastructure, envisioning closer coordination of economic development policies, harmonization of technical standards for infrastructure, removal of investment and trade barriers, establishment of free trade areas, financial cooperation and "people to people bonds" involving cultural and academic exchanges, personnel exchanges and cooperation, media cooperation, youth and women exchanges, and volunteer services.

What could be the impact of the initiative? OBOR could stimulate Asian and global economic growth and make it more sustainable. In particular, countries along the corridor — especially those with underdeveloped infrastructure, low investment rates, and low per-capita incomes — could experience a boost in trade flows and benefit from infrastructure development. China would be able to better secure its energy and raw materials supply — which now predominantly gets shipped through the Strait of Malacca and the South China Sea.

Why OBOR? Some consider the initiative China's plan to ensure markets for its growing excess capacity in the construction industries as economic expansion and domestic investment slow. While it is true that the New Silk Road needs a lot of investment, even the highest estimates would constitute a relatively modest share of China's $5 trillion annual investments back home. Investments of $1 trillion over 10-15 years is not going to absorb a lot of China's overcapacity.

There are at least four reasons why OBOR can succeed better than individual countries fending for themselves: network effects, finance, leadership and China's current stage of economic development.

On network effects, benefits to individual countries accrue if each part of the Belt and Road gets built. It simply does not pay for individual countries to move forward on their own. In addition, the initiative helps individual countries align with each other, and China's finances and leadership provide vital credibility.

In my view, China's current stage of development further bolsters the credibility of OBOR. In the past decade, China has become a major player in foreign investment based on natural resources development. As China's domestic economy is now changing, its overseas investment is gradually shifting toward manufacturing rather than just natural resources. There are good reasons for this transition: at home, China faces rising labor costs and increasing environmental demands on production. Shifting some of its production base overseas makes sense — as long as the infrastructure exists to move the goods produced there. Chinese investment through OBOR provides countries along the Road and Belt an added incentive to join the initiative.

Will it work? China's top planning body, the National Development and Reform Commission, has issued a document on its vision for OBOR that discusses strengthening bilateral cooperation and improving existing regional cooperation mechanisms. However the document stops short of "multilaterilazation" of the initiative, such as a formal treaty or partnership.

The question is whether OBOR would need a more formal agreement at some point — covering trade, investment and business climate issues — to maximize its benefits. For now, countries along the Belt and Road have highly diverse development conditions, and some have challenging governance environment that has made investment in infrastructure hard.

So using the initiative to help countries improve their investment climate, technical standards and customs and logistics procedures through a formal agreement could bring major benefits. If a more formal agreement were to ensue, it would be among the largest of its kind, and similar in size to the just-concluded Trans-Pacific Partnership Agreement (TPP).

THE ECONOMICS OF THE SILK ROAD ECONOMIC BEL T

On 20 October 2015, RUSI held a day-long workshop in Almaty, Kazakhstan, in collaboration with KIMEP University and the Friedrich Ebert Stiftung (FES). The focus of the workshop was the economics behind the Chinese Silk Road Economic Belt (SREB) and its impact in Central Asia.

The key areas of discussion examined the potential benefits that the SREB could bring to participating countries, the integration of the SREB with other economic projects and the various funding mechanisms through which the SREB will be financed. The workshop brought together participants from Almaty, Astana, London, Beijing, Shanghai, New Delhi and Russia, including representatives from academia, the private sector and think tanks.

The first session discussed the real benefits of the SREB to both China and participating countries along the road. There is a risk that the SREB will simply turn Eurasia into a set of transport routes emanating from China, aimed at increasing the volume of Chinese goods going to Europe.

Other than transit fees, China has not made it explicitly clear as to what other value participating in the SREB can add to economic development. Special economic and free-trade zones are one opportunity, such as that of Khorgos on the border of Kazakhstan and China, or those planned for Pakistan.

However, the extent to which these are benefitting Central Asia is still unclear, and those for Pakistan are still under discussion. Kazakhstan's side of this free-trade zone is noticeably less developed than that of China's, highlighting that not all of these projects are implemented to meet maximum potential.

Furthermore, China's emphasis on connectivity as a key goal of the SREB runs the risk of over-emphasising railway development as an end goal, since not all goods are cost-effective to transport by rail. High-value goods are the ideal product: one participant from

Kazakhstan noted that Kazakhstan Temir Zholy, the national railway operator, had begun transporting Apple products from China, cutting down delivery time from sixty days (by sea) to eighteen days (by rail). For the SREB project to be successful, therefore, both Xinjiang, the northwestern Chinese province, and the countries along the Silk Road route need to increase their high-tech manufacturing capacity to produce these high-value goods for transport, neither of which are currently visible.

Understanding of the project has been limited by Beijing's vagueness on practical implementation. The Chinese government's 'Visions and Actions on Jointly Building Silk Road Economic Belt and 21st Century Maritime Silk Road' strategy paper, published by the National Development and Reform Commission (NDRC), emphasises the objectives of the SREB, such as connectivity and greater financial integration.

However, it does not give practical detail on how this will be achieved. This approach of laying out a grand vision without detail is typical of the Chinese government. So far there is not even a formally government-endorsed map of the exact routes of the SREB.

The workshop discussion highlighted a potential explanation for this. China's goal may not be to unpack the details itself but instead to seek ideas and engagement from SREB countries to determine where participation can provide most benefit to them. China does not want to limit its options or jeopardise the project's 'inclusivity' by over-defining its approach.

There is an opportunity, therefore, for countries along the SREB to provide proposals back to China. However, there are some practical questions that China will need to address. Although its openended encouragement of connectivity is central to the SREB, certain political and geographical difficulties in implementing this are so far unresolved. Anyone who has travelled within Central Asia knows the difficulty of flying direct between most regional capitals, while land travel between the countries in the region is hindered by longstanding border disputes.

Although the SREB has broadly been received with enthusiasm by Central and South Asia, the lack of clarity around its planned implementation has led to some suspicion.

India stands out as the country in the region most apprehensive of China's plans. As one workshop participant said, 'there is no Indian perspective at the moment', in part due to a perceived lack of information from Beijing. The suspicions relate to whether there is a broader Chinese geopolitical strategy behind the SREB and whether political strings will become attached to China's infrastructure investment.

India's concerns over a geopolitical strategy are mainly due to the maritime element of the '21st Century Maritime Silk Road', which runs through the Indian Ocean. It covers ports in countries located around India, such as Sri Lanka, Maldives and Pakistan, but not India itself. This has raised alarm bells in New Delhi, who perceive China as encroaching on India's waterways.

China's investment into the China–Pakistan Economic Corridor (CPEC), which cuts through the disputed areas of Kashmir as well as highlighting China's strong connection with Pakistan, is also a challenge for India.

There are areas where India and China can co-operate on this SREB project, such as the Bangladesh–China–India–Burma corridor or areas where both have interests, like Iran. However, India requires more detail and reassurances regarding China's intentions.

A large part of the day's discussion focused on the issue of integrating the SREB with other economic projects. Russia has recently voiced its desire to integrate the SREB with the Eurasian Economic Union (EEU) and Kazakhstan has proposed something similar with its 'Bright Road' (Nurly Zhol) policy.

Although the Bright Road policy, which focuses on infrastructure development, is consistent with the aims of the Chinese project, SREB integration with the EEU is somewhat more complex. As one workshop participant pointed out, the EEU is an organisation with an institutional and regulatory framework, whereas the SREB is more of a 'vision' covering a variety of concrete projects.

'Integrating' these in practice may be difficult. A special economic zone may once again be an answer to this, and the EEU and China are currently exploring this idea. The EEU's external tariffs may present an immediate barrier to increased trade with China, although one benefit is that once this barrier is overcome countries gain access to a significant economic space consisting of five countries. However, to facilitate trade, China and Russia will need to address a number of bilateral trade issues. For example, the Russian–Chinese border currently suffers from excessive bureaucracy that, in particular, prevents cross-border travel and trade.

The third key aspect of the discussions examined the means by which the SREB will be funded. A major tool will be multilateral and national institutions driven by Beijing. China has allocated $29.8 billion to the Asian Infrastructure Investment Bank's (AIIB) overall $100 billion capitalisation and $40 billion to the national Silk Road Fund.

Furthermore, the China Development Bank (CDB) is the lead financial body for the SREB, investing $890 billion into over 900 projects. There are also bilateral funding relations between SREB countries and Chinese provinces.

For example, the recent Tbilisi Silk Road Forum held in Georgia was the first event on the SREB co-sponsored by the Chinese state held outside of China. The principals on the Chinese side were the provincial governments of Xinjiang and Shaanxi.

On top of this, China is seeking to stimulate public–private partnerships to help progress the project finance, as well as exploring opportunities of collaboration with other international financial institutions like the Asian Development Bank (ADB), the European Bank for Reconstruction and Development (EBRD) and the European Investment Bank (EIB).

Most participants agreed, however, that the predominant mechanism for SREB co-operation will continue to be bilateral agreements. As one workshop participant mentioned, China recently pledged $46 billion for the China–Pakistan Economic Corridor alone, a number that puts China's commitment into context when it is compared to the total $100 billion capitalisation of the AIIB.

This highlights the degree to which China is likely to continue to prioritise bilateral agreements over its multilateral financial vehicles. A note of caution was made regarding the enormity of some of the SREB deals announced.

As one participant pointed out, it seems in reality that the CPEC deal included a repackaging – or at least a reinvigoration – of some historical agreements between China and Pakistan, such as the development of Gwadar port and the Karakorum Highway, projects that have been underway for years. This demonstrates a lack of clarity in the detail behind some of these enormous declarations of financial support.

A repeated theme that came up during this discussion related to the broader transparency and governance of the SREB, particularly in participating countries outside of China. One workshop participant highlighted the need for SREB countries to ensure necessary reforms are conducted in the domestic markets to provide a degree of security and flexibility and to avoid an over-reliance on Chinese investment. The slow-down in the Chinese economy may produce constraints on China's ability to meet its ambitious investment programme.

A lack of transparency as regards the relevant information has led to questions over China's asset quality. One workshop participant stated that a 'sudden large injection of external cash could exacerbate existing problems [in the domestic economy] rather than help'. Thus, SREB participants should ensure they protect and reform their own markets in preparation for any large investments from China to maximise returns and protect against a lack of transparency in the deals.

Another question mark surrounding China's funding of the SREB projects is the value this produces for China itself. The divestment opportunities or returns China makes on its infrastructure development projects in, for example, Central Asia, remain unclear.

Much of the historical bilateral projects have been funded through linked loans, where China provides the funding through loans that have stipulations attached to them, such as the requirement that Chinese companies implement the projects on the ground. In other cases where China's Eximbank or CDB has provided loans to fund projects, it is unclear whether there are any short- or medium-term returns or even security on the investment.

One workshop participant pointed out that given the dominance of the state in China's economic policy and the government's long-term vision of investments, China can afford more time to sit on these investments without requiring immediate returns.

Moreover, another participant noted that some projects, such as when Eximbank loaned the money for the high-voltage power line recently unveiled in Kyrgyzstan, provide the Chinese government with foreign investment legitimacy and thus material return is not necessarily the priority.

It is clear that no one wants to be left out of China's SREB initiative. However, questions remain over the implementation plan of the project. For some SREB countries, there are significant concerns over the project's ultimate geostrategic goal as well as the detail of the various routes, both of which need more clarification from Beijing. However, it is clear that while China has ideas for how the SREB should develop, it is also seeking proposals from other countries about its development. This presents an opportunity for SREB countries to take ownership over the direction of their participation and to determine how best to maximise the benefits nationally.

SILK PRODUCTION AND THE SILK TRADE

Silk is a textile of ancient Chinese origin, woven from the protein fibre produced by the silkworm to make its cocoon, and was developed, according to Chinese tradition, sometime around the year 2,700 BC. Regarded as an extremely high value product, it was reserved for the exclusive usage of the Chinese imperial court for the making of cloths, drapes, banners, and other items of prestige.

Its production was kept a fiercely guarded secret within China for some 3,000 years, with imperial decrees sentencing to death anyone who revealed to a foreigner the process of its production. Tombs in the Hubei province dating from the 4th and 3rd centuries BC contain outstanding examples of silk work, including brocade, gauze and embroidered silk, and the first complete silk garments.

The Chinese monopoly on silk production however did not mean that the product was restricted to the Chinese Empire – on the contrary, silk was used as a diplomatic gift, and was also traded extensively, first of all with China's immediate neighbours, and subsequently further afield, becoming one of China's chief exports under the Han dynasty (206 BC –220 AD). Indeed, Chinese cloths from this period have been found in Egypt, in northern Mongolia, and elsewhere.

At some point during the 1st century BC, silk was introduced to the Roman Empire, where it was considered an exotic luxury and became extremely popular, with imperial edicts being issued to control prices.

Its popularity continued throughout the Middle Ages, with detailed Byzantine regulations for the manufacture of silk clothes, illustrating its importance as a quintessentially royal fabric and an important source of revenue for the crown. Additionally, the needs of the Byzantine Church for silk garments and hangings were substantial. This luxury item was thus one of the early impetuses in the development of trading routes from Europe to the Far East.

Knowledge about silk production was very valuable and, despite the efforts of the Chinese emperor to keep it a closely guarded secret, it did eventually spread beyond China, first to India and Japan, then to the Persian Empire and finally to the west in the 6[th]century AD. This was described by the historian Procopius, writing in the 6th century:

Beyond Silk; a diversity of routes and cargos

However, whilst the silk trade was one of the earliest catalysts for the trade routes across Central Asia, it was only one of a wide range of products that was traded between east and west, and which included textiles, spices, grain, vegetables and fruit, animal hides, tools, wood work, metal work, religious objects, art work, precious stones and much more.

Indeed, the Silk Roads became more popular and increasingly well-travelled over the course of the Middle Ages, and were still in use in the 19th century, a testimony not only to their usefulness but also to their flexibility and adaptability to the changing demands of society. Nor did these trading paths follow any one trail – merchants had a wide choice of different routes crossing a variety of regions of Eastern Europe, the Middle East, Central Asia and the Far East, as well as the maritime routes, which transported goods from China and South East Asia through the Indian Ocean to Africa, India and the Near East.

These routes developed over time and according to shifting geopolitical contexts throughout history. For example, merchants from the Roman Empire would try to avoid crossing the territory of the Parthians, Rome's enemies, and therefore took routes to the north, across the Caucasus region and over the Caspian Sea. Similarly, whilst extensive trade took place over the network of rivers that crossed the Central Asian steppes in the early Middle Ages, their water levels rose and fell, and sometimes dried up altogether, and trade routes shifted accordingly.

Maritime trade was another extremely important branch of this global trade network. Most famously used for the transportation of spices, the maritime trade routes have also been known as the Spice Roads, supplying markets across the world with cinnamon, pepper, ginger, cloves and nutmeg from the Moluccas islands in Indonesia (known as the Spice Islands), as well as a wide range of other goods.

Textiles, woodwork, precious stones, metalwork, incense, timber, and saffron were all traded by the merchants travelling these routes, which stretched over 15,000 kilometres, from the west coast of Japan, past the Chinese coast, through South East Asia, and past India to reach the Middle East and so to the Mediterranean. The history of these maritime routes can be traced back thousands of years, to links between the Arabian Peninsula, Mesopotamia and the Indus Valley Civilization.

The early Middle Ages saw an expansion of this network, as sailors from the Arabian Peninsula forged new trading routes across the Arabian Sea and into the Indian Ocean. Indeed, maritime trading links were established between Arabia and China from as early as the 8th century AD.

Technological advances in the science of navigation, in astronomy, and also in the techniques of ship building combined to make long-distance sea travel increasingly practical. Lively coastal cities grew up around the most frequently visited ports along these routes, such as Zanzibar, Alexandria, Muscat, and Goa, and these cities became wealthy centres for the exchange of goods, ideas, languages and beliefs, with large markets and continually changing populations of merchants and sailors.

In the late 15th century, the Portuguese explorer, Vasco da Gama, navigated round the Cape of Good Hope, thereby connecting European sailors with these South East Asian maritime routes for the first time and initiating direct European involvement in this trade. By the 16th and 17th centuries, these routes and their lucrative trade had become subject of fierce rivalries between the Portuguese, Dutch, and British. The conquest of ports along the maritime routes brought both wealth and security, as they effectively governed the passage of maritime trade and also allowed ruling powers to claim monopolies on these exotic and highly sought-after goods, as well as gathering the substantial taxes levied on merchant vessels.

The map above illustrates the great variety of routes that were available to merchants bearing a wide range of goods and travelling from different parts of the world, by both land and sea. Most often, individual merchant caravans would cover specific sections of the routes, pausing to rest and replenish supplies, or stopping altogether and selling on their cargos at points throughout the length of the roads, leading to the growth of lively trading cities and ports. The Silk Roads were dynamic and porous; goods were traded with local populations throughout, and local products were added into merchants' cargos. This process enriched not only the merchants' material wealth and the variety of their cargos, but also allowed for exchanges of culture, language and ideas to take place along the Silk Roads.

Routes of Dialogue

Perhaps the most lasting legacy of the Silk Roads has been their role in bringing cultures and peoples in contact with each other, and facilitating exchange between them.

On a practical level, merchants had to learn the languages and customs of the countries they travelled through, in order to negotiate successfully. Cultural interaction was a vital aspect of material exchange.

Moreover, many travellers ventured onto the Silk Roads in order to partake in this process of intellectual and cultural exchange that was taking place in cities along the routes. Knowledge about science, arts and literature, as well as crafts and technologies was shared across the Silk Roads, and in this way, languages, religions and cultures developed and influenced each other.

One of the most famous technical advances to have been propagated worldwide by the Silk Roads was the technique of making paper, as well as the development of printing press technology. Similarly, irrigation systems across Central Asia share features that were spread by travellers who not only carried their own cultural knowledge, but also absorbed that of the societies in which they found themselves.

Indeed, the man who is often credited with founding the Silk Roads by opening up the first route from China to the West in the 2nd century BC, General Zhang Qian, was on a diplomatic mission rather than a trading expedition.

Sent to the West in 139 BC by the Han Emperor Wudi to ensure alliances against the Xiongnu, the hereditary enemies of the Chinese, Zhang Qian was captured and imprisoned by them. Thirteen years later he escaped and made his way back to China. Pleased with the wealth of detail and accuracy of his reports, the emperor sent Zhang Qian on another mission in 119 BC to visit several neighbouring peoples, establishing early routes from China to Central Asia.

Religion and a quest for knowledge were further inspirations to travel along these routes. Buddhist monks from China made pilgrimages to India to bring back sacred texts, and their travel diaries are an extraordinary source of information. The diary of Xuan Zang (whose 25-year journal lasted from 629 to 654 AD) not only has an enormous historical value, but also inspired a comic novel in the sixteenth century, the 'Pilgrimage to the West', which has become one of the great Chinese classics. During the Middle Ages, European monks undertook diplomatic and religious missions to the east, notably Giovanni da Pian del Carpini, sent by Pope Innocent IV on a mission to the Mongols from 1245 to 1247, and William of Rubruck, a Flemish Franciscan monk sent by King Louis IX of France again to the Mongol hordes from 1253 to 1255.

Perhaps the most famous was the Venetian explorer, Marco Polo, whose travels lasted for more than 20 years between 1271 and 1292, and whose account of his experiences became extremely popular in Europe after his death.

The routes were also fundamental in the dissemination of religions throughout Eurasia. Buddhism is one example of a religion that travelled the Silk Roads, with Buddhist art and shrines being found as far apart as Bamiyan in Afghanistan, Mount Wutai in China, and Borobudur in Indonesia.

Christianity, Islam, Hinduism, Zoroastrianism and Manicheism spread in the same way, as travellers absorbed the cultures they encountered and then carried them back to their homelands with them. Thus, for example, Hinduism and subsequently Islam were introduced into Indonesia and Malaysia by Silk Road merchants travelling the maritime trade routes from India and Arabia.

TRAVELLING THE SILK ROADS

The process of travelling the Silk Roads developed along with the roads themselves. In the Middle Ages, caravans consisting of horses or camels were the standard means of transporting goods across land. Caravanserais, large guest houses or inns designed to welcome travelling merchants, played a vital role in facilitating the passage of people and goods along these routes.

Found along the Silk Roads from Turkey to China, they provided not only a regular opportunity for merchants to eat well, rest and prepare themselves in safety for their onward journey, and also to exchange goods, trade with local markets and buy local products, and to meet other merchant travellers, and in doing so, to exchange cultures, languages and ideas.

As trade routes developed and became more lucrative, caravanserais became more of a necessity, and their construction intensified across Central Asia from the 10th century onwards, and continued until as late as the 19th century. This resulted in a network of caravanserais that stretched from China to the Indian subcontinent, Iran, the Caucasus, Turkey, and as far as North Africa, Russia and Eastern Europe, many of which still stand today.

Caravanserais were ideally positioned within a day's journey of each other, so as to prevent merchants (and more particularly, their precious cargos) from spending days or nights exposed to the dangers of the road. On average, this resulted in a caravanserai every 30 to 40 kilometres in well-maintained areas.

Maritime traders had different challenges to face on their lengthy journeys. The development of sailing technology, and in particular of ship-building knowledge, increased the safety of sea travel throughout the Middle Ages. Ports grew up on coasts along these maritime trading routes, providing vital opportunities for merchants not only to trade and disembark, but also to take on fresh water supplies, with one of the greatest threats to sailors in the Middle Ages being a lack of drinking water. Pirates were another risk faced by all merchant ships along the maritime Silk Roads, as their lucrative cargos made them attractive targets.

The legacy of the Silk Roads

In the nineteenth century, a new type of traveller ventured onto the Silk Roads: archaeologists and geographers, enthusiastic explorers looking for adventure. Coming from France, England, Germany, Russia and Japan, these researchers traversed the Taklamakan desert in western China, in what is now Xinjiang, to explore ancient sites along the Silk Roads, leading to many archaeological discoveries, numerous academic studies, and most of all, a renewed interest in the history of these routes.

Today, many historic buildings and monuments still stand, marking the passage of the Silk Roads through caravanserais, ports and cities. However, the long-standing and ongoing legacy of this remarkable network is reflected in the many distinct but interconnected cultures, languages, customs and religions that have developed over millennia along these routes.

The passage of merchants and travellers of many different nationalities resulted not only in commercial exchange but in a continuous and widespread process of cultural interaction. As such, from their early, exploratory origins, the Silk Roads developed to become a driving force in the formation of diverse societies across Eurasia and far beyond.

THE 21ST CENTURY MARITIME SILK ROAD

The 21st Century Maritime Silk "Road" (MSR) will begin from China, moving on to the South China Sea and then Southeast Asia, the Indian Ocean, Africa, and Europe. The southern extension of the route offers access to the South Pacific.

According to the National Development and Reform Commission of China (2015), the New Silk Road is based on five principles of the United Nations charter: *mutual respect, mutual non-aggression, mutual non-interference, equality and mutual benefit, and peaceful coexistence.* The MSR would play a vital role for development in the seas through regional cooperation based on infrastructure development, financial integration, free trade, and scientific and human exchanges.

The same is supported by academic literature and government reports that how the MSR may evolve newer patterns of regional trade and diplomacy.

China's ambitions support a multilateral approach under international relations where cooperation is promoted on common interests. On similar lines, many experts have raised speculations towards ownership, governance, geo-politics, and prevailing conflicts in the South China Sea.

Can initiatives such as the Asian Infrastructure Investment Bank (AIIB) indicate practical steps from China that defy perceptions limiting political constructs towards hegemony?

What is important to understand in today's context is that development and harmony would fail through a bilateral or a unilateral approach. Collaboration between states through the MSR not only produces economic gains, but results in greater exchange between societies that will promote culture rooted in harmony and cooperation.

A comparative view of the Ancient and 21st Century Maritime Silk Road includes varying perspectives. However, common grounds are based on principles of economic exchanges through peace in a humanistic approach that strengthens regional integration through cooperation and cultural avenues.

The significant difference for MSR today falls under freedom of navigation. International laws and regulations have defined boundaries, which was not the case in ancient times. Another prominent facet of ancient times was the draw of exploration of the seas. Civilizations wanted to get in contact for trade, prosperity, and learning.

What remains a question with regard to today's geo-political dynamics is the following: can great powers co-exist, especially with today's complex political dynamics?

The rhetorical debate over the 21st Century Maritime Silk Road has ambiguities, but participating nations from Europe, Africa and Asia must realize the need for an integrated network. Like ancient times, states need their economic expertise to be promoted, which not only manifests itself in monetary value, but also in mutually cooperative societies that may initiate a sustainable track towards global peace.

Bibliography

Baran, Paul A.: *The Political Economy of Growth,* New York, Modern Reader Paperbacks, 1975.

Bardsley, N., Cubitt: *Assessing Experimental Economics,* Princeton, Princeton University Press, 2009.

Boulnois, Luce: *Silk Road: Monks, Warriors and Merchants on the Silk Road.* Odyssey Publications, 2005.

Elisseeff, Vadime: *The Silk Roads: Highways of Culture and Commerce.* UNESCO Publishing. Paris. 1998

Hansen, Valerie: *The Silk Road: A New History,* Oxford University Press; 2012.

Harding, Harry: *China's Second Revolution.* Washington, DC: Brookings, 1987.

Hayek, F. A. *Individualism and Economic Order,* The University of Chicago Press, Chicago, 1948.

Hunt, E. K. *History of Economic Thought, A Critical Perspective,* New York, HarperCollins, 1992.

Joshi, Vijay and I.M.D. Little: *India: Macroeconomics and Political Economy, 1964-1991.* Washington, DC: World Bank, 1994.

Judy A.: *Feminism, Objectivity and Economics,* London and New York, Routledge, 1996.

Kuzmina, E. E.: *The Prehistory of the Silk Road.* University of Pennsylvania Press, Philadelphia. 2008.

Lieberthal, Kenneth: *Governing China.* New York: WW Norton, 1995.

Link, Albert N.: *Evaluating Economic Damages, A Handbook for Attorneys,* Westport, CT, Quorum Books, 1992.

Loomes, G.: *Current Issues in Microeconomics,* New York: St. Martin's Press, 1989.

Magnussen, L., *Evolutionary and Neo-Schumpeterian Approaches to Economics,* Kluwer, Boston, 1994.

Martin, Gerald D.: *Determining Economic Damages,* Santa Ana, CA: James Publishing, 1995.

Nicholas R.: *China's Unfinished Economic Revolution.* Washington, DC: Brookings, 1998.

Pesendorfer, W.: *The Foundations of Positive and Normative Economics*, New York, Oxford University Press 2008.

Salancik, G. R.: *The External Control of Organizations, A Resource Dependence Perspective*, New York, 1978.

Schotter, A.: *The Foundations of Positive and Normative Economics*, New York, Oxford University Press, 2008.

Scott Rozelle: *Accelerating China's Rural Transformation.* Washington, DC: World Bank, 1999.

Selznick, P.: *Leadership in Administration, A Sociological Interpretation*, New York, Harper & Row, 1957.

Shirk, Susan L.: *The Political Logic of Economic Reform in China.* Berkeley: University of California Press, 1993.

Smith, V. L.: *Papers in Experimental Economics*, Cambridge, Cambridge University Press, 1991.

Taylor, F. W.: *The Principles of Scientific Management*, New York, 1917.

Thubron, C.: *The Silk Road to China*, Hamlyn, 1989.

Tietenberg, Tom, *Environmental Economics and Policy*, New York, HarperCollins, 1994

Tinbergen, Jan.: *On the Theory of Economic Policy*; Amsterdam, North-Holland 1952.

Ullman, D. G.: *Making Robust Decisions*, Trafford, 2006.

Vogel, Ezra: *One Step Ahead in China: Guangdong Under Reform.* Cambridge: Harvard University Press, 1989.

Vogel, Steven K.: *Freer Markets, More Rules: Regulatory Reform in Advanced Industrial Countries.* Ithaca: Cornell University Press, 1996.

Warwick, D. P.: *A Theory of Public Bureaucracy*, Cambridge, MA: Harvard University Press, 1975.

West, Thomas L.: and Jeffrey D. Jones: *Handbook of Business Valuation*, New York: Wiley, 1992.

Wishnick, Elizabeth: *Mending Fences: The Evolution of Moscow's China Policy from Brezhnev to Yeltsin.* Seattle: University of Washington Press, 2001.

Wood, A.: *The Corporate Economy*, London: Macmillan, 1971.

Woodward, J.: *The Oxford Handbook of Philosophy of Economics*, New York, Oxford University Press, 2009.

Index

❑❑❑

.

www.ingramcontent.com/pod-product-compliance
Lightning Source LLC
Chambersburg PA
CBHW031549260326
41914CB00002B/340